As I Remember It

Tara Lee Morin

THEYTUS BOOKS

Library and Archives Canada Cataloguing in Publication

Morin, Tara Lee, 1975-

As I remember it / Tara Lee Morin.

ISBN 978-1-926886-15-2

1. Morin, Tara Lee, 1975-. 2. Indian foster children--

British Columbia--Biography. 3. Indian foster children--

Manitoba--Biography. I. Title.

HV887.C32B72 2012   362.73'3092   C2012-903021-X

Cover Design by Ann Doyon

Printed in Canada

THEYTUS BOOKS

www.theytus.com
In Canada: Theytus Books, Green Mountain Rd., Lot 45, RR#2, Site 50, Comp. 8
Penticton, British Columbia. V2A 6J7, Tel. 250-493-7181
In the USA: Theytus Books, P.O. Box 2890, Oroville, Washington, 98844

 Patrimoine   Canadian
canadien   Heritage

 Canada Council Conseil des Arts
for the Arts   du Canada

 BRITISH COLUMBIA
ARTS COUNCIL
Supported by the Province of British Columbia

Theytus Books acknowledges the support of the following:

We acknowledge the financial support of the Government of Canada through the Canada
Book Fund for our publishing activities.

We acknowledge the support of the Canada Council for the Arts, which last year invested
$154 million to bring the arts to Canadians throughout the country.Nous remercions
le Conseil des arts du Canada de son soutien. L'an dernier, le Conseil a investi 154
millions de dollars pour mettre de l'art dans la vie des Canadiennes et des Canadiens
de tout le pays.

We acknowledge the support of the Province of British Columbia through the British
Columbia Arts Council

As I Remember It

Tara Lee Morin

 # Chapter 1

I WAS BORN BARBARA BRIGHTNOSE on an isolated reserve in northern Manitoba. During my first year of life I became extremely ill. Most travel in those days was via a small four-passenger airplane that flew into the reserve twice a month. My birth mother waited anxiously for a day or two, hoping that my condition would improve, before she packed me up for the arduous journey across a lake and a river followed by a day-long hike to the nearest hospital.

At the hospital, doctors made the decision to transfer me to a children's hospital in Winnipeg. It was there that I first appeared in government records. The files would say that I was a child in immediate danger and that my Native birth mother had ultimately abandoned me at the hospital. Twenty-two years later when we finally met she would tell me of a cunning and devious government that had manipulated her with big words. Just fifteen years old when she had me, she had viewed the government as threatening because it was so powerful. Wanting to avoid the lectures and insinuations of further involvement that she feared would cause trouble for other members of her family, she signed what the government agents placed in front of her. Only later would she discover she had signed away her rights as my mother.

I was soon adopted by a young couple named Janine and Robert Sansowsky. They believed they couldn't have children of their own and were desperate to start a family. They took me home with little understanding of my background, unaware that I had been admitted to the hospital with severe malnutrition and dehydration, showing signs of sexual interference.

I was given a new name—Tara Lee—and a fresh start at just over two years old. I would live with Janine and Robert for the next three years. While I was with them they had twins of their own and we all moved from Winnipeg to the West Coast.

In British Columbia, though, the adoption was reversed and I became a ward of the court.

The social worker who had been assigned to deal with dissolving the adoption had observed that the furniture was covered with plastic and that I was not allowed to go into the room in which his meetings with Janine and Robert took place. His notes from these meetings reflected that Janine thought there was something mentally wrong with me. She claimed I was a threat to her children and cited an instance in which I had tried to hurt the twins by stowing them in a box and throwing the box down the stairs.

Janine described me as being disobedient, deceitful, and argumentative. She said that I had an unnatural affection for men and that she had never been able to form a bond with me because even at three years old I had temper tantrums that were so vicious and violent that by the time I was four she was scared of me. She stated that I seemed to direct most of my rage and anger towards the twins. She believed they were in imminent danger of my seriously harming them.

Janine used words like "seductive," "flirtatious," and "indecent." This horrified the social worker into expediting the paperwork to separate me from her.

Again I ended up in foster care awaiting another permanent placement.

Janine's mom and dad, my grandparents, had met me several times and told the social workers they wanted me to live with them. Arranging for them to get custody of me took time and more paperwork.

While the paperwork was being finalized I moved into a new foster home. Kathy was a single parent who lived with her son on a quiet suburban street outside Vancouver. Sean was quite a bit older than I was and most of the time he ignored me.

The fondest memory I have of living with Kathy begins with her son and I having an argument, which he won by shutting his bedroom door in my face. I cried hysterically until Kathy came to see what the fuss was all about. To help me feel better we huddled in her kitchen baking a cake together. I spilled flour all over her counter when I dropped the bowl. Kathy never skipped a beat in the song she was humming. She just held the bowl under the counter and with her arm shovelled it back into the bowl; then she measured it again into another bowl. That night there was cake for dessert. Even Sean stayed at the table to enjoy it.

I had my first spiritual moment in Kathy's house. She was making spaghetti for dinner and I was sitting at the table with my colouring book when suddenly the floor was on fire.

There was a huge crackling noise and the air became smoky. The smell of burnt plastic invaded my nostrils, almost making me gag. Terrified, I sprang from my chair and ran into my bedroom closet to hide.

After a few minutes of hiding in the dark, the house gone eerily silent, I heard Kathy laugh. I was intrigued because I knew that the floor being on fire was really not funny at all.

I opened my closet and tentatively began to crawl out from my hiding place. I was mesmerized by the sight in front of me.

The sunlight was shining in through the windows and the air seemed to dance and glimmer in a radiant beam leading all the way down to the carpet. I closed my eyes and the faintest breeze swept across my brow. I took a deep breath and felt the panic ease. Serenity filled me.

For that one second in time I knew I was not alone; God was standing right beside me, ready to come out of hiding with me. I stood up, rising into the dancing light.

In that moment I was David, fresh from conquering Goliath, strong and brave.

I finally made my way back into the kitchen and found Kathy still chuckling to herself. When she saw me standing in the doorway she reached out to me and called me over. Holding my hand, she led me over towards the stove. There on her linoleum floor, created by the fire, was a perfect happy face! The black scorch marks had created two eyes, a nose, and a great grin that took up half the perfect circle surrounding it. Suddenly we were both laughing. I felt as if that face was just for me—another note from God.

Kathy threw a party she called "Christmas in July." Half the neighbourhood came to the barbecue in her front yard. We sang songs and played outdoor games. There was a huge cake and gifts for everyone, including me. The one I would treasure most was a rock concert: ten little painted rocks made to look like people carefully placed in front of a stage made of rock with "rock" musicians. I'd take care of that "rock" stage for the next ten years.

Janine's parents pulled their car into Kathy's driveway at the end of the party. They were there to take me home with them to California. Excited, I ran screaming into Kathy's house looking for her. "Kathy! You don't have to take care of me anymore!" I yelled. I found her in my room with its now-bare walls and my already packed suitcases at her feet.

For a split second I thought I saw sadness in her eyes. It was gone when she hugged me and we said our goodbyes.

After that, I took my grandpa's hand. I was ready to go with him and Grandma to my forever house. It would be home for the next four years.

At the time my grandparents lived just outside of San Francisco. It would take us two days to drive there with an overnight stay at the Best Western in Portland, Oregon. I spent most of the drive lying down in the back and either reading or staring out the window at the tops of trees as we cruised down the California coast.

At my grandparents' house I'd wake in the morning and go straight to the shower, then dress in something "smart" Granny would have lain on my bed while I was in the shower. They were strict about appearances and took pride in receiving compliments from strangers about what a polite, well-behaved grandchild they had.

Once dressed I'd race down the stairs to the kitchen for breakfast. If it took me too long Granny would yell in frustration.

Eventually Granny made it into a game to motivate me and I would try to beat my own record for how quickly I could get ready. It was quite fun—sometimes I would even beat Granny to the table. She would give me high praise on those mornings and I would have a spring in my step for the rest of the day.

My grandfather and I had a very special relationship; he was my hero. Every day when he came home from work he would make himself a martini, Granny a Grasshopper, and me a Shirley

Temple. Then he would sit in his chair to read his newspaper and watch *Cheers* or *Family Ties*. Eventually Grandpa taught me how to make those three drinks, and I became an expert at it.

I used to hide behind his chair and wait for him to sit down. Then I'd jump out from behind it onto his lap. One day when I went behind the chair there was the tallest doll I'd ever seen propped up against the wall waiting to be discovered. I don't think it was even my birthday. I was so excited about the doll that I forgot to attack Grandpa when he sat down.

My relationship with Granny was never quite that easy. I know now that she did love me, but she was home with me the most and that made her the disciplinarian. She became the target for my pent-up rage and fear. I would run and hide from her when she called me, and when she caught me I would scream, kick, and wriggle until she had to put me down or drop me.

I found my escape in books. My active imagination made it easy to lose myself in their pages, and sometimes, if it was a really good book, I would have to be physically shaken to get my attention.

I collected and read classic tales such as *Robinson Crusoe* and *Little Women*. I had every Nancy Drew book available. My Hardy Boys and Encyclopedia Brown series occupied their very own bookcase, and I had boxes high up in my closet that housed books by Beverly Cleary and Judy Blume.

My grandparents had to buy new shelves for my room every few months because I would part with none of my books. I cherished them; they comforted me on rainy days.

While living with my grandparents, I went through a stage where I spoke in the third person, narrating everyday life. It was as if my life were a book and my own voice was in my head, stating everything I did and felt. I would give careful thought to how to phrase everything I said.

For some time my grandparents worried about this behavior. They even had me evaluated by a psychiatrist when I was eight years old. I became aware that people were starting to view me as weird, so I made a conscious effort to curb this habit. The voice narrating my life from within my head would never fully go away, but I would learn how to keep it to myself, and I trained myself to speak in the first person.

I was unable to completely squelch my imagination, though, and I began to tell tall tales about where I had come from. My stories never included words like adoption, foster care, or child psychoanalysts. In my world, I was like Cinderella: a soon-to-be-rescued princess.

When my granny overheard my tales she would call me a liar and tell people that I couldn't be trusted. Once, squeezing my shoulders tightly, holding me in place directly in front of her, she angrily informed my listener that if they had any questions about my life they should ask her to get a straight answer.

I wanted her to be happy with me. I was always trying to make her proud. I would tell her tales about what a great day I had had at school; that I had dazzled the teachers with my intelligence at the chalkboard or while reading aloud.

Eventually I began to feel it didn't matter what I said or did, though—my granny always accused me of lying. We would end up in terrible yelling and shouting matches. Later she would refer to them as rows, minimizing the hurt we had spat across the room at each other.

I got the sense that my granny didn't want me there and that I was intruding when I took her away from whatever she was doing. She almost never reached out to me the way my grandpa did, and she yelled at me a lot. Some of my friends were even scared of her. I was terrified of her—not because of her fast hands when she would reach out to slap my face or whack me across the head or backside, but rather because she didn't appear to love me. I knew that meant she would see me gone someday.

When I would get into trouble, which was quite often, she would tell my grandfather what a spoiled rotten little demon I was. I'd be down the hall lying on the floor in my doorway listening to her repeat the day's events. I'd know I was going to bed with no supper. But to me that wasn't the worst of it. On those days my grandfather wouldn't play with me, and I resented Granny for that. I remember thinking that she was jealous of how much my grandfather cared for me.

It never occurred to me that maybe she was jealous of how much I cared for him—that maybe she viewed my kicking and screaming to get away from her as rejection.

We were always moving. My grandfather worked for a large construction company and we always had to go where they were doing the building. Life with them felt frenetic. I'd just make friends and then we would be moving again.

We moved to Burlingame halfway through my grade two school year. My first day was dreadful. The kids were quite nasty to me, making racial comments and wanting to know what colour my blood was. Because my skin was brown, they said my blood must be black. I went home in tears, and Granny told me "Sticks and stones ... " As usual, her words were ineffective. I think parents just say that because they don't know any better way of helping kids cope with bullying.

The next day I arrived at school early. There was a large group of kids playing in the yard and when they saw me they came running over and surrounded me. I found myself in the middle of this large circle of kids screaming and making whooping noises, tapping their hands against their mouths as they danced around me.

I was devastated. I hadn't realized until that day that I was any different physically. I'd been made fun of before because I was adopted—some kids would tell me that that was because my real mother didn't want me. I was used to that. But this, this was new to me, and it hurt. My eyes were filling with tears, blurring my vision. I used my sleeve to wipe my eyes and tried to stumble my way past the group surrounding me.

A girl I recognized from my class, Amber, came out of the crowd that had gathered. She took my hand and began running around in the circle too. She told me to hurry up and do the same, so I did. Before long the crowd had broken up and no one had anything left to say about my being Native. If Amber hadn't come when she did I think things would have gotten much worse.

I learned something that day that I wish I could unlearn. I learned about prejudice. I wish everyone who goes through something like that could have a friend like Amber.

Amber and I quickly became friends and soon we were inseparable. We would have sleepovers almost every weekend, almost always at her house. Her parents were always laughing and kissing. We would make fun of them in her kitchen and then they would chase us, saying they were going to give us a "wet willie." We had no idea what that meant, but whatever it was, it sounded terrifying, so we ran.

All too soon it became obvious we were moving again, this time to Sacramento. Granny had begun to neatly wrap our belongings and pack them into boxes, and pictures were slowly coming off the walls. It was gradual. Like slow torture.

On the day we moved, Amber and her parents came to see us off. We were already in the car when Amber grabbed her mom's hand

and started to cry. I began to cry too and started begging my grandparents to let me live with Amber and her family. I couldn't understand why they wouldn't even consider my request. It seemed that anyone could take care of me if they wanted me, so why couldn't Amber's mom and dad?

I turned in my seat so as to keep eye contact with Amber. With me whimpering in the back seat we began the drive to Sacramento.

It was here that things changed, most noticeably in school. I had more friends in class than I had ever had before. I met a boy who didn't make me want to scream "Cooties" and run, and he liked me too.

There was a quarry in the area behind where we lived. It was overflowing with bushes and trees, and trails wound their way through all the undergrowth. The trench was the perfect setting for the games we played. One of our favourites was pirates, and for the first time I was the damsel in distress. I had never been important enough to get to be the damsel. I liked the feeling, and I didn't want to lose it.

I didn't have to tell a lot of stories to my new friends. I discovered that if I didn't volunteer any information about myself they would rarely ask. I never told my usual tale of how my parents were very important people in the government and that was why I had to live with my grandparents. I had learned to say that so that no one would make fun of me for being adopted.

At home, my granny and I entered an especially bad patch in our relationship.

One afternoon, I stood at the top of the stairs in our house and yelled down to her that I hated her. I remember the frustration in her voice when Granny and her friend yelled back that I was a spoiled rotten little girl who deserved nothing.

I had wanted to hurt her like she hurt me, but it seemed to me that her friend was thwarting my efforts.

In my head a different, softer voice was asking Granny why she was always so angry with me. I wanted to scream that I loved her and really needed her. I never did. I don't remember her ever saying it to me either.

It was around this time that the older girls at school befriended me. I don't remember their names, but I was elated that they were paying attention to me. I had finally become socially acceptable, even to them, and I wasn't going to let anything get in the way when they invited me to a scavenger hunt at the mall.

I called my granny during lunch that day and she gave me permission. Really, how could she say no? I was so excited that I floated through the rest of the day.

On our way to the mall one of the girls lit up a cigarette. I watched in admiration while they passed it around and talked about the game we were going to play. I was quiet when their conversation turned to what the first item should be. They decided on a red knit scarf. I wondered if I was going to have enough money for this game. Talk turned to who was going in first and who was going to "spot."

Now I was confused. Spot what? They decided one of them would go in first; we would all meet up outside the big mall doors and then it would be my turn.

When we had reassembled outside, red scarf successfully scavenged, and my turn came, I no longer had any question in my mind about what we were doing. It was decided that my item was going to be stickers and they would all be joining me to spot. Apparently they were going easy on me because I was new to the game.

I was so nervous that I was actually sweating when I made my way back inside the mall. Seconds later I was standing at a kiosk just inside the mall doors that sold stickers and albums, going through the stickers. I began to casually put them in my pocket. I had stuck in a few handfuls when I felt a hand on my shoulder. Assuming it was one of the girls I turned around with a big grin. My grin became a grimace when I realized it was a mall security officer.

Looking around I saw that my new "friends" were nowhere in sight.

I was no different than any other ten-year-old thief who had graced the holding room in security at the mall. I began to cry. I told them that my grandparents were going to kill me. At the very least I was going to get the beating of my life. I was so scared that when the policeman came I flung myself onto the security guard. The guard then told me that the police officer was only going to take me home. He explained that I was not going to have to go to jail; however, I was never to come to the mall again unless accompanied by an adult.

I remember thinking okay; that's not so bad. He hadn't said that my grandparents had to know.

The police officer was not so reassuring. I think he thought he was doing me a favour by being hard on me.

I thought of the talk my grandfather had had with me a short time before. He had said that I had to start trying harder to get along with Granny because she was running on empty. I knew in my heart that this would be it. Granny would have every reason to send me away, and she would convince him this time.

Back home, sitting on the floor just inside my bedroom listening to my grandparents' muffled voices, I strained to hear what they were saying. The police officer had just left after having had a lengthy conversation with them. The narrator in my head was screaming that I was so sorry. That I really hadn't wanted to play that stupid game in the first place, but I hadn't known how to say no to those girls.

I heard my granny say, "You make things sound so complicated. The bottom line is we are not able to deal with Tara and her problems. She needs more than we can offer. We will go there to see her when we want to and we can still have her come stay with us for visits."

I heard the tone of rejection in her voice. Unable to comprehend, my ten-year-old mind changed her words to something I could understand. I told myself that she hated me, she always had hated me, and that if I had to leave it would be because of her.

Outside the California sun blazed hot and bright while I listened to the silence that followed. The birds still sang outside my window and the clouds still rolled across the sky, creating shapes in the shadows on my floor.

It felt wrong. I felt as if the rest of the world should have stopped to listen to my own world shatter. I was suddenly overcome with the urge to shout. *Stop, you people! Can't you see everything is falling apart?!*

Then it was done. I never did hear my grandfather's response. I did eventually see his face though. The devastation in his eyes was overwhelming and I had to look away. For the very first time he was unapproachable.

It was always on the tip of my tongue but I never found the nerve to tell him what I was really thinking. I wanted to tell him that I was going to be okay and that I understood why I had to leave. I wanted to tell him that I was sorry and that I loved him fiercely with all my heart and always would. Most of all I wanted to beg him to forgive me. Not to let me stay but just to not look so sad, so lost. I never said these things. They just echoed in my head.

On one of the last nights I spent at their place my grandfather was taking my bike apart in the garage, and as I stood watching him I realized he looked older to me somehow. I was so forlorn.

I knew that I had let him down more than I could ever make up for, but I just wanted his love. I thought I had lost him and that Granny had finally won. To my ten-year-old mind, she got what she wanted.

After that there were social workers coming over for tea, and more packing. Only this time it wasn't so gradual. This time it was very quick.

In the past I had always enjoyed going to my Aunt May and Uncle Soren's place. They lived in a large house in North Vancouver, BC, with my baby cousin, Jake. Jake won my heart easily with his crystal blue eyes and chubby little baby body. Whenever he saw me he would stretch out his arms and reach out to me. He wanted me to play with him or even just to pick him up for a cuddle. I always knew I existed when he was in the room.

My aunt and uncle were more lenient than my grandparents were, and I had had more freedom at their house to play and explore.

There was often takeout for dinner when I was with them because we would be out all day at the aquarium, or taking long drives to beautiful desolate beaches or exciting new parks. So there were lots of burgers and french fries, yummy finger food that was extremely rare at my grandparents' house. I felt as if I were breaking the rules by not eating with a fork. Those nights I felt a special camaraderie with my aunt and uncle. We were all being naughty.

One rainy afternoon, my uncle had crawled down on his living room floor with me and hooked up his stereo. He handed me the earphones and I listened to Dolly Parton sing "9 to 5" over and over again. I wanted to learn the lyrics so eventually I could imitate her. She definitely sounded different from Nana Mouskouri and Crystal Gayle, my grandparents' music of choice.

Another afternoon, during Jake's nap, Aunt May had shown me how to make paper using lint from the dryer. The process was messy and sticky but the end result was thick, coarse grey paper. We toasted our accomplishment with hot chocolate and cookies.

They were both always so wonderful to me.

This trip, however, was destined not to be like the others. It was a terrible week. A sadness hung in the air. My aunt and uncle both seemed angry, and briefly I thought that they were angry with *me*. I was terrified of what was going to happen next.

At some point during that week my grandfather called. After talking to Uncle Soren for some time he asked to speak with me. When I took the phone he told me that they had changed their minds and the house was empty without me. I could go back home to them. Everything was happening so quickly, I really didn't know what was going on anymore. I was very confused and also a little worried that it wasn't Granny who had called me. It was she who had wanted me gone. I told him that I needed time to think about it. I think he was surprised.

When I hung up the phone Aunt May and Uncle Soren explained to me that I had little time to think about it as the social worker was finalizing everything very soon. They already had a foster home for me in a town called Squamish. They talked to me about some of the problems at my grandparents' house and explained to me that my grandparents, being the age they were, didn't have the ability to deal with me as a teenager. I would be better off with a new family that was equipped to deal with children like me.

I never asked, who *were* children like me? Although I wondered what that meant—especially after I made the decision not to go back to California.

A few days later Aunt May packed up the car with all my stuff and we began the drive to Squamish, a town north of Vancouver with about 10,000 people at that time. It was on the commute to Whistler, which would eventually make it prime real estate for fast-food chains. But when I first moved there it still had a small-town feel.

As it turned out, we were actually heading about ten kilometres past Squamish, to Brackendale.

There were about 1500 houses in Brackendale at that time. Most of the properties were spread out over acres and were single-family homes. Trailer parks lined the old road into downtown Squamish.

Aunt May had a long talk with me while we drove to the small town that I would call home. "You should look at this as an opportunity for a new life, Tara Lee," she told me. "Your new foster parents are very nice to be willing to take you into their home. You need to give them a chance." She was silent for a time, gazing out at the road unwinding ahead of us, her hands gripping the steering wheel. "Remember, everyone loves you. Sometimes people just get too old to remember what it's like to be a youngster. You're growing up now—soon you'll be a teenager, and you'll need someone a bit closer to your own age to relate to." Aunt May fell silent again. I suspected that she wasn't entirely sure either that this was the right thing for me.

I wanted my aunt and uncle to be proud of me so I decided I wouldn't cry in front of them. I was going to be strong because if they did have doubts, I didn't want them to feel bad. So I told myself to buck up and take it on the chin, and as Aunt May drove I fought with a frog deep in my throat.

After driving in silence for the last leg of our journey we turned off the highway and headed towards this great opportunity that had been given to me. I didn't tell my aunt that I was having trouble breathing.

At that moment I heard my grandmother whispering to me sternly, telling me to straighten up.

We made a few turns on some quiet streets and pulled over in a cul-de-sac. We sat in the car and waited, for what, I didn't know. My aunt was drumming her fingers nervously on the dash. She kept craning her neck to look out my window at a large two-storey house. I knew from the way she was looking at it that it was the house where I was going to live.

A red car came up the cul-de-sac and parked in the driveway behind us. We climbed out of Aunt May's car and went over to greet the driver. A short stout man climbed out, struggling with a big thick briefcase. He had short curly black hair and a kind face. I could tell he was trying to look reassuring as he introduced himself to Aunt May, who shook his hand.

Aunt May turned to me expectantly. I in turn smiled as best I could. I imagine I was very pale. I could hear nothing but my heart pounding, faster than I had ever heard it beat before.

The man's name was Freddie Lavin. He was a jovial type, and when he smiled his whole face crinkled into one large laugh line. I was almost unable to help but smile back. As we walked up to the house, he explained that he was a social worker and that he and I were going to be good friends. He said he would be the one in charge of my file, and that he would be pleased to answer any questions I might have. Then he knocked on the door.

The terror I felt while standing there holding my bags waiting for the door to open is unimaginable to anyone who hasn't been there. I thought here I am, knocking on the door of a stranger's house where children go who have nowhere else to turn.

I gripped my bags as tightly as I could and waited. I could hear the pounding of someone descending stairs on the other side of the door, and then the door was open and she was standing there.

"Tara Lee, this is Deanna Peters. Deanna, this is Tara Lee," Freddie said.

Deanna had tightly curled short reddish-blond hair that framed a puffy-cheeked face. Her clothes didn't quite fit. She was wearing very baggy jeans and a long oversized T-shirt. She looked me over curiously. Seeming to approve, she smiled slightly in my direction, then turned her attention to Freddie.

It was obvious from the way she and Freddie shared pleasantries that they already knew each other quite well. A sudden awkwardness descended. There was nothing for me to say or do except stand there gripping my bags waiting for someone to tell me what to do next.

Then Freddie turned to Aunt May and told her that the time had come, hinting that it was time: time for her to leave me.

I wanted to run and climb back into her car. I wanted to forget the whole thing. But I didn't. I turned to Aunt May and hugged her. Oddly enough I was the one who said, "It's okay."

Then she was gone, leaving me clutching my bags, standing on the stoop of a stranger named Deanna Peters.

Deanna opened the door all the way and invited us in. We were standing on a landing with stairs leading up to the main part of the house and down to the basement. I stood on that landing debating whether to take my shoes off or not, and then decided that I should. It was the polite thing to do, and that day I needed to be polite. Following Deanna up the green-carpeted stairs, I got my first glimpse of her living room.

There were family pictures all over the walls, even overtop of the large bay window that overlooked the street below. There was an ivy plant that wound its way around the pictures, embracing them. I thought that was nice. She must either have a lot of family or really love the family she had, I thought, to have so many pictures of them gracing her walls.

We followed her into the kitchen. I didn't know it then, but soon the kitchen, with its yellow walls covered in mushrooms, would be my favourite place in the house. I would sit with Deanna at the table in it and we would have deep, heart-to-heart conversations that would come to mean the world to me.

She would sit on her chair in the corner between the wall and the table, one leg up, her chin resting on her knee, and smoke while we talked. We would have family meetings and play games at this table, not to mention devour home-cooked meals that I would be told were old secret family recipes. But all that would come later. At that moment I wanted nothing to do with Deanna's ugly kitchen table or her ugly yellow mushroom walls. I wanted nothing more than just to sink into the floor and disappear. Too much was happening to me all at once and I was really tired.

I took my cue as Freddie and Deanna both chose seats at the table, and sat on the next available chair. I ended up in the opposite corner to Deanna.

Freddie took a file and a writing pad from his briefcase and placed them softly on the table, making small talk with Deanna. When either of them included me in their idle chatter I had to force myself to answer. I just wanted to sit quietly and not think for a while.

Freddie was rustling his papers beside me, distracting me. I wondered what was written about me on them. It couldn't be good—it was going to make Deanna hate me before she knew me. What difference did it make? Today, tomorrow, next week, later, it always ended the same. At the age of ten I understood that nothing was forever.

I looked past Deanna into the living room. Freddie began talking about my schooling with her and Deanna said there was a school up the road that was within walking distance. It took me a minute to realize she was talking to me. She was describing the route, which would apparently take me further down the street we had driven in on. She explained that there was a trail beside the train tracks that led straight to the school. On Monday she would show me it.

Moving on, Freddie explained that on his papers it said I was a capable student who received good grades. I began to slowly zone out; their voices faded into the background of my own swirling thoughts. I remember thinking, why am I here? They could talk about me much better if I wasn't still sitting here.

As if reading my mind, Deanna suddenly stood up and asked if I wanted to see my room and maybe try to get organized while they chatted. I followed her down the hall to a room on the right. She explained that my room was directly across the hall from her and her husband's. Taking in my surroundings, I found myself alone in a room that felt empty.

I sat on the bed. Without straining too hard I could hear everything Freddie and Deanna were saying quite clearly.

I heard Freddie telling Deanna about my grandparents. Freddie had never met us in California. He didn't really know what my life had been like with them. That was when it hit me that it was I who was the stranger, probably just passing through their lives— why should they get to know me or *like* me? Suddenly I didn't feel like listening anymore.

I met Deanna's husband that night at dinner. Larry was a husky man with peppered hair. I knew he worked with his hands because even from where I sat across the table I could see his large hands were callused and stained. They weren't dirty, just dyed black around the nails and knuckles.

He mumbled a hello to me and went back to eating his meal. I understood that he was just a quiet man, and I liked him almost right away.

Deanna and Larry had one natural son, Alex. He was older than me by 11 years and no longer lived at home, so I wouldn't meet him for a while. Eventually Larry and Deanna would take me into Vancouver to see him play hockey as a goalie, a sport he excelled at.

When I went to bed that first night I didn't get a lot of sleep. I sat staring up at the strange constellation of stars and trying to find something in the night sky that I recognized. I spent a long time gazing up into that vastness of space, talking to God. I begged him to fix my life. I told him that I knew I could be like the normal kids out there; he just had to help me find a ... what? What could God help me find that would make it all better?

I didn't even know what to ask for, I felt so hopeless and desolate. I cried so hard that night, great wracking sobs that shook my entire soul. I fell asleep eventually but my sleep was invaded by dreams of strangers in shadows.

I didn't have to go to school that first week, and Deanna took the opportunity to take me shopping for clothes appropriate for school, or maybe it was clothes adequate for a small town. Either way apparently the frilly dress clothes I had would not do. I think she had been leaning towards jeans and Ts but I didn't get it. I kept grabbing things that Deanna would talk me out of—I showed her a bright silver raincoat that looked like it was made of tinfoil. Deanna just shook her head. I grabbed a shirt that had holes all over it; again Deanna shook her head. It took us all day to gather a wardrobe for me. In the end though we went home successful, with three full shopping bags.

Deanna was very nice to me. She talked to me a lot, about everything and nothing: what we were going to have for dinner, or when she was going to go to ceramics class next. I began to feel less invisible, less like a distraction.

Soon it was time for my first day at the new school. It was doomed from the night before.

I had a red dress with white lace overtop, really quite beautiful, that I took scissors to. When I was done I had a cut-up lace shirt. Going to my dresser, I took out a black tank top and put that with the shirt on top of the dresser. From the closet I took a pair of red jeans that Deanna had just bought me and added that to the pile. Now my outfit was almost complete. I had a pair of beige boots from my grandparents that were still in the box; I took them out, sat on the bed, and tried them on. They still fit. These found their way to the foot of the dresser.

Deanna came in at some point and saw what I planning to wear to my first day at my new school. She didn't say anything specific but she did ask me if I had really thought out my choices. After she left the room I sat on my bed. Maybe what I had chosen was a bit much. Instead of changing my mind, though, I reached into my jewellery box and took out my dangle bracelets. There, I thought, now I'm ready for my first day of school.

The next day came swiftly. Deanna and I ran distractedly through the house getting this and that, then finally made our exit. Deanna had planned to arrive at the school extra early to meet the staff in the office and help make sure that the registration was all taken care of.

The elementary school sat at the foot of a high wooded hill just on the outskirts of town. I would be entering midway through grade five. I mentally prepared myself for joining a class that already had established friendships and groups.

When Deanna and I arrived we were introduced to Mr. Barnes, who would be my teacher for the rest of the year. He was a round man with a large build and a round face, who was really smiley and seemed genuinely happy to have me in his class.

Deanna joined us for the walk to the classroom. The classroom had two doors, the one we entered through from the corridor, and one on the opposite wall that led outside. When Mr. Barnes turned the lights on I heard a boy's voice yelling that he thought there was a new student in there. That did it. Other voices chimed in, egging him on to climb the wall.

Mr. Barnes told us that it was almost time to open the doors anyway and that when the warning bell sounded they should quiet down. He and Deanna talked quietly. I sat, unable to concentrate on anything other than the disturbance outside. I knew that someone was climbing the outside wall trying to get a view of me through the windows.

Deanna patted me on the head and asked if I remembered the way home. Assuring her that I would be fine, I said goodbye as she turned and stepped into the hall.

I was alone with Mr. Barnes. He tried to talk with me but I just wanted to sit quietly and collect myself. He was saying something about recess when all of a sudden a much louder clearer voice from outside yelled out, "It's a new girl in the class." Then a pause and in astonishment, "She looks like Madonna!"

I looked up to the windows just in time to see a boy with curly brown hair peeping through, and then he was gone. I could hear other students laughing at him and realized he must have fallen down the last few feet. I was upset about his reaction to seeing me. It was definitely not the one I'd been going for.

Suddenly I started shaking with nervousness. I told myself not to let them see that I was intimidated. But for the first time, putting myself into the storyland in my head failed me. I couldn't focus on being Davey from *Tiger Eyes* or Ramona Quimby. I was lost. There was no book I had read that had anything resembling this situation.

At last the doors swung open and my new classmates poured in. As always, some openly stared at me; others casually glanced my way. But everyone got a good look at the new kid. There were whispers about my clothes throughout the room. By now I was bright red and near tears.

Mr. Barnes called the class to attention and motioned for me to stand up. Obligingly I rose, feeling my face get even hotter.

At recess that first day one of the girls—the first one in my class to talk to me—asked me if that was how they dressed in the United States. I said I didn't know. The next day I went to school in jeans and a T-shirt. No one stared at me. I guess even though I was still the new girl, my clothing just wasn't as interesting as the day before.

I imagine it was hard for Deanna and Larry when I first moved in with them. I wet my pants all the time, day and night. Nightmares plagued my sleep, and I would awaken Larry and Deanna with my screams. Sometimes they heard me crying myself to sleep at night.

On one of those nights Deanna crept into my room and told me to come with her. She took me into the dimly lit kitchen and invited me to take a chair at the table. She made us warm milk and we just sat at the table together in that ugly kitchen. I think she was waiting for me to make the first move and talk to her, but I didn't know what to say. No one had ever let me just sit with them like that before, long past bedtime.

It was the nights that I didn't cry myself to sleep or make my way to the windowsill that were the most damaging to me. On those nights I hated myself. I would look in the mirror, in the dark, when my face was all in shadows, and remind myself that I was useless. I would tell myself that there was never going to be a place for me in this world because I was unlovable. I would crawl real close to the mirror so I could look deep into my eyes and tell myself that I was a mistake no one wanted because no one wanted the devil's spawn. I told myself that soon Deanna and Larry would see me for the ugly, filthy, disgusting little girl I was, and then they would be gone too.

Some nights I would have to clench my hands into tight fists and hold them stiffly at my sides to keep from giving in to the urge to attack the mirror and gouge out my eyes—it was so intense. The vision played itself out over and over again in my mind. After a while it would almost have been a relief if I had actually done it.

Spent, as if I had been through an ordeal, I would climb back into bed and seek the solace of sleep.

Today, I know those nights were a sign of past abuse.

 # Chapter 2

I QUICKLY GREW TO LOVE Deanna. She seemed to understand me, and to be genuinely interested in my life.

I could tell she didn't think highly of my grandparents but I think that was mostly because of how much I cried those first few days.

My eleventh birthday came and Deanna got me a perm as a gift. It was the worst perm in the history of all hair-kind. I was appreciative and polite, but the resulting plunge in social acceptability made me slip further into the abyss of loneliness.

After my hair was done, Deanna and Larry were going to let me rent a movie. While we were walking to the video store I accidentally called Deanna "Mom." I was really taken aback at my *faux pas* and hoped she hadn't heard it. After a few minutes she told me that she liked the sound of it and didn't mind at all if I called her Mom. She said that I was going to be with her and Larry for a long time and that if I was ready they would be happy if I wanted to call them Mom and Dad.

Larry looked less than thrilled about it. I think he was worried about Deanna getting too close to me. Like me, he knew that there was no such thing as forever in this world.

But from that moment on Deanna and Larry were "Mom" and "Dad" to me.

Now don't get me wrong; I wasn't moving in with the Brady Bunch. Deanna—I mean Mom—and I did argue. But with her it was different. I really cared what she thought. For a while I tested her. I discovered swearing. I would shout swear words and no one would come running to wash my mouth out. It was confusing, and I kept waiting for the carpet to be pulled out from under me.

Most days though were pretty good. I was Mom's shadow. I followed her all around the house. I helped with laundry, supper, and other housework. I liked it. She was very generous with her praise and would tell me after every chore that I was a great help to have around, even if she had to redo what I had just done. Mom would say that she was just "backing my job up with a double." I didn't quite understand at the time. Maybe you don't until you have kids of your own.

One afternoon I came home from school and could hear music blaring from up the road. There was someone singing about the spirit in the sky and how they were going on up to see him. It was a fast song with a really catchy beat, and I was smiling when I came through the front door. When I saw Mom dancing with one of their pet birds on her shoulder in the living room, I couldn't stop myself laughing. Mom saw me standing there watching her and for the second time in my life that I can remember, a woman reached out to me. I paused for only a second before taking her hand and dancing with her. I copied her sideways boogie and we danced for over an hour, just letting the music play, Mom with the bird jumping up and down on her shoulder.

My grandparents still called quite often, and every time I talked to them I would have nightmares afterwards. I felt as if I was betraying them by getting to like Deanna and Larry. I could hear the regret in my grandfather's voice and the relief in my granny's.

I was still having the same nightmare, full of shadows and fear.

Someone enters a room I'm unaccustomed to. It's dark outside and I am in a bed by a window. Moonlight casts shadows all across the room, but it's the sound of the door creaking as it closes that stops my breath and makes my heart rage in my chest.

A male figure moves closer to the bed and stands over me. I have my eyes shut tight, desperately pretending to sleep. The only sound in the room is the short, deep breaths the figure takes and the rhythm of the movement of his hands. He reaches through the darkness and places a grotesque hand all over my chest, rubbing and caressing me almost tenderly as he works his way down past my belly. I can taste bile in the back of my throat. When I hear him grunt, low and guttural, I know that I have only seconds more to endure until he leaves. Afterwards, when I am sure he's left the room, I open my eyes and stare into the darkness, scanning the shadows to make sure that I am indeed alone.

Even in my dreams I wouldn't open my eyes because I was too afraid I would see what they were doing and then I would know; there would be no way to hide anymore, and I would have to live with knowing.

Eventually I wouldn't even scream from this nightmare. I would wake up and turn my lights back on so that my room would no longer be in darkness. I would tell myself that it was only a nightmare and try to go back to sleep, but the lights would stay on until the brightness of the morning engulfed the room. Only then would I feel safe enough to turn them out.

I walked home after school almost every day. One afternoon when I came around the corner into sight of the house I saw a brown Oldsmobile in the driveway. I began to run towards the house, warning myself that I could be wrong because I knew the disappointment would be crushing if it wasn't actually my grandparents' car. I flew through the front door and up the stairs without taking my shoes off and there they were, sitting at the kitchen table with Mom. I threw myself at my grandfather and kissed Granny's cheek. I was so happy to see both of them.

They took me out to dinner that night, and when they dropped me back at home they made arrangements with Mom and Dad to come and take me out for the day that coming Saturday. I was so excited. Not only was I going to see my grandparents, I was also going to get to go into Vancouver. Back then the city was a fascinating world of change to me. I was meant to be in that city. I just knew it.

The drive to Vancouver with Grandpa and Granny was fast and smooth. I barely noticed the windy curves of the road through my excited chatter. I had lots to fill them in on and I wanted to cover everything before the drive ended.

Granny and I went to an afternoon session of bingo in a North Vancouver private school gym. This time we actually won, so afterwards we went shopping at the mall. I spent all the money we won in a store I had never shopped in before that carried hip and trendy clothing. It was a very exciting afternoon, and I was skipping when we left the mall.

At the restaurant during dinner I looked out the window and asked God to stop the end of the evening from coming, just for a little minute. I'd have given all my Barbies for just ten more minutes of that feeling of being with both of them, and of them being happy.

The nightmares came almost every night for quite some time after that.

That was also when I began to hurt myself physically. Alone in my room at night I would take apart razors and use the blades to slice through my skin until I bled. I would take things that I found around my room, remove my underwear, and touch myself with them. The need to hurt myself was almost desperate. The world around me would fade. I was left with only me and whatever I was holding. Staring into the mirror I would silently scream at myself. I wanted to ruin my body. When I did hurt myself I wouldn't allow myself to feel the pain; I would just attack myself even more brutally.

Afterwards, when reality would start to slowly come back into focus, I would cry in shame and horror, wondering what was wrong with me.

Deanna found my bag of bloody Kleenex under my bed and when she asked me about it I had to show her my legs and arms. There were deep gouges in my legs and tiny cuts on both my arms. Deanna slumped down into the closest chair.

When she asked me why I would do such a thing, I could only cry that I didn't know. Strangely, around the same time I had stopped wetting myself.

I was sent to see a child psychiatrist. His office was dusty and he kept the lighting low. He was a thin man who wore a light brown polyester suit. His beard had thick abrasive-looking red and brown hair. I have this image of him in a chair with one leg crossed over the other, resting his foot on his knee, a yellow notepad sitting on his lap. He seemed uninterested in anything I might have said, and made me feel very uncomfortable. This did not go unnoticed by the adults in my life; thankfully, I didn't have to see him for very long.

That was how I met Edna Cimpini, a child psychologist who would be in my life for the next three years. She was a tall woman who appeared to be in her early fifties. She had all-white, medium-length hair that she wore brushed back off her face, a very clear complexion, and deep laugh lines around her eyes and crinkles around her lips. I imagined that when she was a teenager she would have looked like Marilyn Monroe; she had a classic beauty, and I was captivated by her piercing grey eyes. I was floored when I learned her true age—she was so graceful and lovely, she really didn't look it.

From the moment I sat down with her it was difficult for me to lie to her, so I gave up trying. I wasn't ready to get dirty with anyone yet so I told her what I thought all psych docs wanted to hear. I told her right away about the nightmares in a sarcastic sad way that stank like a lie. I thought to myself, there; now no one can say I didn't try to tell someone.

It wasn't until our second visit that she told me she believed the nightmares really did wake me and that she would like to talk about them. I sat stone-like on her couch and we remained in silence for most of that session. On my way out I told her that I would see her next time. I liked her, if only to stare at her for an hour, but I liked her.

On the third or fourth visit Edna took me out to a local diner for a side of fries. She said she thought that maybe a more relaxed atmosphere would be better for me, and besides she liked the coffee at the café compared to the slurp at her office.

That would be the way we would spend our hours together. I would find myself divulging many stories of my life to this woman who really not only appeared interested but almost as if she couldn't wait to hear what I would have to say next.

I kept most of my secrets to myself even though there were moments when I would look across at her and see how much she truly cared. It was then that I knew I couldn't ever tell her. I didn't want her to know how sick and twisted I really was. I didn't want her to stop getting better coffee with me.

It was around this time that Ellena came to live with us.

Mom and I spent a lot of time preparing the spare room for her arrival. We put fresh sheets on her bed and we dusted and vacuumed her new room. I didn't want her room to feel empty, so I added some finishing touches such as stuffed animals that I carefully propped up against her new pillows.

Mom sat me down and told me that she didn't want to have any jealousy issues going on between Ellena and me. She said that I needed to remember that the other children who came to live with us also had a story to tell and that they were just as desperate as I was to tell their tales. At the time I didn't understand what she was getting at.

Ellena was about four years old, maybe five, when she moved in. She had exotic features that almost looked Hawaiian. She had thick black hair, bronzed skin, and a brilliant smile.

She was shy at first. I kept waiting for the shyness to go away, but it never did, and after a while it became endearing. Mom spent extra time with Ellena trying to help her to feel comfortable living with us. I wanted to be like her big sister, and for a while we got on really well, but then Mellanie moved in.

I really wasn't happy about having yet another foster sister. I remember I yelled that Mom kept getting children and it didn't seem fair that I couldn't even get a cat. Not only were we getting another foster child for me to compete with for attention, but to make it even worse, Ellena was going to have to move into my room. I had never shared a room before.

I was really angry with Ellena for this, as if it were somehow her fault that she had to move into my room. In protest against the change she was bringing I slammed the door behind her every time she left the room to get more of her stuff.

Mellanie was around fifteen when she first arrived. She was fascinating to me, with her oversized tassel purses and makeup-covered face. She was very slender and wore skin-tight jeans showing off her long legs. Her big Eighties hairdo needed an entire arsenal of hair products and an hour a day to achieve.

Mellanie and Ellena became very close very quickly, which made me once again feel like an intruder. At times Mom would talk about how helpful it was having Mellanie around. It felt like a slight against me as at the time I was in a less-than-helpful phase.

What did they need me for, when Mellanie was good at everything and helpful enough for all of us?

At school I was a social outcast. I had very few friends and I wasn't really interested in making any. I was different. I was Native and in foster care. Other kids were curious about me, though. I once again began making up stories about where I came from. Everyone must have seen through me, because eventually they stopped asking.

Around this time I got a report card that wasn't good. A great big C and D stood out loudly from its pages. I felt my heart sink. There was no way I could take this home. Thoughts of what my grandparents would do when they saw my report card haunted me the whole way home. By the time I got there I was so worked up that I didn't have it in me to face the music.

On this particular day Mom was not at home when I arrived after school. She had left me a note to keep an eye on Ellena for her until she came home.

I quickly sprang into action. I emptied my backpack and began to stuff it with clothes, pictures, and my favourite stuffed animals. For protection, I went into the kitchen and shoved a steak knife in my jacket pocket, just in case.

When Ellena came home I told her to grab her Glo Worm because we were going on an outing. Soon we were running down the street heading for the woods. I wanted to get out of view of the street in case someone saw us.

We were walking along the trail behind the general store when I heard Mellanie calling my name. My heart racing, I grabbed Ellena's hand and began to run blindly through the trees. In that moment I hated Mellanie. I didn't want her to find me—us. It was more than that, though: I was scared. Had I kidnapped Ellena?

Somehow Ellena and I became separated and I could hear her crying somewhere close behind me. I stopped running. I didn't want Ellena stuck in the bushes alone so I hid where I could still hear her and waited for Mellanie to find her. When she did, she called out to Mom, "I found Ellena!"

I waited until I thought Mellanie was gone and then crept as quietly as I could from under the bush I was hiding in. Twigs snapped under my feet, breaking the silence and giving my location away. Then Mellanie was right behind me and she looked angry. I mustered all the strength from every villain I had ever read about, and at that exact moment I felt capable of overpowering her.

I reached into my pocket and pulled out the knife, my heart racing. Panicked, I stood holding the knife in her direction. "Don't come near me," I growled, and started to back away from her.

There was nowhere for me to go. I was in this small clearing surrounded by bushes and dense trees. I realized that Mellanie had me trapped. She must have seen the malevolence in my eyes because she hesitated and tried to reason with me. "Tara ... drop the knife. You don't want to do anything that's gonna ruin the rest of your life. C'mon. I promise I'll try harder to get along with you. Just give me the chance."

I didn't budge.

She jumped me. In the heat of our struggle I was thinking please don't let me accidentally cut her. I made only a halfhearted effort to prevent her from grabbing the knife. Mostly I just tried to keep either of us from being cut in the skirmish. Mercifully neither of us was injured before she managed to wrest the knife away from me. We both walked out of the trail area towards where Mom was parked behind the general store.

When we arrived back at the house I went quietly to my room and began to pack. I knew what was coming. I had endangered both of my foster sisters. I was going to have to go.

After some time Mom came into my room. She sat on the edge of my bed and hugged me. She didn't say anything at first; she just sat there hugging me, and I cried.

I had really messed up this time, and I didn't know why I had done it. Mom wasn't really that scary, and my grandparents were so far away that only a few harsh words from them could have reached me.

I didn't know why I had taken Ellena with me either. At the time I stated that it was because I hadn't wanted to leave a five-year-old alone. I suspect it was more that I hadn't wanted to be alone while I ran away.

I don't remember all of what Mom said to me that day but she didn't make me leave. I had to apologize to Mellanie and Ellena. Mellanie was hard to say sorry to. It felt hollow—how do you apologize for pulling a knife on someone?

I knew the afternoon could have ended very differently. There would have been no way for Mom to have helped me if any of us had been hurt. I knew that what I had done was somewhere beyond dangerous, bordering on criminal.

That night I sat on my windowsill for extra long. I fell asleep leaning against the sill as I had many times before, with no answers to the questions swimming in my head and no insights into my behaviour.

It was around this time that Danny moved in next door. The first time I ever saw him I recognized something tragic in him. It drew me to him. He was good-looking in a very mature way—he had unique brown eyes, and he was muscular, as if he had done manual labour. I imagined he had lived on a ranch. He seemed older to me than our eleven and twelve years.

I think he and I became friends because I never asked him anything about his life, and he didn't ask me about mine either. He was my first friend I didn't lie to in that small town. But then neither of us talked much. Sometimes we would just sit on the swings in the park near where we lived. We would meet up silently and hang out together silently, swaying back and forth, just listening to the silence.

Then one day not very long after he had moved in, he was gone. I watched him leave from my window; he looked up at me as he climbed into his dad's truck, and then they backed out of their driveway for the last time. I never did see his mother, nor do I recall ever seeing his father's face. I never saw them move in or out; they just drove off one day.

Summer came and with it came free time.

We spent most of it at Alice Lake, a provincial park just north of Brackendale. Mom was a sun worshipper and would spend hours lounging in its rays. Us kids would swim. I loved it. Mom would let me try to swim across the lake, but that first summer I couldn't quite manage it.

Expo 86, the World's Fair, was taking place in Vancouver that summer, and we drove down to take it in almost every weekend. It was a lot of fun. I could tell that Dad especially loved going. We would wander through exhibit after exhibit, and Dad would tell us what he had read and learned about everything he saw. His eyes lit up and there was a definite jig in his step even as we stood in line waiting to see more.

Then we would go on a few rides. Now that I was tall enough to be allowed on even the most extreme ones, I agreed to go on one that went upside down. Dad said he would sit with me. I think he was relieved when it was over that I hadn't been sick on him, although I had come very close. After that I stuck to the tamer rides, preferring to spin and swing instead of going upside down or speeding across anything that resembled a track.

Sometimes we would stay for fireworks. On those nights we would arrive home long after midnight. Dad would carry Ellena up the stairs and tuck her carefully into bed. He would poke his head in our rooms and whisper good night. Not long after that the house would fall silent.

I would lie awake and talk to God. I would thank him for the moments in the day when I had forgotten who I was. I would thank him for the peace I felt when I forgot that I was a foster child, a permanent ward of the court who truly belonged to no one.

For those few intermittent hours I felt a sense of belonging. I knew that I was wanted and even enjoyed on afternoons like that.

When the summer was over and school began again my classmates were still mostly the same, but we had a different teacher. That year we discovered hormones. Grade six would see notes being passed all through the class asking the receiver to check yes if you liked the sender or no if you didn't.

After the incident where I ran away with Ellena, Mom had decided that Mellanie and Ellena would room together so that I could have a bedroom to myself again.

But I had to move into Mellanie's old room, and the windowsill in it wasn't the same as my perch in the room next door. Some nights I would hide in the closet instead. Closing the doors behind me, I would sit on the floor and stare into the darkness. Sometimes I would fall asleep like that and wake up when the house was silent except for Larry's snoring.

I met Tanis later that year. She was a fiery redhead with as much attitude as I had. We hated each other instantly, and our snide comments soon turned to threats and eventually a lunchtime date in the field.

By the time the lunch bell rang the whole school had found out there was going to be a fight. We each had allies who came and stood by our sides. I met my rival in the middle of all these screaming kids.

We were yelling obscenities at each other when she lunged at me. I put my foot up to ward her off, and then she was on the ground coughing and sputtering. The whole thing was over in seconds but when it replayed later in my mind it felt as if it had happened in slow motion. I heard the voice of a teacher shouting for us both to get to the office.

Tanis and I found ourselves sitting out in the hallway outside the principal's office waiting as the teacher briefed him on our big brawl. With nothing else to do, we began to talk. We discovered that we actually had a lot in common and from then on we were good friends.

I moved on with the rest of the class to having boyfriends, which consisted mostly of note passing and silent lunches in the woods. Some of the boys had reputations for making out and they became the most sought after, as well as boys from other schools whom we would meet at preteen dances and the arcade. We were always keeping a watchful eye out for any good-looking boy who might also be looking our way.

My friends, like Tanis's, were mostly boys. Not boys we made out with; it was just that boys were easier to get along with.

When summer once again came, we spent it out riding our bikes, playing by the river, and exploring the mountains.

That summer, my mom and dad were really into music and dances. My dad began to DJ for pre-teen dances, which meant that I went to them all with a full chaperone. So we were forced to sneak out the back and wander off to have our cigarettes.

My first kiss happened at one of these dances. His name was Richard Hart. He was from another school, and we had been going out for over a week. Tanis had started going steady with his best friend, and after a short time it had seemed only natural that I should go steady with Richard.

Tanis had already been to first base with a boy. She told me how great it had been and that I should really try it myself. I hung on her every word—so far I had only been with my pillow.

During the dance, Richard and his friends led us outside and into the tall yellow grass fields. We all stood in a circle just laughing and smoking. When everyone else began to go back inside, Richard and I snuck off seemingly unnoticed. He held my hand and we giggled as we crouched down to crawl under a large bush that was perfect for providing privacy.

We sat so close to each other that I could feel him breathing in the darkness. He became a silhouette in the moonlight, moving closer and closer. I felt him put his hands on the back of my head to pull me closer. I shuddered when he brushed his fingers across my neck and cupped my cheeks, feeling tingles all down my back. I was soaring with the moment.

Then he stuck his tongue out, aiming for my mouth. I hadn't expected it, and he salivated all over my face. I tried not to show my disgust when I pulled away fast. I wiped the kiss away with my sleeve and broke up with him that same night.

Mellanie was in and out of trouble that summer. She had come home drunk once or twice. Many a time I would be sent to watch television because she and Mom were having an argument.

One hot boring summer night Mellanie asked me if I would let her do my makeup. I obliged. When she was done I was stunned at how much older it made me look. I didn't really like the purple eyeshadow she'd used, but my eyes had a new definition and I liked it. My lips were now pink, which made them appear bigger. I would lose the purple eyeshadow, but from then on I wore a hint of blue eyeliner and pink lipstick every day.

Mellanie gave me her old makeup that she no longer used, and I would spend many mornings that summer hanging out with her. We would sit in her bedroom listening to her stereo and hovering in front of her mirror.

When Mom and Dad had to go out at night they would get Mellanie to stay in to watch Ellena and me. Mellanie objected bitterly. She had a lot of friends and almost never planned to stay in. One night in particular she was especially upset because she would not get to see her boyfriend. She just sat on the couch silently. I felt sorry for her. When I was sure Ellena was asleep I went to Mellanie to tell her to invite her boyfriend over. At first she was wary because she thought I might tell on her, but I promised I would keep it secret and take the blame if we got caught.

Her boyfriend knocked on our door later, and he wasn't alone. He had a friend named Eli Kerban, who got stuck with me in the basement watching television. Mellanie and her boyfriend were upstairs in my room.

Eli sat in the chair next to mine and began to make small talk. He asked me about being in foster care and what it was like to have different parents. It wasn't the usual curiosity I heard in his voice so I answered his questions.

Eli was older by three years and was in high school with Mellanie. He wasn't the most handsome boy I had seen. He had a big nose and acne scars on his round, part-Native face, but he had an encompassing presence that dominated the room. He seemed very sincere and leaned in real close to me while we talked, giving me his full attention.

I must have won Mellanie over that night because she started to introduce me to some of her friends. She even stopped kicking me out of her room when they came over. I met Cora, her best friend. I was privy to their gossip and occasionally included in the giggling.

I was sitting on Mellanie's bed one night chatting with her and Cora when they began to dance to the music on the stereo. I watched in awe as they wiggled their hips in an exotic, almost dirty way, twirling their bodies in a small circle, barely moving their feet. I asked them to show me how they did that.

Mellanie responded by telling me that virgins couldn't dance that way because we didn't know how to move our hips. I decided I would ask her every night until she gave in and at least tried to show me how.

That summer I made it across Alice Lake. My triumph was a letdown. I remember making it across and thinking that until I could make it back I had technically not swum the whole lake. So I began swimming laps along the shore for long periods before starting my swim across the lake. I figured if it took me roughly thirty minutes to go one way then I needed to swim one hour with ease to make it there and back. Once again I did not make the goal I had set for myself before summer ended.

Grade seven would be very different. Mom and I would argue and shout our way through the year. I didn't wash the dishes properly; she didn't listen to me while I was explaining; I didn't talk, I yelled; she put words in my mouth. I called her names and punched walls; she would threaten to call Social Services. Sometimes we were extremely combative, but it almost always ended the same, with me crying hysterically as we sat at the kitchen table. Gradually I would calm down. She would drink coffee and I would drink juice while she listened to me rattle on about my grandparents.

Back then my grandparents were still very important to me. I wasn't sure why they had suddenly taken a massive step back from my life. They called sparingly by then, and I hadn't seen them since that time we went to bingo. It seemed so long ago.

We had a new teacher for grade seven. Her name was Mrs. Rhodin. At first I thought she was mean and nasty, as she made it perfectly clear from the beginning that I would get no special attention because of my "situation." I hadn't asked her for any, but I knew what she meant by "situation," and I was offended. Later, though, the way she always kept a caring and watchful eye on me made it clear she was actually a big softy and had probably given more thought to my "situation" than she would ever admit to.

Tanis was dating a guy from the junior high school named Dolf. We began to hang around his place with his friends, and that's how we came to smoke our first joint. We were sitting on Dolf's roof in the afternoon heat. I was leaning back on my arms with my eyes closed to the sun when I smelled it: a sweet aroma that passed quickly and faded. I really liked it. Tanis was first in line and sucked it like a cigarette. She coughed until her eyes watered.

The guys all started laughing, and Dolf told us that if we didn't cough we weren't going to get off. Tanis held the joint out to me and with little hesitation I reached for it. I sucked slowly and was pleasantly surprised when I didn't cough until I cried. One of the guys whispered that that was a little too dainty for him and I should have a real toke to get the full effect. So obligingly I took another. I was coughing and choking when I passed it on.

We all went in shortly after and I remember hoping no one would talk to me because my mouth was so dry I was sure it wouldn't open. The rest of the afternoon passed by in a blur.

The introduction of the one-dollar coin ("the loonie") had been prosperous for me—I had been stealing change and cigarettes from Mom's purse fairly often by this time and partway through grade seven she caught me stealing some of her cigarettes.

She sent me to my bedroom where I convinced myself that she was going to phone Social Services and get rid of me. I wasn't going to let some social worker come and tell me where to live again.

I packed a bag with my favourite photographs and my notebook of poems I was currently writing, one change of clothes, and a good book. I would take no kitchen knife. In fact I would never hold a weapon of any kind in my hands again. I never wanted to be that close to hurting anybody ever again.

I knew I was making a big mistake. I knew I could get hurt. Briefly, I thought of apologizing to Mom and asking her to give me another chance.

Ignoring the battle of voices in my head I quietly went out the front door and began to run. I ran straight to Tanis's house. I was hunched in Tanis's closet in the dark when her stepdad came in, walked straight to the door, and opened it. He informed me in a clipped voice that my dad was at the door to get me. When I came out I imagine I resembled a deer in the headlights. Tanis and I exchanged glances. I knew her look was meant to encourage me. I quietly grabbed my bag and trudged down the hall and out their front door.

Dad opened his truck door and waited for me to get inside before slamming it shut. Getting in beside me, he said, "We're going to have a talk, Tara Lee. And I don't want any arguments from you. Just listen to what I have to say." It was the first of what would be many such talks. He may not have thought I was listening, as I rarely acted on what he said, but even today I remember those talks and some of the things he said to me.

This being the first one, I remember it well. He started by asking me, "Why do you do such things?" I had no answer for him. "Surely you know, or else you wouldn't do it."

I thought of what had been going on in my head just before I had run away. Still nothing came to mind.

"We want you to be a member of the family, Tara. Just try. We'll meet you halfway. But you have to make the effort."

I just stared at him. He had said that they wanted me to be a member of their family. Mom had said it before, but until that day I had thought that Dad mostly tolerated having foster kids around. Maybe I was wrong—maybe there was something in me, if these people really wanted me around.

I felt much better by the time Dad pulled into the driveway. Mom didn't say much when I apologized to her. She told me I would pay for the cigarettes out of my allowance and to please not do it again.

For some time we would coast along and things would go well, but it would always begin with a small argument that would escalate to both of us shouting and her reminding me that a new home was a phone call away. But we had a strange relationship, she and I: despite the turmoil, neither of us ever really questioned how much we meant to each other.

Tanis figured out how we could buy cigarettes at the local general store. Our parents would sometimes send us with money and a note stating that we could buy one package that was being purchased for them. If we kept those notes our parents had written, we could use them later to buy our own packs. We were on our way to the store one day when Tanis realized she had left her mother's note on her dresser.

I volunteered to go into the store instead. I told the clerk that I wanted to purchase a package of cigarettes for my mother and that I had lost the note that said it was okay somewhere between our house and the store.

The clerk asked for me to just give him a second. He picked up the phone from behind the counter, dialled, and said, "Deanna, how are you dear?" Living in a small town definitely had its pitfalls.

It wasn't long though before Tanis moved away. She went to live in with her dad somewhere in Vancouver. I didn't see her again after that. My mother would ask her mom about her but she really didn't tell us much. I told myself to add Tanis's name to my mental roster of goodbyes and move on. No one was forever.

Joe joined our class about halfway through the year. He and I became fast friends when I learned that he too was in foster care. There was a few of us who always hung out. We could usually be found exploring this big area of brush behind our cul-de-sac. The cracked pavement of abandoned roads that wound through the area were giving way to bushes. I asked Mom once why it was like that and I think she said something to the effect that the area had once been a trailer park.

I was hurting myself more often at night by this time. There was a new brutality in my eyes when I looked in the mirror. If I looked long enough I couldn't see myself at all. I would lose myself behind my skin and all I saw was the blackness of my eyes. I would wait for the nothingness to steal me away forever, never to find my way out.

I would take off my underwear and attack my body with things I found around my room. I even used a small pair of scissors once. I was disappointed that they didn't destroy my body or cause me any memorable pain, just humiliation. Sometimes I would cry helplessly and pray that someone would catch me and lock me away where I was sure I belonged.

I would only stop when I bled and then I would look in the mirror and remind myself that I deserved it. Later I would shrink into myself wishing I wasn't me, knowing there was definitely something perversely wrong with me.

I was caught shoplifting again that year. I stole a package of cigarettes from Shoppers Drug Mart. When Mom asked me why I did it, I told her it was because I couldn't buy them. She bought me the odd pack now and then after that, I think because she was hoping that would keep me out of trouble. It did—that kind of trouble, anyway. But I could always find new trouble to get into.

In court I shook visibly when the judge told me that stealing was a crime and that I was to be on probation for six months. He gave me a curfew of 10 p.m. I was to be in good standing in my foster home, and not to obey would put me in breach of probation, which was a whole new charge that would mean I'd have to stand before him again.

For a while I did obey.

 # Chapter 3

S CHOOL WAS OUT FOR the summer and Joe and I spent our days together, until Joe began dating a girl from school named Ashley.

For the first time I realized that I had more feelings for Joe than I had previously admitted. I was lost when Joe wasn't around, and I found myself plotting to break him and Ashley up.

One day Ashley and I were alone in her garage talking about Joe. I took the opportunity to imply that Joe had a crush on someone we both knew. Ashley was heartbroken by what I said, and they broke up that same afternoon.

It didn't take long for Ashley to suspect that I had lied to her. She never told Joe but her eyes reflected genuine hurt when I looked at her. It startled me to realize that she had been my friend as well.

Then, one simmering afternoon, Joe kissed me.

He and I were at the sand flats by the river trying to escape the torture of the sun. The river was roaring meters away from where we were seated. We had found a small pool of still water about waist deep. We were sitting on a branch that jutted out over the pool, our toes dangling in the cool water underneath.

Joe and I were giggling over something he had just said when he became uncharacteristically pensive. He took my hands in his and said he was going to kiss me. He said it so casually I almost laughed, but I heard the hesitation in his voice and said nothing.

He brought my hands up to his chest and close to his heart as he leaned closer to me—so close that I could taste his breath. Then he paused and looked straight into my eyes. I didn't even dare breathe, I was so afraid of breaking the spell. Then Joe grazed my lips with his and pulled away. When I opened my eyes he leaned in and kissed me again. This kiss was deeper and longer than the first. Gentle and soft, his lips felt like silk brushing across my cheek as they left my slightly open mouth.

Later, when I was riding my bike home I decided I was going to remember that kiss with Joe as my first kiss.

Joe came over one morning after he had a fight with his foster parents. They had threatened to call Social Services and have them move Joe out.

Joe explained that he was going to run away because he wasn't going to let *them* move him again. In the next breath he asked me to go with him. I was momentarily speechless. Things were okay with Mom and me, and I hadn't thought about running away in some time. Yet I knew that I would go. I wasn't going to let Joe down when he needed me.

I told him we could go to California, either to my grandparents' house or to Amber's. He was excited at the idea and we made a plan to meet at the end of my driveway at 3 a.m.

Later that night I picked a fight with my mother. I was good at pushing her buttons, and that night I was on a mission.

It was quarter to three in the morning when I tiptoed down the hall to the kitchen and found Mom's purse sitting by the microwave where I had known it would be. I slipped out two twenties and silently apologized. Then I made my way back to my bedroom.

I reached behind my dresser, removed my already packed bag, and went to my bedroom window. Joe was already waiting for me in the driveway. He motioned for me to hurry up. I opened my window and threw my bag down to him before positioning myself to drop down feet first.

I hadn't realized how precarious it would feel hanging from the second-floor window. I found myself hanging onto the window ledge by my hands with my feet dangling in the air. I was waiting to get up the nerve to let go. When I finally did, it was more because my hands hurt than from a conscious decision to jump. Laughing, we made our way down the road. We were one day away from an experience that would change both our lives forever.

After hitchhiking into downtown Vancouver we took the SkyTrain to Surrey, a suburb about 40 minutes southeast of the city. It was the second time I had taken the SkyTrain. The first time had been at Expo 86 with Mom and Dad. I pushed the memory from my mind and concentrated on the motion of the train.

I stared out the window as the train glided past normal peoples' houses in perfect rows, and wondered who lived in them.

Joe was taking me to meet his real father. We were both nervous and there were long lapses in our conversation when we were lost in thought. Joe had told me very little about his father. I knew Joe missed living with him a lot and that he loved him. I could hear the longing in his voice and see the admiration in his eyes when he talked about him.

Joe and I took the train to the very last stop and headed for a parking lot at the bottom of some stairs. His father was waiting for us in a beat-up green Chrysler. He was a tall thin man with a strong acrid odour coming through his pores. Later I would recognize that as the smell of alcoholism.

He was a little gullible too. We told him we were going to a concert in Seattle and that neither of our foster parents had agreed to take us, so we had to make our own way there. He gave Joe some money and told us we could get a good night's sleep at his place.

After we ate dinner I excused myself to the bedroom Joe's father had said was ours for the night. I wanted to give Joe some time alone with his dad. I fell asleep listening to him tell his father how great everything was.

Morning came and after a good breakfast of bacon and eggs we said our goodbyes. Joe was very quiet. I just held his hand as we made our way to the bus stop.

We continued on to Aldergrove, BC, where Joe said we had to find a trucker willing to hide us in the back so we could get across the border. It had occurred to me that sneaking two kids across the border couldn't be legal. However, Joe's confidence in this plan paid off and soon we were both hiding under blankets in the cab of a truck as the driver made his way across the border. My heart was beating so hard I was sure the customs officer would hear it.

Dusk was turning into night when we parked in Bellingham for burgers and fries at a roadside café. During dinner the trucker talked to us about his family, and what it was like leaving them for so long while he was on the road. He said the money was good, though, and that Joe should consider driving a truck for living if he aimed to be a travelling man.

The conversation turned to his children and the driver's whole face lit up.

Then he threw some money on the table and shook each of our hands goodbye. We mumbled our thanks for the ride, and he paid his bill and left.

Joe paid for our share of the bill with the money he'd left us and we made our exit soon after. Outside, I was surprised to find that it had started to rain.

In the dark, in the rain, walking along the side of the road, I was overcome with a feeling of dread. Ignoring it, I stuck my thumb out and prayed that a ride would come quickly.

Joe was tired and it showed as we trudged towards the distant highway on-ramp. His head hung low and his eyes were puffy and red. I told him that next time we got picked up he was to ride in the back and get some sleep; I would keep watch over the road and us. I was tired too but I had this prickling feeling in my stomach—I felt nervous and on edge. I couldn't have slept even if he had taken watch instead of me.

We still hadn't managed a ride when we reached the on-ramp for the highway. I could feel the darkness moving in, surrounding us. The rain coming down in sheets made the atmosphere even more ominous. We were soaked. I remember thinking that I would have to take my jacket off before getting into a car; I was that wet.

Lights came down the road and continued to move past us. Time passed with them.

Joe and I decided that we might have better luck getting a ride if we headed up the ramp to the highway. A sign ahead was illuminated with each passing car and when we were able to piece together what it said we were overcome with laughter: PICKING UP HITCHIKERS PROHIBITED BY LAW.

The sound of a horn beeping caught our attention. We were relieved to see a car had finally pulled over for us. We quickly gathered our bags and ran to the little yellow two-seater hatchback that had pulled over.

A large, Egyptian-looking man leaned over and told Joe to go ahead and hop into the hatchback area with the bags, and to hurry as we were only getting wetter. I threw the bags at Joe once he was in and remembered to remove my jacket before I sat down in the front seat.

The man introduced himself as John Moralice. He said he lived in Seattle and that he was going home, and could take us that far. Joe and I told John we were going to the imaginary concert in Seattle. "We really appreciate the ride, sir," Joe added.

After a while John and I were the only ones talking as we drove through the night. I realized Joe had fallen asleep in the back.

We could see the lights of Seattle when John pulled into a gas station.

He asked me if I wanted something from the store and I asked for a Coke. He came back with sandwiches, cigarettes, chips, and Coke for both Joe and me. We didn't wake Joe to give them to him; he was snoring quietly in the back and even drooling a little.

"Where are you going to drop us off?" I asked John. That was when his demeanour changed.

He pulled the car over and turned in his seat so he could look fully at me. He looked angry. He said he knew that we were runaways and that he had seen this before. He reached past me and opened his glovebox, showing me what was inside. He took out a gun, and a wallet that had a badge in it. He said he was a police officer and that he was going to take me for a drive to show me something.

I couldn't move. In my head I was yelling at myself because now that he mentioned it he did look like a police officer—he was clean-cut and dressed in a suit. No tie though.

I sat and stared out the window as we got closer and closer to those city lights. The sparkle of the city was suddenly gone to my eyes, and as we headed into a less savoury area all I saw was sadness and despair.

"You wanna know what happens to little girls like you?" John shouted. "Just look out the window: they grow up to become whores!"

I felt my eyes welling up and knew that I was going to break down if he didn't stop yelling at me. I tried taking a deep breath but I was scared and my breathing was shaky and uneven. I wondered if he was taking us to the police station where he worked. I decided that he must work this area because of how angry he seemed to be.

We drove those blocks for what was probably only a short time, but it seemed like an eternity as John raved about where Joe and I were headed if we kept the same attitude that we had. By the time he stopped talking I was almost wailing. I had both my hands over my head covering my ears as if I could block his voice with my arms.

Then just as quickly as he had gotten angry he became very tender and caring. He reached across the seat to stroke my hair and told me to stop crying. He said that it hadn't happened to Joe and me, yet. He added that he could help us if I let him.

Grateful that he had calmed himself down and didn't appear to be as agitated as he had been, I almost begged him. "Yes—please help us!"

While all this was going on Joe was still snoring quietly in the back, undisturbed by the drama taking place in the front seat.

I listened and nodded as John devised a plan for what to do with Joe and me for the night. He said his wife would have a fit if he just showed up with two runaway kids; he needed to explain things to her first. He drove silently for a few minutes before saying that he would pay for a hotel room for both of us, then come back the next morning and take us to his house.

I tried to hold still while I snaked my right arm between my seat and the door, frantically trying to reach Joe's hand. I needed to wake him up. A voice in my head was screaming that something wasn't right with the situation. It felt like time was running out. And it did, because right then we arrived at our destination. John pulled the car into the parking lot of a dark, one-level motel.

When he stopped the engine I thought that Joe would wake up for sure. He didn't even shift position.

John turned to me and said that I needed to go with him to get the room and that I was not to say anything to the night manager. John would do all the talking and pay for the room.

It was very late and we had to ring the night bell to wake the manager. As we stood and waited for someone to come to the door, John grabbed my hand and pulled me in close to him and held my elbows, forcing me to hug him too. I could feel his hot breath against the back of my neck he was so close. It made me really uncomfortable but I was too afraid to pull away from him.

I tried to peek past him to see if there was any movement from the car. There wasn't.

The manager came and John pushed me in behind himself, concealing me. I didn't even really get a glance at the guy. John turned to me when he had the key. He said we should go into the room and take a look around before we got Joe up, just in case.

In case what? I wondered.

I let him take me by the arm to the room.

When we got inside, I was excited there was a television. I knew Joe would like that. Turning it on, I found the music channel and cranked up the volume so the music filled the room. I looked around and realized there was nowhere to sit but on the bed.

I looked up at John and saw that he looked angry again. He said for me to sit on the bed and that he wouldn't harm me.

I sat.

Then he asked, "Are you still a virgin?"

My blood suddenly charged and I felt light-headed. This whole thing was wrong.

I didn't dare not answer him. I forced a muffled yes from my throat.

I knew that I had made a mistake in trusting this man and that he was going to hurt me. I just didn't know how much.

"I like virgins most because of their tight pussies," he replied. "Did you know that virgins have tight pussies?"

His words were so harsh and vulgar that I was rendered powerless with shame. My mouth would no longer open.

I rose and began trying to ease my way towards the door. He grabbed my wrist, and with his other hand grabbed my face and forced me to look at him.

He reminded me that he had a gun in the glovebox and Joe in the back seat of his car. He pointed out that I would not be able to get Joe out of the car faster than he could get to his gun.

Then he began to rub my bum and felt all over my chest. I threw my head back and cried. He told me to stop crying; that he was doing me a favour. He brought his lips to my ear and whispered that it was only going to hurt a little, which only made me cry harder.

Then he told me to take off my pants.

With tears streaming down my face and snot running from my nose I began to fumble with the button on my jeans. He lowered his gaze and glowered at me. "Just pretend you're getting ready for the shower," he ordered.

This sent me into hysterics and I couldn't see through the endless curtain of my tears. I knew I wasn't getting ready for the shower. I knew what was really about to happen and yet I couldn't get my head around it. I couldn't focus; my heart was beating too fast, too loudly, and it took all my concentration to stay on my feet.

Then he said for me not to think about my friend in the car who was depending on me to keep him in a good mood. I knew Joe was trapped and in real trouble, just like me.

What if John did take Joe away?

I managed to get my jeans off and was standing there in my shirt and underwear when he sat down on the bed, grabbed me, and pulled me onto his lap. He began to touch me everywhere.

I could feel his hardness through his pants and my underwear. I was suddenly overcome with the urge to vomit but somehow I managed to hold back.

I listened to him grunt and groan as he took off the rest of my clothes, and struggled to keep my legs together in one more valiant effort to make it stop happening.

I tried to lose myself in Edie Brickell & New Bohemians on TV as they sang their way through "What I Am." It didn't work.

I cried hysterically while he split my body in two. I prayed for it to be over. I remember begging for somebody, anybody to please hear my mumbled pleas. He looked at me with disgust and snarled that I was no virgin.

When he was done he crawled off me and reached for his shirt. I just lay there naked, feeling broken and raw.

He kept talking while he dressed. "Sluts who aren't virgins only get what's owed to them," he said in a clipped tone of voice. I turned over, managing to cover my backside with a pillow, and hid behind my long hair and cried.

Moments later I heard the door close. I leaped from the bed and ran to the washroom. I threw up immediately, nearly missing the toilet. I couldn't stop retching. I don't know how much time had passed when I finally managed to crawl over to the bed. I stopped short of climbing onto it and instead hovered on the floor beside it, hugging myself, unable to stop writhing with disgust and despair. I didn't even think about what was happening with Joe.

I don't know how much time passed before Joe came through the door with our bags. When he saw me on the floor he dropped the bags and ran to me. I was so embarrassed; I didn't want him to see me naked and on the floor like I was. But I couldn't pull myself together.

I kept hearing John saying, "You're no virgin." I thought about all those nights that I had lain awake and tortured my body. He must have seen it in me. He must have seen the perverseness in me.

Stunned and hysterical as I was, Joe managed to get me into the shower. When he saw that I was starting to bruise between my legs, he turned from me in what I interpreted as disgust and left the washroom. I finished my shower and tried to pull myself together as best I could.

I thought of my mother and of how I had picked a fight with her on purpose. This brought on a new wave of tears and once again I had to wash my face. When I came out of the bathroom Joe turned to me with a handful of US bills. He said he had found the money on the dresser. John must have left it there.

Shame and humiliation coursed through my veins when I remembered how he had said, "Sluts who aren't virgins only get what's coming to them." Suddenly I couldn't let Joe see my face. I just curled up on the other side of the bed from where I'd been lying before and closed my eyes.

Morning came. Surprisingly, I had managed to sleep. Joe was already awake—I could hear him in the shower. Thankfully he had not touched me since helping me into the shower the night before, and I hoped he wouldn't.

I quickly put on my jeans and grabbed a new shirt from my bag. I was ready with my jacket on when he came out also dressed and ready. We grabbed breakfast at a small roadside café. My thighs ached when I sat down at the table, a brutal reminder of the previous night's events. Joe asked me if I wanted to go to the police. "To tell them what?" I said numbly.

So we continued on. I remember thinking that nothing could be worse than what had already happened.

We arrived in Portland, Oregon, just after midnight. It had rained all day and Joe and I were exhausted, wet, and miserable.

We found shelter by crawling and shoving our way into a large bush. For the first time that day I let Joe wrap his arms and legs around me. I understood that it was for warmth but it made me feel trapped. I surprised us both when I burst into tears. Joe put his head against my back and I knew that he was crying too.

In the earliest hours of the morning we made the decision to go home. We told each other it was because the bitter cold from the ground had made it impossible to sleep and we desperately needed showers to warm our bones. In truth we both knew that it was more than the cold making us long for home.

We went to a small business and waited until someone showed up to open for the day. Joe made a few phone calls, and it didn't take long for the police to arrive. By early afternoon Joe and I had been taken to a Portland group home and given beds for an overnight stay.

I was in the living room curled up on the couch with a book when I heard someone calling my name. I looked up to see a woman standing in the hallway motioning for me to follow her. I knew she was a staff member. Her grim expression unsettled me. She led me to an office where another staff member was sitting with Joe.

All at once I knew that Joe had told them what had happened at the motel.

I couldn't speak. I tried to stare Joe down but he wouldn't even look at me. I felt so betrayed. It had been *my* secret to tell; it had happened to me, not to him. I pulled my gaze from Joe and looked at the other faces in the room. Now everyone would know my shame. I didn't understand why Joe would tell on me.

One of the staff members sat with me when the police came and took my statement. Then I was taken to the hospital where I was made naked and exposed again.

Before we left a staff member pulled me aside and said that Joe was also very affected by what had happened. She said that Joe had needed to talk about it and that they were obligated to report all crimes involving children. I was surprised that she referred to what had happened to me as a crime. It must have shown on my face because she continued, "Rape is a crime, you know, and so is impersonating a police officer."

The word "rape" sounded foreign to me. I hadn't even thought of the possibility that John was not really a police officer at all. I took off my own pants, I thought.

Joe and I were returned to Canada the next day, where we were separated because they couldn't get a group home with two beds. We had to wait for them to make arrangements for us to be taken back to Squamish.

After being so close to someone who knew so much about what had happened to me, I was thankful for some time alone. Night came and then morning. After a subdued breakfast I caught a bus to Squamish.

That night, sitting at the kitchen table with Mom, she told me of the plans for our family vacation. Dad had just bought a new truck and we were going to break it in with a long drive to Michigan.

We would be staying with Mom's dad, who lived in Luddington, just a few blocks from the beach on Lake Michigan. I felt a twinge of excitement when I thought of spending my days lounging by the water of the Great Lake.

Mom stressed that they couldn't take me if they had to worry about me running away. In a low voice I assured her that I was not a flight risk, repeating what I had heard the social workers say the night before.

Mom put her coffee cup down and placed her hand gently over mine.

"Is there anything else you'd like to talk about, Tara Lee?"

I knew she was asking if I needed to talk about that night in Seattle. I couldn't bring myself to repeat those horrible ugly words that replayed over and over in my head. My eyes never meeting hers, I shook my head no, and, keeping my head down, walked out of the kitchen, seeking the solitude of my bedroom.

Mellanie and Ellena were naturally curious about my travels but Mom must have said something to them because they asked very little about my trip. I told them about meeting Joe's dad and having lunch with the truck driver but revealed nothing after Bellingham.

By running away I had breached my probation, and so I had to appear in youth court on that charge. I received a stern talking-to from the judge, but apart from that I remember very little of this visit to court. Maybe it was just overshadowed by the more traumatic events around that time.

Joe and I stayed friends but it was never the same again. We were no longer united. I had changed. Something deep inside me was now untouchable. Something unique and beautiful was now hidden deep within my soul, and it would be a long time before I would even know it was still there.

Not long after my court date, we pulled out of our driveway, setting off on our journey to Michigan—farther than I had travelled in a long time. I smiled to myself at the thought that if I had stayed on the road with Joe perhaps we could have met my family there.

We drove and camped, and drove and camped some more. We stopped everywhere along the way—we visited Mount Rushmore; we went to Yellowstone; we stopped for ice cream in Detroit, and drove through fingers coming down from the sky. Later I would learn they had been tornadoes, but it was amazing. I really loved being on the road. I was scared to sleep in the back for fear of missing something. Maybe I needed to consider becoming a truck driver.

Our stay in Michigan left me with many happy memories. I eased back into being a young teenager, and once again started to look at boys. But Mom and I began to argue again when we arrived in Michigan. We tried to stifle our harsh words when we were around others but I could tell that her family could see it wasn't easy to raise foster kids.

I became friends with my cousins Amy and Heather, my mom's sister's daughters. One night I accompanied them to a movie, and they introduced to me a boy from their school. I sat in the back of the theatre with him and let him touch me under my shirt. His hands felt foreign and my body felt detached, but getting him excited made me feel powerful. I knew that people could see what we were doing, and I met the eyes that turned our way with defiance. Amy and Heather were embarrassed for me—or maybe by me. They didn't take me out with them anymore after that.

We spent a lot of time on the beach on Lake Michigan. Dad tried to teach us how to bodysurf. Mellanie got it right away, but the first time I tried, a mighty wave caught me and slammed me into the sandy bottom, scraping the skin from my cheek like sandpaper. After that I just watched from the shore. Dad was especially fun to watch. He would disappear in the waves and come back up laughing. It felt good to see him having such a good time.

Mellanie told me she had heard Mom and Dad talk of Disneyland. No wonder Mom had been so worried about me trying to run away; they were taking me where I most wanted to go.

Surrounded in hugs and drenched in kisses, we had a tearful goodbye with our relatives on the morning we left Michigan. By then we had been told of the Disneyland plan, and everyone was excited. Once again we drove and camped, eventually arriving in Anaheim.

We found a campground, and Mellanie and I helped set up the tent and site. Then the two of us headed straight to the pool.

We hadn't been swimming long before two guys around our ages approached us. One of them asked if they could hang out with us, and explained they were there on vacation from Colorado. The one doing the talking was Nick; he was older than Mellanie by almost two years, and his younger brother was Shane. Nick was quiet and laid-back. He had a tall, muscular, athletic build, blond hair, and bright blue eyes. Shane was like his older brother but his smile was warmer and more inviting. His hair was cut rougher than his brother's and was a darker shade of blond. He had a clear complexion with a hint of shadowing facial hair just under his nose. His eyes were also blue, glinting with mischievous shades of grey in different light. Mellanie and I stayed at the pool with them until long past sunset. Mom was forced to come and get us.

Mellanie had made plans for us to sneak out of our tents and meet up with them when our parents went to bed. When she told me about the arrangements I readily agreed.

Later that night when Mom and Dad's tent had fallen silent we crept out of ours and ran to meet Nick and Shane back by the pool. Nick and Mellanie went off somewhere by themselves, leaving Shane and me to talk. We sat with our feet dangling in the pool and talked until the early morning. When the sun started to come up I was disappointed to have to return to our tent. I walked Shane back to his tent first and was surprised to find Mellanie and Nick in Nick's sleeping bag, naked. Shane and I waited outside the tent for Mellanie to come out.

Back in our tent, Mellanie and I quietly whispered about how in love we both were. By the time our parents got up she and I were planning her wedding in Colorado.

Mellanie and I were allowed to go off together in Disneyland for the day. Excited and voracious for experience, we explored everywhere. We went on the rides, looked in the stores, and took in the parade. It made for a very long day.

Nick and Shane were still there when we got back to camp, and we were happy to hear they'd be there for one more night.

Once again when silence fell Mellanie and I crawled out of our tents and went to meet the boys. Mellanie and Nick went off to do their own thing. Shane and I talked on into the night again. This time, though, I told him about what had happened to me in Seattle. He was very kind. He just listened to me talk and work it all out in my mind, and then he just hugged me. He never tried to reach through my shirt or anything. I liked him even more after that.

Before we went our separate ways that night we exchanged phone numbers and promised to keep in touch, vowing we would never forget each other and would love each other forever. Walking backwards, we waved our last farewell.

When Mellanie and I returned to our tent, Mom was up and making coffee for herself and Dad. Very little was said but we knew we were in for it eventually. It was obvious we had been gone all night, and I'm sure Mom knew where we had been.

Sadly, when Mellanie and I got back to the site that night Nick and Shane's campsite housed completely different people. Mellanie and I spent a quiet evening by the pool, both of us staring off into space, lost in our own thoughts.

A day or so later we were all piled into the truck for the drive back up the coast. We had one final stop to make in Seattle, to visit Mom's niece, June, and her husband, Mick.

Mom and I argued all the way up there. She was angry about the night we had snuck out, and I was angry that she didn't understand. I retaliated by doing nothing to help along the way and by replying with sarcasm and snippy remarks when I had to respond to anything she said. I could tell she was losing patience but I kept pushing.

We had been visiting with June and Mick for two days when Mom and Dad began to pack up Mellanie and Ellena's stuff. Mom explained to me that they thought since June and I seemed to get on so well, maybe I would like to stay with them for an extra week. They would arrange for me to come home on the bus later if I would like to stay. I jumped at the chance. It would be fun.

I spent most of the week riding around the mud flats on their ATV and getting to know the boy next door. Soon enough, though, conflict arose between me and June.

I had broken their ATV by putting a stick in the gas tank to check how much gas was left. I dropped it and lost it in the tank.

Worse still, the boy next door's parents caught me necking with him in their shed, and they confronted June about it.

So my home going was a shameful, nerve-wracking journey. I wondered what to expect from my parents when they picked me up from the bus.

When I arrived home, though, little was said.

I think I somehow ruined the relationship my mother had had with her niece. I know that my mother didn't talk to her that often after my return, and that that made her sad.

I was extra well behaved for the next while, but as we know nothing lasts forever.

 # Chapter 4

M ONTHS HAD PASSED SINCE Joe and I had run away, and I still hadn't spoken with any of the adults in my life about what had happened to me on that trip. Mom was especially concerned, and my visits with Edna Cimpini became more frequent.

One afternoon, with a large plate of french fries between us, I startled us both with a sudden outburst of tears.

I had been staring at the globs of ketchup drenching the fries. I had been wondering which fries were the luckiest. The ones drowning in ketchup, or the lone and untouched fries with nothing to do except wait to be eaten as if they had never existed?

Edna reached across the table and placed her hand over mine. I heard her whisper quietly that it was good for me to cry and that I would feel better if I talked to her and told her what happened. That made me angry and I began to pull back into myself again.

I told myself that crying made me look weak. A few tears falling would never change who I was, where I had come from, or where I was going. I took the Kleenex Edna offered and dried my eyes. *Don't ever let anyone see that again.*

I stuck out my chin and stared evenly at Edna. She looked me over and opened her mouth as if to say something. Instead she reached into her wallet to get the money for the uneaten french fries.

Around this time I bought my first bottle of Nytol. It was not an easy purchase to make because the pharmacist kept the bottles behind the counter, forcing customers to ask for it. I was nervous—I knew I was being deceptive. I told myself it was none of the pharmacist's business why I was buying it, and met her eyes when she looked me over. I left the store with the bottle in hand and a smile on my lips.

It became my most prized possession, my secret. A silent weapon I kept hidden high in my closet. I envisioned going to bed early one night, arranging myself peacefully, closing my eyes, and waiting for the Sandman to put me to sleep and the Angel of Death to take me away.

I started junior high school that year. I was both excited and scared. It was a relief to leave my elementary years behind. I hoped junior high would be different. I imagined new friends who didn't know about me and hadn't already decided that I was different from them; a class that didn't start off with the teacher giving me a warning at the beginning of the year.

When the first day of grade eight came, though, I was completely unprepared for the change in how things worked. We had schedules and different teachers for every subject, and we spent a good part of the day wandering the halls from class to class.

I met Jana Cavans that first day. She was dressed in a long brown skirt and a baggy green sweatshirt. She looked a little frumpy and had a large build, but she had a beautiful fresh face—Noxzema could have used her face for its ads. She was sitting on the floor in the hallway among all the chaos of everyone trying to figure out where their lockers were, where their homeroom was, and how to get to where they were supposed to be now.

Jana started talking to me first, and I found myself joining her on the floor and watching everyone panic around us. We met up after school that first day and walked home together.

Jana lived just down the road from me and I was surprised that I hadn't seen her around, but my family had had a very busy summer and when I had been home I had spent most of my time grounded.

I was already sleeping late and ignoring my mom's orders to get up and go to school. It didn't take long for me and Jana to skip our first class together, and eventually we were skipping whole days of school. We would go back to her house because no one was there. Her mother worked outside the home, so the house was ours during the day.

I had started writing poems about suicide, and Mom found them. I could tell that it scared her but I was unable to talk to her about it. She turned the poems over to Edna Cimpini, who told me that if they thought I was suicidal they would have to place me into a treatment centre for troubled youth. I retorted that it was my private poetry and that I hadn't been the one to share it with her in the first place. Her words reinforced my decision to never tell her what I did to myself at night. If they would send me away for poetry, they would definitely send me away—maybe for longer—if they knew how disgusting I was at night.

Jana and her mother had a volatile relationship as well, and her mother didn't like me. I was not a good influence: I fuelled Jana's rebelliousness.

One afternoon, Jana and I found the key to her mother's liquor cabinet and helped ourselves. Her mother came home from work one day to find both of us drunk and giggling our way through *Charles in Charge* on TV.

Her mom yelled for me to leave her home and warned me that she would be in touch with my parents that night.

Jana and her mother must have had an exceptionally bitter argument because Jana came over in the morning and said that we needed to talk on the way to school. When Jana realized things weren't going much better at my house she decided to wait for me outside.

My own mom had spent a few hours on the phone with Jana's mother the night before, and in the morning we had argued over the incident ourselves. She said that she was going to be left with little choice but to call my probation officer and report that things were not going well.

"Go ahead and make the call then," I challenged. "We both know they won't do anything to me."

I left, slamming the door behind me, and crossed the road to where Jana was waiting for me. We headed off into the woods, silently agreeing that there was no reason for us to go to school when everyone was already so mad at us. And we couldn't go to her house anymore because her mother, now wise to us, had locked Jana out for the day.

Jana and I sat in the forest and listened to the silence for some time before she spoke. "I heard you ran away with Joe. Were you scared?"

"No, not really," I said, but my heart was beating faster and I realized I was holding my breath. I knew she didn't know what had happened in Seattle. Joe had his own reasons for keeping his silence, aside from his loyalty to me. He would never tell anyone about that night.

Joe and I avoided each other so we didn't even have to do the customary nod in the halls at school. It was strange: we didn't talk to each other, yet I found it comforting to know he was there. A few people who were curious about what had happened between us told me he had asked after me. They knew that for a long time we had been inseparable.

Jana wasn't one of them. Even as the rumours had occasionally passed her way she had never asked me about Joe. She never allowed her own curiosity to surface about anything that I didn't want to share with her.

There we sat in the forest with not a cloud in the sky. We could see our breath in the crisp morning air as we talked. Jana brought up her pen pal, a boy who lived in a small town in Alberta. They had been writing to each other for over a year and had become very close through their letters, and she wanted to meet him.

In the end once again a friend was asking me to run away with them. Even before Jana asked I knew that I would go. I didn't care where we went. For me it was about the adventure.

I don't know why it always had to be three in the morning, but again I found myself sneaking out my window and jumping to the ground at that wee hour.

Jana was waiting for me at the end of the road, sitting on the curb when I came running down the street. Together we made our way to the highway, destination: Alberta.

Getting into cars with strangers now had an aura of danger that was almost inviting. I was nervous but keenly aware. This time I was prepared. I told myself that I would fight if we ever met anyone again who was like John Moralice. This time no one was going to slip into the trunk or the back seat of any two-door cars. This time there would be four doors on all the cars that we climbed into.

Jana didn't ask me why or try to change my mind. She just pulled her thumb back for vans and waved off people who pulled over with two-door cars.

It rained a lot that first day on the road. Jana and I were fairly lucky, though, and got picked up quickly.

That night we met a woman who lived with her two sons in a large log cabin. When she had pulled her car over she had looked us over and told us that she had a hot meal waiting for us at her cabin. I'm sure she knew we were runaways and felt sorry for us. She took us to her cabin and let us sleep in a spare room. In the morning she made us pancakes and bacon; then drove us back to the highway once we had eaten. Jana and I never did meet her two boys but we saw photos of them on her walls. They looked like a nice family.

Later the same day, Jana and I went to grab a coffee at a roadside café. We started talking to two men who introduced themselves as Frank and Jeff. Frank was tall, slender, and blue-eyed while Jeff had a smaller frame and a darker complexion. They were both significantly older than us.

Frank explained that they were working on a freight train that was going in the same direction we were heading. They offered to let us ride along if we agreed to sneak onto the train since they weren't supposed to have any ride-alongs in their room.

Once on the train, the men hurriedly ushered us into their room. They explained that they had to work for twenty minutes but would come back as soon as they could.

The room they left us in was no bigger than a broom closet. It had space enough for two bunks and the men's bags, and that was it. Jana and I sat on one of the beds and listened as the train started moving.

For a moment we acknowledged that maybe getting on a train with two strange men was not the wisest thing we could have done. We quickly talked each other out of our misgivings, though.

They came back with a bottle of vodka, sat down on the opposite bunk, and offered us a drink. We gladly accepted. Before too long Jeff and I traded places. Jana and I were laughing at jokes and falling back onto the beds periodically in our drunken stupor, but we were having fun. More time passed and we were no longer laughing as we found ourselves kissing the strange men and letting them kiss us everywhere. At some point I looked over and saw that Jana had her pants down and was lying back on the bed with her eyes closed, moaning. Jeff had his hands down her pants; her shirt was open and his head was bowed to her chest.

It wasn't long before my own shirt was splayed open. I didn't react when Frank undid my pants. I felt his hands sliding down past my stomach, and I made no protest when he pulled my pants down.

I felt sick afterwards and I knew it was more than the alcohol that was making me queasy.

When Jana and I got off the train we were still drunk and tipsy, laughing at everything, and disoriented.

We made our way to a road that looked busier than the rest and began to hitchhike again.

Finally we arrived in her pen pal's hometown and found a pay phone. Jana began to make calls, trying to contact him. Only at that point did she tell me his name was Stuart. I know the town was named after a river that ran through it, but its name eludes me. It was the smallest, quietest town I'd ever been in: the school was in a house, and the daycare attached to it was also a church. The pay phone we were using was the only one in town; it was in a grocery store that doubled as a gas station. No cars lined any of the dirt roads and the only sound was the distant whoosh of traffic on the highway.

Before long we were climbing into the back of a station wagon. The only person in the car was Stuart's sister, Stella. While she drove she lit a joint and offered us a toke, which we gladly accepted. She explained that Stuart was having a shower because he had only just arrived home from work when Jana had called.

It wasn't far to their tiny cottage-like home. We climbed out of the car with our bags and followed Stella inside.

Stuart turned out to be very hard to read. I couldn't tell if he was happy to see Jana or not. I didn't find him very good-looking or very friendly. He seemed to radiate this aura that said don't talk to me. He was tall and very clean-looking. Not clean-cut-looking; just clean, as if he had scrubbed his whole body with a floor brush. Jana spent a lot of time trying to please him. I didn't see much of her during the two days we spent at Stuart and Stella's.

I went to a lakeside party that first night with Stella where I spent most of my time separate from the crowd that had gathered. They had built a large fire not far from a marshy lake. The lake didn't appear suitable for swimming; however, it was hospitable to a large array of bugs. Mud wasps buzzed along the shoreline and blackflies flew around me, mostly unnoticed until they bit my scalp, taking chunks from my head.

Eventually I found a picnic bench where I could hide from both the flies and the curious who wanted to know more about the young runaway from "the city." I found it amusing that to people in that town, Squamish was a city.

After a few days at Stuart's spent watching soap operas and game shows mixed with smoking the occasional cigarette outside, Jana came to me and said that we needed to head back to Squamish. That afternoon we said goodbye, thanked everyone for having us, and left.

Hitchhiking home was less eventful and not any fun at all. We got rained on again. It felt rather fitting considering that we still had to face our parents when we did get home.

Back home, Mom said nothing to me the first night. She watched me walk down the hall to my room, where I immediately climbed into bed. I slept deeply for what felt like days. The following morning Mom informed me that my probation officer had been notified of the recent events and that there would be consequences to what Jana and I had done.

I talked to my probation officer that afternoon. He told me there was a warrant for my arrest and urged me to turn myself in to the police station on my own. He advised me that it would look better in court the next day.

Later that evening I did just that. The police gave me a small cell for the night. I lay on the wire cot and listened to the clanging of the bars and the occasional squawking of a police radio.

There were messages on the walls from previous cell occupants who had managed to get a pen or pencil past the searches. Most of the messages were derogatory comments targeting the police; otherwise the graffiti mimicked that in most public washrooms.

I thought about the criminals before me who had occupied this cell. Were they home with their families by now, or had they moved on to other cells in different prisons? I knew that everyone who had lain on these cots had also had a first time, a first night there. They each had wanted to go home as badly as I did in that moment. They each got through it and so would I. I just had to wait for time to somehow pass. My tears were unstoppable as I turned to the wall, placing my back to the door.

The next morning I stood in front of the grumpy judge who by this time knew me quite well. He added another year to my probation and told me that if I stood before him again I would be going to juvenile detention. By then what had started out as six months' probation had turned into two years' probation. Still, my attitude was pretty cavalier. "They'll never send a teen to jail for simply running away," I figured.

My nights were harder than ever after the trip with Jana. My nightmares seemed almost vengeful. They had a face now. Sometimes I wasn't even conscious of having been asleep before I'd be startled awake by a deep, dark voice whispering in my ear, "It's only going to hurt a little."

I would lie in the dark too petrified to move, concentrating on breathing.

One night, I crept up to my closet, slid the door open as quietly as I could, and reached up onto the shelf. Finding my bottle of Nytol, I kissed it as I made my way back to the bed. I planned to take ten but I got scared while I was holding the last four in my hand and put them back in the bottle. I crawled back into my bed and imagined that my heart was slowing, like a clock winding down.

I woke up in the morning feeling sick to my stomach. My mouth was pasted shut and I felt dizzy and groggy. The room seemed to tilt away from me as I made my way to the shower.

In the shower I leaned against the wall and cried. My tears mixed with the shower water and I might not even have noticed them if I hadn't been whimpering too. I was angry with myself, disappointed that I was too scared to follow through. I felt like a coward.

Later that night I cut myself deep enough to leave scars that would last a lifetime. I cut into the skin of my legs horizontally, slicing deep, trying to find bone. Once the facecloth was covered in my blood I threw it under my bed and grabbed another one. I began to slice through my arm, picking at one spot until I had soaked the fresh cloth in my blood.

I was disappointed in myself. It seemed I really did have no control, even over myself.

My mom had given up trying to wake me for school and I was getting up long past noon almost every day. I was becoming more and more withdrawn and wouldn't talk to anyone anymore.

One afternoon I was walking with Dad to the car from the video store in Squamish. He looked me over quizzically while we walked. "Tara, why do you always walk looking down at the ground?"

I didn't know how to answer his question. I had never really thought about the way I walked. "You should walk with your head held high, you know. Confidence is learned. You need some."

I was silence the entire drive back to Brackendale, thinking about what he had said.

Melanie and I were still getting on quite well as long as I stayed out of her room and didn't ask her any questions. She was almost always in trouble and quite often came home drunk.

One night she had to stay in with Ellena and me while Mom and Dad went into Vancouver. They would be an hour to drive into the city, an hour for errands, and another hour for the drive home. I calculated that they would be gone for at least three hours.

Mellanie invited her boyfriend and Eli over after Mom and Dad were gone. She told me that Eli had really liked me when we had met the last time and that if I wanted to hang out with him in my bedroom she wouldn't tell on me.

I knew what she was getting at. She wanted me to have sex with him. She thought I was still a virgin. She had told me that I couldn't stay a virgin forever, and that I should give it away to someone who at least liked me.

Her words stung. I hadn't given anything away. Hadn't she noticed that I wasn't asking her to show me how to wiggle anymore? I wasn't asking her about anything anymore.

Eli came over that night with Mellanie's boyfriend and as expected Mellanie and her boyfriend slipped off to be alone.

Eli and I made small talk. Then he asked me if I would let him kiss me. I was flattered that he liked me. He was in high school; I was still in junior high, and only the popular girls had boyfriends who were in high school. Feeling somewhat mystified, I let him place his sloppy goober kisses all over my neck and eventually lower.

We didn't actually have sex but we were naked under a blanket. I got scared, though, and thankfully he was nice enough not to push me. If he had, I'd have done it. Back then I didn't have it in me to say no. I always just considered myself lucky that people even saw me, much less talked to me.

It wasn't long after this that my parents had a big fight. I don't know what caused it but whatever it was, it must have been major. Dad moved onto his boat for almost two weeks.

During that time Mellanie, Ellena, and I stayed with Mom. We would visit Dad on his boat and he would ask how Mom was doing. I wanted to tell him to come and see her; then she could tell him herself, but I never found the nerve to come out and say it. Instead I would tell him that she was doing fine and then we would talk about something else.

I knew that Mom was not fine. I knew she cried every day because she missed Dad. I also knew she wasn't sleeping because I could hear her puttering around the house late into the night.

It scared me that they were fighting like that. They had said that family always stays together, but they weren't even talking to each other.

One day while Dad was living on the boat I came home from riding my bike with friends to find Mom at the kitchen table. She was crying and very drunk.

My parents didn't drink or do drugs. At the time they were both smokers but other than that they led clean, healthy lives. I knew Mom was hurting deep inside, and that there was only one person she wanted to comfort her.

I wanted to make her feel better because it hurt me to see her so upset and I knew what it was like to feel all alone. Since there was nothing else I could do for her, I did the only thing I knew how to. I got down on my knees and crawled to her. Putting my head on her lap, I told her I loved her and that she would always have me. I put my arms around her legs and hugged her as best I could from the floor. She cried harder, but she put her arms around me and held me close.

Mellanie came in shortly afterwards and sprang into action. She took the rest of Mom's alcohol away and dumped it down the sink. She called Mom's best friend, Rhae, who came over with her husband, Tom. Rhae took Mom to her house and Tom stayed at our house for the night.

Later that night Mellanie went out in a fit of rage and I stood on the porch steps crying for her to come back, to please not leave me. Mellanie just kept on walking. As I watched her turn the corner at the end of the block I thought "Things are never going to be the same again." Mellanie never even looked back, not once.

Mom came home the next day and she and I had a long talk at the kitchen table. She told me that she was sorry that we had seen her that way, and that she remembered what I had said to her. I told her that there was nothing to apologize to us for. Mom cried again but this time not out of sadness—I think it was at the camaraderie we shared. I loved my mother more than anyone could love anyone at that moment. She was my mom, and she loved me. I decided right then that until Dad came home I would take care of her.

Mellanie did come back home after a few days but she was different. She was meaner and, as Mom had once said about me, she had a chip on her shoulder. She was harder to get along with and wouldn't talk to anyone unless she had to. Her music blared loudly from her room as if warning us to stay away from her door. I didn't dare knock and when I passed her in the hallway I was careful to avoid her eyes and keep my head down. She was angry and was looking for an excuse to take it out on someone. I didn't want to be that someone.

I still wanted Mellanie to feel better and happier so I reached out to her in other ways. I offered to do her chores, let her watch what she wanted on the TV we shared, and even made her breakfast once or twice.

Soon after Mellanie returned, Dad came back home. It was wonderful to have Dad back at the supper table. I looked around the table that first night we were all back together and smiled, just happy that everyone was in their rightful chairs.

I couldn't understand why I wasn't okay. There seemed to be nothing wrong: my parents were both home together; my foster sisters, though one was sad and morose, were in the room next to mine safely snoring. I could hear them occasionally through the walls. Yet to me, life felt so wrong and chaotic. I felt scrambled, and had no words for anything I was feeling. Just confused and alone and lots in between.

During one of our sessions Edna Cimpini asked me, "Why do you feel you're so different from everyone else?"

"Because they treat me differently."

"Who are *they?*"

"Everyone else."

"How do they treat you differently?"

I stopped fidgeting with my thumbnails and stared straight into her eyes, and asked her if she had these kinds of conversations with any of the children in her own family.

She shook her head no, a questioning look in her eyes. I smiled at her, still looking her in the eyes. I said very quietly, "I have conversations like this with my mom all the time." Sitting back, I held her gaze, struggling to keep from fidgeting again.

Edna said nothing to me for a moment. She just stared at me, digesting what I had said. Then she smiled—slowly at first, then wider—and thanked me. I didn't know why she was thanking me. Now I think it was because that was the most I had said all that week.

It was around this time that I began to hang around with a new boy, Shaye. He and I met at the arcade. After chatting, we discovered we didn't live that far away from each other.

Jana and Shaye didn't get along so I had to try to divide my time between them. That didn't work very well, and Jana and I slowly began to part ways.

It was an easy transition to make because Jana was so angry with me over something to do with our trip. She had unjustly accused me of stealing from Stella or Stuart, or maybe it was Stuart's mother. Anyway, that had caused a rift between us. Angry with her for not believing me, I decided she wasn't much different from everyone else.

Jana and I planned a farewell party for two. We had managed to get our hands on a two-litre bottle of Rockaberry Cooler. We decided the night before that we would drink it on our way to school the next day.

I secretly planned to take the Nytol that I had hidden high up in my closet. This time I would make sure I got the job done—the medication mixed with the alcohol would definitely work. I took four Nytols with my breakfast and with my juice I downed the last five that had been in the bottle. Not trusting that alone to do the trick, I took apart a razor in the shower and used the blades to slice deep across my wrists. I wrapped Kleenex around my wrists and put on a long shirt to keep them hidden, then left to meet Jana on the trail.

I was startled by how lightheaded I felt. I could feel my heart struggling in my chest.

I realized I'd neglected to write a note. I decided to tell Jana what I had done and asked her to tell Mom and Dad that I was sorry I was such a difficult child.

Jana panicked. She took off running down the trail to school. Minutes later, I was soon surrounded by other students and one of the teachers. They had called an ambulance, and they said I would have to have my stomach pumped at the hospital. I almost laughed when the teacher added that I would be welcome back at school as soon as I felt better. *There's no such thing as "better." Better just gives them something to take away.*

I thought maybe I should've just ducked into the bushes and gone to sleep instead of meeting up with Jana.

A nurse at the hospital gave me a concoction that made me sick to my stomach. It tasted awful.

After the nurses left me I was able to get some sleep. The nurse had told me on her way out of the room that Mom was going to come and see me soon. I hadn't picked up on the fact she had said see me, not get me ... otherwise I might not have been able to sleep.

I was awakened by Edna Cimpini. I could smell her before I opened my eyes and saw her standing beside my bed.

She sat with me for some time while I talked. I told her I was so sorry for what I had done. If I had done it right then I wouldn't have caused anyone any more trouble, I added. She replied that it was that kind of thinking that had made them decide I needed help—help Mom and Dad couldn't give me.

Edna had arranged for me to go to a youth treatment centre in Vancouver. She explained that it was a thirty-day session in a closed facility. Meaning that for thirty days I would be locked up.

At this, I turned my back to her and refused to say another word. I don't know when she left, but I know she stood there for some time, waiting for me to say or do something.

Mom came in shortly after that and told me I would be going to the centre in the morning. She said she and Dad would drive me there together and that if I gave it a chance this could be a really good thing. I just lay there and cried silently while she spoke.

This time I had gone too far and now everyone agreed that something needed to be done. I wished I had just done it right; then everyone could just go live their lives without all the turmoil I brought wherever I went.

Thirteen was proving to be a very tough year.

The next morning, true to their word, Mom and Dad came to pick me up. I saw they had packed my bags for me as I climbed into the back seat of the car. I resented that I didn't even get to choose what I was going to wear while away. I pursed my lips and said nothing as the car began to move. Although the treatment centre was in Burnaby, just past Vancouver, this particular drive was excruciatingly long and quiet.

In the centre we went to an office with a big sign that said Intake. My mom filled in the papers they thrust at her, and sat with me until a youth worker came and said they were ready to show me to my room. Mom gave me a package of cigarettes. "Make them last until the weekend—I'll see you again then," she told me.

In the treatment centre I was introduced to the other kids. Some were almost done their time there; others, like me, had just started. The rooms were cell-like, with only a bed and a counter. There was no dresser. We were to live out of our suitcases.

There were six of us in the centre when I first arrived. I spent a lot of my time out in the smoke area with the other kids.

There was also Louie Childer. Apparently he had been hanging around the treatment centre for a long time. He lived nearby and would come by in the early afternoons and chat with us through the fence. I didn't really give him much thought. He was tall, about 5'7", older than us by a few years. He had short dirty blond hair and acne scars on his face, but he always appeared friendly.

Most of us were there for depression, some because of eating disorders, and some because they were just plain angry. We had group sessions and one-on-one therapy. I had been with Edna for almost two years now and I had never told her my real secrets. What would be different about thirty days with these people, I wondered.

When I had first arrived at the centre the staff had had me fill in questionnaires and complete a psychological assessment. They determined that I was a "follower." They said I had a rescue complex. That would be proven much more dramatically than they bargained for, I'm sure.

I was told that if you had an incident-free week you could get a trip pass if you were accompanied by a family member, and you were allowed to go to the store with a buddy from the centre. It was supposed to be a staff member but quite often we went out with just each other.

I had befriended three of the other kids in particular, two girls, Erica and Heather, and a boy named Jim. I had been there for almost three weeks and was looking forward to my last week, when I would be able to count the days till I left. Then Erica and Heather went AWOL. They told the staff members that they were going out for a pack of smokes and didn't come back.

Jim and I were careful to eavesdrop on the staff when they talked to the police officer who came and when they talked among themselves.

Erica and Heather had been missing for at least a whole day when Jim saw Erica coming down the road towards the centre. I knew something was wrong when I heard Jim scream for staff to hurry to the gate. I never really got a glimpse of Erica, but I was told she was a mess. Her clothes had been torn and she had what appeared to be blood between her legs. Back outside, while the other kids chatted, Jim and I shared a knowing glance and watched through the gate as the second police car that week came up the driveway.

We sat together in silence, smoking and waiting. The police car left with Erica inside, taking her to the hospital, and that was the last time I saw her.

Jim and I were called into the staff lounge, where the staff leader asked us if we knew Louie Childer. We revealed what we knew of him. He lived somewhere near the facility. He always showed up when there were no staff sitting outside with us, so perhaps he knew the schedule. We knew what he looked like and what he said he drove. After we were done talking to the staff we knew Louie was responsible for what had happened to Erica. Worse, we knew that Heather was still with him.

I couldn't just sit there. I had to help Heather. I had heard Louie give directions to the 7-Eleven before. He'd said that you passed his house on the way. I decided I would have to go because I was the one who had overheard the directions, and my being a girl made it more likely that Louie wouldn't suspect me of anything. I would find him and then find Heather.

While I tried to devise a plan to get out of the facility, it actually devised itself. Mellanie happened to call a few minutes after I decided that I had to find a way out.

We didn't talk long, but I stayed on the phone after she hung up. I said things that implied that she needed help looking for a dress in Metrotown mall, which was only one bus away. I asked a distracted staff worker if I could go meet my sister at Metrotown. "Are you going with a family member?" he asked. I let out an exasperated sigh. "I'm meeting my older sister at Metrotown," I repeated, all the while holding a dead phone line.

A few minutes later they opened the gate and I was free. I said a silent thank you to Mellanie for her timing and began to make tracks towards a local high-rise hotel. Louie said that on the other side of the hotel was a convenience store and beside that a pathway between houses that led to his street. I found the trail easily enough and carefully checked all the back windows in the houses I passed. Seeing no sign of Louie, I continued on.

I had been walking for about thirty minutes when I heard someone calling my name. It was Heather. She was standing outside a beat-up blue van, waving and calling my name. I was surprised to see that she was smiling and looked no worse for wear. I waved back and returned her smile.

As I approached, Louie stepped out of the van. He too was smiling. He didn't look like a man who had just hurt someone.

When I started talking to Heather, I could tell she'd been drinking. Louie asked if I would like a drink as well. All thoughts of rescuing my friend forgotten, I said yes, and we all climbed into the van together.

Louie reached behind the seat and produced a bottle of vodka—no mix; we just drank it straight from the bottle. I saw Heather had gotten together with one of Louie's friends. He was naked in a sleeping bag in the van. He didn't say much and seemed somewhat irritated at my arrival.

The van hadn't moved when at some point we went into Louie's house. I suppose you could call it a house, anyway. It was more like a shack, with only one window.

I don't remember everything that took place after that—alcohol has a way of stealing your memory away. What I do remember is being in Louie's room. I was lying on his very smelly bed. Louie was on top of me, pounding into me, and I was crying. At some point there was a boy I recognized from the treatment centre; he had opened the bedroom door and was standing in the doorway. I screamed for him to please help me. He just shut the door. Later he would tell the police that he had seen what Louie was doing to me but that he didn't want to upset Louie because he was such a violent person.

When Louie was done he acted as if nothing had happened. I remember I thought that if it was going to hurt this bad, I would have to stop fighting.

Louie said he had some running around to do and that he would be back in a few minutes. As soon as he left I ran to the front door and was shocked to find that it locked from the outside. I was locked in. I couldn't get through the one tiny little window. I sat back down on the bed and hugged myself, trying to think of something I could do. At a loss, I began to scream. I screamed and screamed and screamed.

Soon there was the sound of someone outside the door. I immediately shut up, afraid it was Louie. Whoever it was kicked the door in. There stood a police officer. Scrutinizing me, he asked if I was Tara.

He took me to the hospital, where they checked me head to toe and took something they called a rape kit. Then the officer returned me to the treatment centre.

Unbeknownst to me, the staff there had their hands full with Mom and Dad, who had been told what had happened. They blamed the centre—they said I should never have been allowed to leave, especially after what had happened to Erica.

I was taken to my room and given a sedative to help me calm down. I had been shaking almost uncontrollably since Louie had left his house. It was adrenaline and nerves.

After a short time I heard a commotion in the hallway. Before I could even turn towards the door my foster brother's wife, Angela, came storming into my room. She ran to me and held me real close while my brother, Alex, stayed in the hall. I heard him telling the staff that he was leaving with me. Within minutes of their arrival he scooped me up and carried me out of there.

At Alex and Angela's place I waited for Mom and Dad to come and get me. They must have driven like the wind because in no time at all they were there.

Up until then I had assumed Alex thought of me as just another of the many foster children Mom and Dad had taken into their home: a big pain in the butt that Mom and Dad wouldn't have to deal with if they hadn't chosen to. But from that day on Alex was a real hero to me. I will forever remember the way he and Angela came bursting through the doors and stole me away.

I had been waiting for a moment like that so many times. This time it actually happened. Maybe I had been born for a purpose.

 # Chapter 5

PARTWAY THROUGH GRADE EIGHT I learned that Freddie Lavin was no longer my social worker. He had been promoted and my file had been passed on to a new man, TJ Kwan. He was younger than Freddie and appeared to be new at his job.

When I met him he seemed nervous and disorganized. He was trying to be friendly but it came across as forced, and he kept stalling for time to read his notes.

He wanted me to learn about my Native heritage, and offered to take me to a powwow. I wasn't interested in going, but I did listen more carefully when he talked about the possibility of funds being held in trust for me somewhere in Manitoba.

He applied for Native status for me. We waited over a month for a response, but then the application was denied. I was disappointed. One look at me made it obvious I was Native, but apparently I didn't belong in that world either.

I was almost never at school anymore, and when I did show up the teachers mostly ignored me, probably because they never knew if I would be there the next day.

One afternoon when I had graced eighth-grade English with my presence, my teacher asked me to stay after class. He said that he believed I was smarter than the grades he was forced to give me. He produced a report from his desk and placed it in front of me.

I stared at a large red A with 96% written next to my name. It was rare for me to see what my grades actually were because I completed so few assignments. I sat back in my chair and listened to him plead with me not to rob myself of the education that could give me so many opportunities. I was waiting for him to let me leave.

I didn't want to hear that I was smart or that there was a chance I had something to offer, because it was too painful to even picture such a possibility. It felt as if he was slapping me while he spoke of the opportunities my intelligence could bring me.

He was frustrated when I left the classroom—he never said so, but it was in the way he gathered his papers into his briefcase and stood to dismiss me. I felt banished from his class and didn't go back for some time.

After spring break that year Cara transferred to my school. She was a year older than I was and a grade higher in most of her subjects.

She was beautiful. She had shoulder-length red hair with blond highlights, and bangs framing the freckles across her cheeks and nose. She wore tight clothing that accentuated her slender frame. Her brightly coloured outfits always matched, from her hair ties to her socks.

I ran into her quite literally in the bathroom on her third or fourth day and we started talking. She invited me to the smoke pit after school to join her and her friends. "It'll be fun," she added over her shoulder as the door shut behind her.

I stayed in school for the rest of that day, which meant that for the first time in months I completed a whole day at school.

I'd never been to the smoke pit before. It was exactly what its name suggested. There were three large rocks that acted as a barrier between the forest and the school. In behind the rocks it was littered with cigarette butts, empty lighters, and lunchtime debris.

When I got there, Cara was standing with a group of students I had never talked to before. I almost turned to leave but Cara saw me and waved me over to her.

I felt awkward standing among this older group. They were talking about people I didn't know and weekend parties I wouldn't be attending.

Eventually only Cara and I were left sitting on the rocks. We lost track of time that first day, talking and laughing. We had a lot in common and I knew I had found a kindred spirit in my new friend.

From then on I could be found there after school. Some of the other kids even began to talk to me and include me in their discussions.

On weekends Shaye and I would explore the mountain on the other side of the highway. We fantasized about living up in the trees. We would climb up the steep rocks and head past the trees towards the cliffs. There was a ledge high up above the cliffs that we were determined to get to. The day we first tackled the climb we discovered that it was a lot harder than it appeared from the ground. It took us a few attempts on subsequent afternoons, but eventually we resorted to rope and found a way up to the ledge.

Jack London was a favourite author of ours. We laughed when we thought that if he were with us that day he could have written a tale about us, about how we would live and conquer up there on those giant boulders of the earth.

We were always quiet when it was time to head home, neither of us wanting to return to the lives waiting for us at the bottom of the mountain.

When summer came I was disappointed but not surprised to see that I had failed grade eight French and math. I was going to have to take French again, and spend next year in the Math 9m (modified) class.

Mom and I were starting to argue again. Our hostilities seemed to come in phases. We would fight and argue, then have a major blowup that usually ended with me leaving the house in a fit of rage. I would storm down the street with Cher's song about Jesse James blaring from my Walkman.

I had started throwing things at my bedroom walls and trashing my bedroom on a regular basis. I would pick up anything within arm's reach and start throwing my weapons at the walls. Even my ghetto blaster had dents in the speakers and chips off the dials from hitting the walls or being kicked and stomped on.

Every time I acted like that I would end up wondering what it was Mom saw in me that she wouldn't just give up and send me away.

My chats with Dad were becoming a regular occurrence. I could tell he was running out of things to say. He had stopped asking me why I was the way I was; I think he didn't know what to say anymore.

Still, he never put his foot down and said I had to go. We would talk and then he would take me out for breakfast or lunch. He would make a point of saying that he didn't want to hear another word about it—we were to enjoy our treat.

I think he wanted to soften the blow of my getting into trouble yet again. For that hour over breakfast Dad would smile and nod knowingly while I chatted to him about school, friends, and virtually anything that seemed mentionable over pancakes.

Cara's parents were almost never at home and left her to fend for herself most of the time. She would invite me over for bacon and eggs and we would make a big mess of the kitchen and never clean up after ourselves. I think that was her only way of communicating with her parents.

Cara stopped calling one day and I didn't hear from her again for almost a week. Which may not sound like long but when you're a teenager, it's an eon. When she reappeared it was in an unexpected locale.

Shaye and I hitchhiked into Squamish fairly regularly to share a side of fries at either the Mountain Burger House or the Lotus Gardens. It was on a lazy afternoon at the Lotus Gardens that Cara found us. She came through the front door with two guys who were obviously from the big city. They were older than us by a few years, and they looked like trouble.

Cara introduced us to Jeff and Mick. Jeff had a large muscular build and short, spiky blond hair that framed an oval face. He did not smile when he greeted us. He just sat in the booth across from us looking bored and impatient.

Mick seemed friendlier and smiled in my direction. Mick had long curly black hair and olive skin. He had a smaller frame than Jeff; he was quite thin. He had Native features with dark brown eyes that emanated wisdom beyond his seventeen years.

Cara informed us that I was going with them into Vancouver, and offered to drive Shaye home. I felt the stirrings of excitement, knowing there was an adventure ahead. I ignored the warnings of the other voice that begged me to go home, ordering me to stay in town with Shaye.

Outside the café, we all clambered into a large black SUV Jeff was driving. At the time I thought it was odd that he started the engine with a screwdriver, but I didn't ask about it.

We dropped Shaye off at his house and headed back to the highway. As we passed my house I noticed there were no cars in the driveway. I asked Jeff if he would stop the truck. I wanted to pick up my notebook and pack a change of clothes. Cara followed me into the house and called to me from Mom's room. She was in my parents' closet taking my mom's clothes out and admiring them. She didn't have to say what she was thinking.

I thought about it for a minute before I grabbed a few outfits and stuck them in my bag. By stealing Mom's clothes I was crossing an invisible line, sealing my fate.

On the drive into Vancouver I was told that we were going to the Hunchback Hotel. I had never stayed in a hotel in Vancouver before and was excited at the idea.

Jeff asked if we wanted to get anything on the way there and Cara immediately spoke up. She wanted some blotter. I had heard about LSD and what it can do to you—mostly stories of people who never sobered up or who hurt themselves or other people while they were high. The idea of trying it made me nervous; I didn't really want to. I knew it wasn't like marijuana. I leaned farther back into my seat as if to disappear.

We made all the necessary stops, and then Jeff parked the truck two blocks away from the "hotel." We were in a residential neighbourhood. I reasoned that with a name like the Hunchback Hotel maybe it was a bed-and-breakfast type of place.

Two blocks later, I was disappointed to find that the Hunchback Hotel was in the basement of a tiny grey house. Its name came from the fact the ceiling was a mere five and a half feet high. Cara and I were the only ones who didn't have to duck on the way in.

I could smell fresh paint and was told they had just painted some lime green on the black walls so that it would glow in the dark. I was both appalled and curious. Who would want to paint their walls black and want them to glow in the dark?

Four guys were stuffed into this den-like suite that really couldn't be called a suite at all. There were three bedrooms the size of large walk-in closets, a large recreation room with a couch and TV, and a bathroom. A hotplate and a small brown fridge in a hallway served as the kitchen.

Besides Jeff and Mick there were RJ and Chris. When we arrived RJ jumped up and kissed Cara in greeting. Up until then I had thought Cara was with Mick—it had been so clear to me that Mick was smitten with Cara.

RJ was short, with a heavy-set, muscular build. He was Cuban with darker skin and sharp, keen golden eyes. He had an air of danger to him. I felt a warning prickle down my spine when we were introduced: this wasn't someone you wanted for an enemy.

I would not meet Chris, the fifth Hotelmate, until much later. He was almost never there and he never hung out with us.

That first night there we all dropped acid.I couldn't wait for it to be over. The walls seemed to be breathing and the neon lights swaying, making me feel sick. There was an overpowering taste of tin in my mouth that I could not get rid of no matter how many cigarettes I smoked. When anyone spoke, including myself, I had to play the words over in my head in an attempt to make some sense of them. Even just trying to express anything required a supreme effort. I was laughing and crying at the same time, completely unable to control my emotions. It was an awful feeling because the high was persistent, increasingly stronger and more intense.

"Keep a hold on yourself or you'll just make yourself have a bad trip," I heard someone tell me. I tried to remind myself that I had taken a drug and that everything I was seeing and feeling was not real, that it was just caused by a little square of paper I had placed on my tongue earlier.

Colours caused me to break into tears. We told each other stories of how colours became memories, and they made perfect sense. When Jeff touched my hands during the early part of the night I swore I could feel his thoughts. We chatted quietly with each other for a while.

At some point I insisted on getting out of that stuffy house into the fresh night air. I was having trouble catching my breath and everyone was chain-smoking, which was causing a haze that kept getting thicker and thicker until it was a dense fog that threatened to envelop us all. Jeff stood up to join me.

The warm night air and the outside world immediately comforted me. I was sure I was in a different dimension than the Hunchback Hotel. With only Jeff and me there, conversation was less confusing. By the end of that night I was Jeff's girlfriend.

Jeff had a sadness in his eyes that held something deeper than the pain of abandonment—more a vulnerability caused by hopelessness. Immediately I felt as if I could help him: in some way I could touch his life and save him from being completely lost. That night I set about making him laugh. I liked his smile. It was awkward yet spontaneous. His eyes crinkled when he guffawed, and I decided that his was a face I could love.

The first time we had sex, Jeff was very gentle with me. It didn't feel great or even good but for a change it wasn't awful. Jeff talked to me the whole time, asking me if this hand felt good there or if it was okay to take my shirt off. I had never had anyone talk to me before during sex and it almost made me giggle with self-consciousness. I responded mostly by nodding but I looked into his eyes when he asked me to and held him tightly in my arms.

We had been there a full week when Jeff and Mick decided that they needed to go out to work. Cara and I knew what they were doing, and we were worried about what would happen if they were arrested. We followed them throughout the house while they were collecting their tools: wire cutters, dent pullers, and big black bags. We pleaded with them not to do it, promising we'd find a way to collect welfare, but the guys ignored us, leaving us staring at the closed door after they left.

They came back hours later and dumped two duffle bags full of electronics and jewellery onto the rec room floor. Cara and I immediately began to rifle through the jewellery until Jeff told us not to touch it. He said they would sort it and that we could have whatever was worthless.

I watched as they began to make small piles, discussing certain pieces before tossing them onto a pile. I realized that none of the pieces were worthless to those who had cherished them. We were sorting through people's memories. There was even a baby soother that had found its way onto the garbage pile. I stared at that soother for a long time, imagining the reasons a soother would become someone's treasure.

I knew then that I never wanted to be sitting on the floor watching them sort people's hopes and dreams again. It made me feel sick.

The following night we all went to Granville Street for a movie. During the movie, Jeff whispered in my ear that he had to do something and would be right back.

It wasn't until we had left the theatre and were outside having a cigarette that he rejoined us. I was so relieved to see him. I don't know what I thought could have happened but I had been worried.

When Jeff and I were alone in his room later that same night he took something out of his pocket and showed it to me. It was a flap of what I assumed to be cocaine. I was learning a lot there at the Hunchback Hotel. I still hadn't done any myself but by then I knew what it looked like and had seen someone do it.

Jeff explained to me that it was peyote, not cocaine. Did I want some? Why not? I had tried LSD; what was another name on the list? I didn't even bother to ask what peyote was.

He showed me how to do it by taking the straw first. Minutes later we had to run to the bathroom because my nose started to bleed, causing me to throw up. In hindsight I think I was lucky—it must have stopped the drug from getting into my system, because I felt nothing.

Jeff definitely got something from it, though, because he mellowed right down, and we talked late into the night lying on his bed.

Up till then Jeff hadn't talked about himself at all, so I was eager to hear about his life. I learned that he came from a broken home. He had a brother whom his mother was proud of, but she really didn't bother with Jeff. Jeff had a foster father he saw all the time; he just couldn't live with him anymore. He had been basically on his own since he was twelve. He had been in jail five times by the time I met him, and even he thought that he hadn't seen the last of the inside.

Jeff explained to me that the Hunchback Hotel was actually a halfway house for youth. He was supposed to be actively looking for work and/or going to school. The man who ran the house lived upstairs, and he also owned the property. He was not at all interested in what happened downstairs and left the guys alone as long as they kept their dealings away from the house.

I pictured the stolen goods that had been sprawled across his basement floor earlier that week but said nothing. I just lay there and listened as Jeff talked.

When I woke in the morning Jeff had his arms wrapped firmly around me. I felt really safe and secure. No one could hurt me when I was with Jeff. He was huge—no one would mess with him. It was more than his size though. It was his demeanour, an unspoken promise that he would take care of me.

Later that morning he told me he loved me. Even though we were so young, I believe he really did love me at that moment in the only way he knew how to.

It wasn't long before the guys were talking about going back out for another night's work. We were running low on money and weed, so RJ was tense and irritable. He had an unpredictable temper, and one night he snapped.

Cara and RJ had been in RJ's room for some time and Jeff and I were in bed when their raised voices became audible.

Jeff and I quickly arose and made our way down the hall. Jeff grabbed me from behind to stop me banging on their door. He stepped in front of me and was going to just walk right in when suddenly RJ opened the door. He had Cara by the neck and was yelling at her almost incoherently.

Cara was sobbing and coughing as she tried to right herself while RJ dragged her past us down the hallway. He threw her tiny frame brutally into the bathroom. Following close behind, I caught a glimpse of his menacing face as he slammed the door shut.

Jeff shoved his way past me and began to throw himself against the bathroom door. It came splintering apart on the second try.

RJ had Cara by the back of her neck, forcing her to her knees. He was threatening to put her head into the toilet when Jeff grabbed RJ by the back of his shirt. He seemed startled to see Jeff there. I think he'd forgotten there was anyone else in the house.

RJ gave Cara one final shove. Her hair swung into the toilet water. Cara let out a shriek and then continued to wail as if her heart were broken. I knelt down and helped her up.

Jeff was just getting RJ under control when we heard a commotion in the living room. There was a big bang, followed by another one. I could hear someone yelling through the walls. I saw the couch suddenly lurch forward and realized for the first time that there was a door behind it. Jeff once again sprang into action, moving the couch away from the door.

My first glimpse of the owner of the house revealed a man wearing tight-fitting jeans and a black leather jacket over a white T-shirt. Derek was about 30 years old, with short curly black hair, a moustache, and at that moment a rather large scowl on his face. He looked angry.

Derek raved that it had sounded as if the house was coming down. He said he knew the guys had girls living with them and he had been willing to overlook it in the name of keeping the peace in the house. However, we had proven we couldn't handle playing house yet, and Cara and I were no longer welcome to spend the night, starting right away.

Jeff started to say he was going to leave with us, but Derek interrupted him saying that based on what he'd heard, maybe us girls should separate ourselves from the guys for the night. "You're still on probation," he said to Jeff, "and this time I'm gonna hold you to it."

I agreed with Derek that Cara and RJ could use a break but at the time I couldn't understand why Jeff had to stay behind.

Cara and I decided we were going to go home to Squamish. We'd been gone for ten days—that was the longest I had gone without leaving a message on the answering machine at home. I was missing Mom. She was bound to be worried. Plus, I knew I had breached my probation again. If the police picked me up I would definitely be spending some time in a cell. My only chance was to go home of my own accord and go to the courthouse first thing in the morning.

Cara and I packed what little we had into one backpack and told the guys they could call us. The Hunchback Hotel had no telephone. The guys could use Derek's to call out but they couldn't receive calls.

By the time Cara and I began to hitchhike on Joyce, the nearest major street, it was almost 2 a.m.

It was 5:30 when we got back into Squamish. After we said our goodbyes I hitched another ride to take me home to Brackendale.

It was 6:30 by the time I arrived back on my parents' doorstep.

Dad was the one who opened the door. He said nothing, just shook his head at me and walked away, leaving the door open for me to go in. I felt my face go hot with shame as I made my way inside and down the hall to my room. Closing the door behind me, I stood at the window and watched as minutes later he climbed into his truck and drove off down the street on his way to work.

I could hear Mom walking through the house as she got herself ready for her own day. I was exhausted but I knew I needed to make an appearance. So I took another deep breath and opened my door.

Mom was sitting at the kitchen table drinking her morning coffee and smoking a cigarette. She looked up at me when I came in and motioned for me to sit at the table with her. Until that moment I had forgotten about stealing her clothes on our way out the door. It came to me as I sat down across from her. After I remembered I couldn't look at her.

"When I realized you were gone, Tara, I had to call TJ," she started.

"When we didn't hear from you, we had no choice. What if you'd been in the States again?"

Defensively I sniped, "It wouldn't have mattered if I were in California. I always come home!"

I told myself it was her fault if I went to jail because she didn't trust me to come home.

Mom and I argued at the table for some time. Then we began moving through the house, still at each other's throat. I ran into my room; she stayed standing in the hallway. She watched as I grabbed another bag from my closet and began to stuff it with my belongings.

When I finally did look up at her she was leaning against the doorjamb. She looked weary. I heard her say very quietly, "I love you Tara."

Then she turned and walked away.

Her words deflated my anger in seconds and suddenly I was completely drained. Not knowing what else to do, I followed her into the kitchen and very quietly sat at the table. After making herself a fresh coffee she too sat down and we talked for some time.

Mom shared some of her own life story, which was not unlike my own, and I realized that she saw something of herself in me. It gave me hope. Despite her rough beginnings, her life now wasn't so bad. Maybe I too just had to make it to somewhere I didn't know yet.

Later that day she drove me to the courthouse where I met with my probation officer. He told me that I would have to go stand before the judge later that afternoon. He also said that I should prepare to spend some time in youth detention because he was strongly considering making such a recommendation to crown counsel.

Mom sat with me as we waited for me to be called to the bench. A lawyer came and talked to Mom for a few minutes; then they both came and talked to me. The lawyer thought that the best thing for me to do was to say that I was guilty of the breach. Then maybe the judge would take it easy on me. But the reality was that I might be looking at serving some jail time.

I was the last case before the judge that day. He glowered down at me and warned me that if I stood before him again I would no longer be on probation—I was going to be sentenced to jail, and he would remove the probation order to save taxpayers money. This time he was just giving me community service hours. When he was done he asked me if I understood all of what he had just said.

He left no room for confusion. My knees buckling under his gaze, I managed to state that I understood completely.

I knew I was very lucky and that he had taken mercy on me for the last time. I think he was getting tired of always seeing me for the same thing. I was starting to understand that they really might throw a runaway in jail.

I hadn't heard from Cara since our return from Vancouver and I was scared to call her. I thought her parents might blame me for our escapades. When I did hear something about her it wasn't good.

Squamish being a small town, it was hard to keep anything under wraps, and Mom came home one night to tell me that Cara had been placed in a group home in West Vancouver.

I was confused. They were her natural family. Didn't having a family mean that you always had a home? I felt panicked for Cara. It seemed so unfair.

My social worker made the decision to move me into an alternative school. It was on the outskirts of Squamish and I had to get a ride in to school every day. There were no classrooms to speak of, just large rooms, one with computers lining one wall and science equipment lining the other wall. Another room had cubicles with room dividers; the workspaces there had been personally claimed with posters and notes. There were three teachers there all day long available for questions if we ran into trouble. We followed individual self-paced programs designed to get us caught up within that one year so that ideally we could rejoin our peers the following year. I liked the self-paced program and began to race through my lessons, grateful for the distraction.

Ellena moved out during this time. Mom and Dad were very sad to see her go. Dad had to say his goodbye the night before because she would be gone by the time he got home from work the next day. He hugged her close and told her that she was a great kid. He smiled at her and patted her head before sending her off to bed.

The next morning, I watched as Mom carefully packed her stuff up into boxes and suitcases. When she was done we began to carry them down the hall to the door. A social worker came to fetch her minutes after we had placed the last box down.

Mom cried openly when she said goodbye and Ellena did too. They clung to each other and then Mom pulled away. I never really said goodbye to her. We hugged and then I told her that she had a real family waiting for her to come home.

That afternoon I decided I needed to go find Cara. I knew she was supposed to be in a group home but I was willing to bet she was actually at the Hunchback Hotel. Why was she taking so long to get in touch with me?

After a late lunch with Mom, I made my way to the highway, telling myself that I would just look in on her. I would turn right around and be back home by curfew.

When I arrived at the Hunchback Hotel, Jeff was the only one there. He was happy to see me. He had been on his way out to meet RJ. He said I could join him; then we could go to Cara's group home to see her, and then he would drive me back to Squamish.

We left the Hunchback, walked towards a beige Mazda RX7, and climbed in. Jeff started the ignition with a screwdriver. By now I knew what that meant. It made me feel nervous and a little excited to be in a stolen car.

We met up with RJ, who was with a girl named Alice. I liked her almost on sight. Someday we would come to be good friends but at this point we would just spend a brief two days together.

RJ was also driving an RX7, only his was black. Both the cars only had two seats. I should have seen the omen for what it was but I ignored the voice in my head.

Jeff and RJ raced each other, taking off from every red light, and we swerved and sped our way through city streets. We came to a screeching halt in front of a yellow house on Fifteenth Street in West Vancouver. RJ motioned to Jeff that he would go and get her. We were to sit tight and wait. Before long Cara and RJ came running down the alley to their car.

When I looked past them down the alley I could see a rather large black-haired woman chasing them. She was shouting something and waving her hands around wildly. Jeff laughed and told me to hold on. Then we were zooming up towards the highway with RJ, Alice, and Cara poured into the car beside us. I don't think any of us had our seat belts on.

RJ and Jeff were racing each other again as we headed down the main highway towards Squamish. Jeff was laughing and cheering, tenaciously keeping the lead. I was watching straight ahead of us doing my best not to scream for him to stop the car and let me out. Suddenly Jeff exclaimed, "What the—? Where did they disappear off the highway?" I didn't know—I hadn't been watching them; I was too busy praying that the road ahead stayed horizontal.

Jeff was swearing and cursing as we turned off at the next ramp and made our way back up the other side of the highway. We went back to the previous off-ramp and circled back, retracing our path.

We almost missed the car because it was upside down in the ditch on the side of the highway. Our friends were lucky: it had landed not that far from the edge of a steep ravine.

There was no sign of them at all. Jeff yelled, "Hurry up, Tara! Grab your jacket and get out here!"

I didn't really want to get out of the car. I was scared that someone would see me and say that I had been driving the car that flipped. Reluctantly I emerged and headed over to Jeff.

He used my jacket to wipe down all the surfaces on RJ's car that might have had fingerprints on them. "Who knows if RJ had the presence of mind to do this, being stuck with two hysterical women?" he snickered. We got back into our own car and headed for the side streets of West Vancouver to search for our friends. Squamish was no longer a priority.

We didn't find them, though, and eventually, heading back to the Hunchback Hotel seemed to be the best bet.

Jeff parked the car a ways away from the Hunchback, wiping it down to make sure there were no signs of us left in it. I knew he wouldn't be using it anymore.

When we did finally arrive at the Hunchback we were surprised to find RJ, Cara, and Alice already there. Alice had hit her head in the accident and was lying on the couch moaning and groaning. Cara and RJ seemed none the worse for wear and were laughing and joking as they explained the events that led up to the accident and how they had come back to the Hunchback.

I don't know how they managed to make public transit sound so exciting, but they pulled us in with their tales of passengers staring at the spectacle they must have made in their travels. Alice was the only one who seemed unamused. She just lay listlessly on the couch.

There was still no telephone at the Hunchback Hotel; the closest phone was a few blocks away. My curfew was fast approaching. I had to get to that telephone and buy myself an hour to get home. Once again, what I considered to be fate stepped in when Derek from upstairs came down. He said that under the circumstances Cara and I could spend the night there at the Hunchback. I was dumbfounded. Where had this come from? "They should have the highway to Squamish open again in the morning," he added.

Jeff turned on the TV and we saw that a landslide had closed the highway. It would take road crews until the early hours to clean it up. I looked heavenward and thanked the man upstairs for my good fortune.

Derek was kind enough to let me use his phone to call my parents and tell them what had happened.

I thought that if I called them they would see that what had happened had been beyond my control, and maybe they wouldn't call my probation officer about my delinquency. Conveniently, I was forgetting that I wasn't supposed to be in Vancouver in the first place. My mother was angry and said little as I explained myself to her, but I thought when I hung up with her that I was in the clear.

I had really been diving into my work at the alternative school. My parents and my social worker and parole officer seemed happy with the feedback they were getting from the school, and so I thought I would make sure that if the highway opened in time I would attend school the next day. I would call Mom from the school before she would have time to call the probation officer. My plan was that Mom would be so impressed at my having gone to school that she would not call.

Alice had managed to nod off and we were watching for signs that she was not okay when I got a chance to talk to Cara. I explained I was going to have to go.

Cara told me she had no intention of leaving. I was okay with that. Where was she going to go? I was sad for her and a little for Jeff and RJ too. I sat and listened as they let the adrenaline propel them into animated chat about rolling the car.

Later that night I kissed Jeff as he slept and stole away from the Hunchback. I had the feeling that was the last time I would see that place and perhaps even the people it housed. Something had changed in me the moment we'd realized the RX7 had left the road. Suddenly it wasn't all play anymore.

They had closed the highway farther back, past Horseshoe Bay, and I walked in alone. I perched myself on a rock beside the deserted roadway. It was eerie, yet I found it peaceful too. I sat and listened to the crickets and stared at the rock walls that lined the highway. I stayed like that, lost in thought as the hours ticked by.

I came to the realization that I did want a better life than I was giving myself a chance at. There had to be something in the world for me because I had been saved from myself too many times. Why was I so special that I never slipped through the cracks?

The highway opened that morning just after 5 a.m. I was at the school before any of the staff. I sat on the stoop and let my eyelids droop. I was falling asleep when one of the teachers arrived.

Surprised to see me there, he let me in with him. I went straight to the phone and called home.

Mom was less enthused. She said it was good that I had gone to school but that some lessons in life were harder to learn than others. I gave little thought to the comment, and when I hung up I was actually feeling pretty good about myself. I went to the couch in the teachers' lounge and lay down. I was asleep within seconds.

Percy, one of my schoolmates, woke me up. He was saying something about going out the back door when I heard the sound of a police radio. I knew instinctively that they were there for me.

They arrested me in the school. I was embarrassed at being in handcuffs in front of my peers. But none of them seemed vindictive. Most were either curious or looking at the police officers with open hostility as I was ushered past them to the waiting car. I caught Percy's eye and tried to silently convey a thank you for his attempt to warn me. He looked sad as he stared at me through the windows of the school. I thought wow ... I'm an after-school special.

How could Mom have done this to me? Didn't she see that I was trying? Didn't she know that I could have gone home to bed instead?

I knew I was in big trouble this time because I was one of the first cases on the docket that very morning. They wanted me dealt with. I had been sitting in holding for only a short wait and was hoping against hope the judge would take mercy on me one final time.

I waited for the stern talking-to, for the lecture on behaviour, for him to say anything to me. After my initial plea—guilty—he said nothing directly to me.

True to his word, he took me off probation and sentenced me to thirty days in juvenile detention. I began to cry, panic setting in with the awareness that I was losing my freedom.

I wasn't hurting anybody. I never participated in the thievery of my friends. I was not a criminal. I really didn't understand at the time what they were thinking. I felt wronged and misunderstood. It fuelled my anger.

I spotted Mom sitting in a pew watching the proceedings as they opened the door leading back to holding and shot her a look I hoped would make her see how deeply she had hurt me. I thought I would never forgive her for what she'd done to me.

I was transferred here and there as we made our way from Squamish to Burnaby, where the facility was located. I was going to Willingdon Youth Detention Centre, otherwise known as YDC.

Rage overtook me; my resolve from that morning to change my ways fled. I was going to show them that they couldn't control me. I told myself that after the 30 days were over I could run away freely. They had lost me.

I had lost me.

 # Chapter 6

MY FIRST GLIMPSE OF YDC was through the tiny windows from my seat in the back of a police paddy wagon. The thick double Plexiglas windows distorted the view but I could see barbed wire on all the fencing that surrounded the buildings. We entered through what appeared to be a gate and came to a stop after a few more feet. Voices outside the vehicle were shouting orders.

There was only one other occupant of the wagon. Having already seen her scowling face and seething eyes, I didn't want to make eye contact again so I was careful to stare only out my own window or at my feet on the floor.

Soon our turn came. The door to the paddy wagon swung open and a guard climbed in. We held our hands out in front of us and she silently removed our handcuffs. She was a very large, sour-faced woman with bright red lips and big rosy red cheeks. Her blue uniform had patches that mimicked police badges, and she stood straight-backed and square. She looked grumpy enough to be the judge's mate. She yelled for me to step off the truck. As I slid past her I heard her mutter, "Looks like you're good at following the crowd." Stung by her obvious disdain, I moved over to the waiting group of teens.

We were all taken into separate rooms and told to remove our clothes. After they strip-searched us they gave us new duds to wear: a pair of baggy grey sweatpants, a baby blue T-shirt, and a matching sweatshirt. Once the preliminaries were over we were all taken to our assigned areas. I was going to a place called Magnolia. They told us that Magnolia was where they put the short-timers and the ones they suspected of being trouble.

I was shown to a small cell. Fortunately there was no toilet like they have in the movies, just four walls and a really uncomfortable wire cot. That first night we ate dinner, and then we were going to go to the arcade for rec night.

We were lined up by the front door for a head count before we left. I had barely noticed the blond girl with the big build who stood near the back of the line. As I walked by her she spat in my face.

Horrified and stunned, I stared open-mouthed at her. She made a gesture with her fingers down her face, signalling tears, and pointed at me. She and her friends shared a laugh as the line moved on.

I wiped my face and began to follow the line down the walkway. Another girl fell into step beside me. She said I would have to rebut what the other girl had done or I would become Magnolia's newest punching bag.

Apparently, because I had the least amount of time to serve, I was the one they were going to single out if I didn't retaliate. She went on to say that this was no place for tears and weakness.

I listened, but I didn't like what I was hearing. I was not the fighting kind.

At the arcade it continued. The blond girl and her friends stood snickering and went ahead of me on every game I tried to play. In the end I sat down by the pool table and pretended to intently watch the game that was being played.

I learned the blond girl's name was Chelsea and that she had been at Magnolia the longest. She was a gang member of some kind in the real world. In Magnolia she was the leader.

The guards, it seemed, just wanted to get through their shifts without incident. They would turn a blind eye to much of what went on in the centre.

I made it through that evening, though. It wasn't until the following day that Chelsea and I had it out.

I was sitting on a chair in the main room reading a book when she and her posse of five came into the lounge. At first I just sat there, hoping they hadn't seen me. I was out of luck.

They came and sat down across from me with Chelsea standing in front of them, looming over me. I realized that from my position in the chair I had no room to maneuver. I started to stand up and Chelsea pushed me back down. I felt adrenaline rise in me, but a voice in my head said not yet. I prayed she would give me a chance to strike first. My heart thundered as I sat and waited.

Chelsea yelled, "You don't know how things work here in Magnolia. But you're lucky, 'cause I'm the perfect one to show you how things are gonna be." I said nothing as she spat out her tirade. I could tell she was enjoying herself, and I figured that was to my advantage. She clearly didn't think I was a threat.

Springing into action, I jumped out of the chair and turned it around at the same time. Now it was between us. Chelsea had a gleam in her eye as she deked from left to right. I matched her every move by darting in the opposite direction.

"Look at the scared rabbit!" she taunted me. "I bet I know how to make the rabbit cry." I wondered what was so fascinating to her about people crying.

She took a sudden leap over the chair. I stepped back and kicked with all my might.

I felt it before I heard it—my foot made a sickening crunching sound as it connected with her face. I knocked out one of her teeth with that first kick, but I didn't stop; I just kept kicking. Then I was on top of her, grabbing her by the hair and grinding her face into the ground.

I don't know if Chelsea was screaming or not—I didn't even notice the guards starting to gather around. They made no move to break up our fight until the head guard came in. Then there was nothing but hands and arms as they began to pry us apart. They dragged me off of her and I saw that her face was covered in blood.

Chelsea was taken to the medic room and I was returned to my cell, unharmed. The guard who accompanied me sternly told me I would be there for the rest of the afternoon and the following day.

At some point the same girl who had told me that I needed to stand up for myself came and stood outside my door. She told me her name was Midget and that I would be Rabbit from now on. She said Chelsea wouldn't mess with me again.

I was disgusted. I hadn't wanted to fight, but now that I had, it seemed I had somehow bought myself some freedom, even within those walls.

I cried quietly to myself those first few nights. I was counting every day as it passed. For the first while I even counted the minutes of the days. Halloween was the big day I was looking forward to. After October 31 I would have only three more days till my release.

I finally called my parents after that first week. Mom told me that TJ had been there to see her and Dad, and that he thought their home wasn't working. TJ suspected that I would need more structure once I got out of YDC because I would no longer be on probation.

I knew she was looking for me to reassure her that I wasn't going to run away anymore. But that was a promise I could not make. "We're your parents," she finally said. "We're never going to give up on you. You need to remember we love you."

Although I had no idea how far-reaching the consequences of that conversation would be, I was crying when I hung up. Maybe Chelsea was right and I was a bit of a baby.

Nighttime was the most miserable in that place. There was nothing to do but think once the lights went out. No way to sneak books into your room to read at night; no tiptoeing down the hall to the washroom. Only the four walls and the occasional clanging of doors. The only indication that time was really passing was the beam of the guard's flashlight when they looked in on you every hour.

Midget and I became friends. We did everything together. The guards seemed to know this because they assigned us the same duties. We were paired up for almost all our activities.

One afternoon, we were in the laundry room folding clothes when I finally got up the nerve to ask her what it was she was in there for. She went on to tell me a story that would change my life. From her I would finally understand what Dad had been trying to tell me about responsibility.

He had said sometimes things just happened and you might think you had no control over the outcome. But you were always guilty of relinquishing control in the first place, and that made you responsible for the entire outcome.

Until I heard Midget's story, I'd never really understood what Dad meant.

Midget had been living on a beach in Vancouver with some friends. One day they'd been drinking and smoking pot when they came on a man's clothing neatly folded over a log.

One of Midget's friends had grabbed the pants, hoping for a wallet, when a pair of hands grabbed the pants from the other side of the log. A man stood up, still holding the pant leg, and a tug-of-war over the pants ensued. Watching, Midget realized the man was getting the upper hand, jumped over the log, and kicked him in the chest.

She just meant to make him let go of the pants, but her kick caused him to lose his balance, and her friend let go of the pants at the same time. The man fell with enough force to be speared by a branch that was sticking out from another nearby log. Her friends ran, leaving her behind. She stayed to try to help the man, but he died.

Now she was serving a three-year sentence for his murder and the rest of her life would be haunted by what ifs and if onlys.

I thought back to all the times I had been about to get into trouble—how the voice in my head would try to warn me, and I would ignore it. I eyed Midget closely and realized that she believed it was a tragic accident. I felt sorry for her, but even sorrier for the man. I saw the series of events that could and should have been prevented.

October 31 was fast approaching and an air of excitement charged the YDC. On Halloween there would be pizza, candy, and activities in the gym. Not only that—the event would be co-ed. I think that was what was causing most of the excitement.

Occasionally, we would catch glimpses of the boys who were being held in another part of the facility, but the staff at YDC were pretty good at keeping us all separated. One day, though, we were making our way back to Magnolia from an activity when I heard a voice calling my name. It took me a minute to realize someone was calling me because I hadn't heard my name in some time. I looked around and saw Mick standing on the boys' side. He was smiling, happy to see me. Mick shouted at me that Jeff had gone to Squamish to look for me and that everyone had been worried. He said they would get a kick out of it when he told them that he had seen me in there.

I talked to him for about two minutes before the guards made it clear our moment was up. "I'll go see Jeff as soon as I'm out!" I shouted after him.

That was a very exciting day. Something had happened to break the monotony. I thought about Midget. I was serving thirty days and it was really hard to manage. Three years seemed like an eternity.

I was also attending school during the week. That helped pass the time, but otherwise days were spent mostly the same. You woke up, you showered, you ate breakfast, and then you had exercises. After exercises depending on what day it was you either had school or art class.

When November 3 came I was almost sorry to leave. Most of the girls had actually turned out to be quite nice, and even Chelsea managed a half-snort when I said goodbye. The guards escorted me all the way through the gates to where TJ stood waiting for me. It was so exhilarating to see open skies without wires that I almost felt happy to see him. I climbed into his Jeep, and he surprised me with a package of cigarettes. He even let me smoke in the Jeep. Later it would dawn on me that he'd been softening me up for the blow to come.

He asked if I would like some lunch. I readily agreed. I hadn't had a juicy burger and fries in at least thirty days.

He said little as we headed to the restaurant, and I thought about finally spending an evening in my own bed. I made secret plans to read a book late into the night and sit on the windowsill no matter how uncomfortable it was getting for my growing body. I was also going to go to the bathroom at least ten times, just because I could.

We were sitting in the restaurant digesting a great lunch when he hit me with the news. He was not taking me home to Squamish. I was going to live in a group home in West Vancouver. He explained to me that the structure and rules of a group home environment were exactly what I needed.

I couldn't believe it. I told TJ it couldn't be true because I had talked to my parents two days ago and they had said nothing to me.

TJ said that was because the decision had only been carried through the day before. It had been TJ's call. He said my parents were both upset by it, but that given time, he was sure we'd all see that this was for the best.

My mind raced while he paid our waitress. I imagined punching him; I imagined jumping out of the Jeep as it roared along; I imagined many things, but I knew that in the end nothing I could do would hurt him. He would just keep driving, carefully keeping his eyes on the street ahead.

I settled for shouting in the parking lot. "You must feel like a god, being able to mess with real lives like this! Are you proud you've finally gotten to do something with your social worker status?!"

He nodded, almost sage-like, as if he had thought that was what I would say. I tried switching tactics. I tried reason. I told him that I had had a lot of time to think in YDC and that if he gave me a chance I would prove that Mom and Dad were the best thing for me.

None of it worked. We climbed back into the Jeep and began the journey to my new home. Shocked into silence, I didn't say another word to him the whole way there.

The group home stood on a corner high up on the hill, just below the highway in West Vancouver. I remember thinking it looked familiar as we pulled into the alley and parked behind a small red Fiat.

The first staff member I met there told me they prefer to be called counsellors in this home, and that I was to talk to them if I ever needed to. She was a round-bellied lady with black curly hair. She looked familiar too.

TJ was talking to the counsellor, Joan. I interrupted to ask about my belongings. I wanted to get what I needed from that place and leave as quickly as possible. Joan told me that my belongings had been brought in the day before by TJ and that when I finished the orientation she would take me down to my new room.

Orientation was time-consuming and boring. It mostly consisted of the counsellors telling me the rules of the home and asking me a series of questions geared towards getting to know me: what grade I had completed; what school I had last attended; what my goals were for later in life; that sort of thing. TJ stayed and listened as I answered them. I resented his presence and wanted him to leave.

Tracy, another counsellor, came in while I was answering Joan's questions. He was tall with long blond hair, quite good-looking. He kept in shape by riding his bike everywhere.

When I had answered all the questions on Joan's list Tracy asked if I wanted to go down now. I didn't even say goodbye to TJ before following him down the stairs. My room was half below street level in the basement. Three other girls also had rooms down there. I was told that there were two boys living upstairs.

Left to myself I began to go through my stuff. My mom had painstakingly wrapped everything that was breakable, which really wasn't much, and had neatly folded my clothes. I no longer needed my trunk. My belongings now fit into two suitcases. I realized that I had lost a lot my stuff in my travelling adventures. I sat heavily on the bed and looked around the near-empty room. It looked cold to me. I knew I wasn't at home and would never really live there.

I fell asleep and was awakened by a girl who was dressed in hippie-inspired clothes and wore her hair long and loose. Her name was Skye. There was something very gentle about her movements; I thought she would make a good mother someday. She led me upstairs for supper.

As I got closer to the kitchen I heard a very familiar voice. I didn't dare believe the evidence of my ears. I had to see her with my own eyes.

When I rounded the corner into the kitchen I saw that it was Cara's voice I had heard. She was standing at the kitchen sink rinsing vegetables for salad.

When she saw me she dropped what she was doing and came screaming over to me. We must have looked a sight as we jumped up and down holding hands, hers all wet and slimy. I didn't care. I was so happy to see a familiar face. We danced around like that for some time before Joan said enough was enough and that there was work to be done if we were to sit down for supper.

While I helped Cara with the salad she told me that RJ was living there too, although he wasn't home at the moment. She whispered that she and RJ were still together. He had come to live there after the Hunchback Hotel had been closed down for some reason. Jeff had gone back to live with his father but was rarely seen now because his father had very strict rules.

While we ate dinner, I found myself getting involved in the group conversation. In fact Cara and I dominated the table chatter reminiscing about our past escapades. When I had arrived at the group home that day I'd had no intention of spending even one night there. Discovering that Cara was there changed all my plans to leave. I knew I wouldn't be leaving unless she and I left together.

RJ never did come home that first week that I was there, but he did call. He put Jeff on the line too so I was finally able to talk to him. It was the first time I had spoken to him since I had left YDC, so it was a long conversation. Jeff hung up after telling me he would come by and get me soon. I probably should have clarified what he meant by "soon," because I spent the next three days afraid to leave my room in case I missed him.

Eventually RJ and Jeff did come for us. That evening I had already said good night to Cara and was alone in my room when she came creeping in. A few minutes later we were sneaking out my window and running through the front yard to where RJ and Jeff were waiting for us.

That night we must have driven up Robson Street in Vancouver about fifty times. We were all happy and high on life. I was just relieved to be with Jeff. We stayed out until the wee hours when Jeff said that he had to get back to his dad's.

Cara and I crept back through my window, our absence seemingly unnoticed. It was weird coming back the same night we had left. It felt as if we had been gone a lot longer.

Christmas came and for the first time I was a guest in my parents' home. My brother and his wife came for Christmas that year as well. Mom and Dad decided that Mellanie and I would room together in the basement on the fold-out couch. I was staying for two days. It didn't seem like long enough.

Christmas was always really big and important to our family. There was a lot of love in our house all year round, but at Christmas it overflowed. Mom and Dad would start preparing for it in November. They always had a huge tree that would dominate the living room. The decorations were carefully hung, each carrying its own special meaning. Many had been in the family for years and had such sentimental value that us kids were forbidden to touch them.

My parents didn't stop with the tree, though. As the month slipped by and December approached, Mom would put up decorations all over the entire house. She would take down the regular occupants of each surface and replace them with angels, Santas, and snowmen.

Dad was in charge of the outside lights and decorations. He would hang lights from the roof, and all the trees in the front yard would be covered in lights. We would have ornaments on our lawn; one year we even had a reindeer on the roof.

Mom would start her Christmas baking in late November. The wonderful aroma of fresh-baked chocolate permeated the house from then right through to New Year's.

On Christmas morning I sat in one of the living room chairs and watched as everyone celebrated and opened gifts. For some time I opened none of mine. I felt like an outsider again, like I wasn't really there. I felt invisible. Mom must have seen something in my face because she came over to me and sat near me while handing gifts out.

That year my parents gave me a typewriter. It was a testament to how well they knew me, and I felt overwhelmed with gratitude. Not even so much at the gift itself, but at the recognition that it was their way of telling me that they knew I wanted to write and that they thought

I could. I felt an odd sense of responsibility holding that typewriter in my lap.

Later that night Mellanie and I were alone in the basement. We started to talk. I told her about living in the group home and what that was like. I talked to her about Jeff and his family life, or lack thereof.

I was crying on her shoulder when she did something really weird. She kissed me very deeply, as you would a lover, and when I went to pull away she told me to hold still; that I would like it. She began to touch me in my private places and I cried harder. Finally she must have realized that I wasn't going to enjoy it because she stopped, and asked me not to tell anyone. I was horrified. To me if felt as if my home was gone. Nothing was the same anymore.

Mellanie seemed embarrassed the next day and barely said a word to me. I know that Mom knew something was going on between us but I'm sure that she thought that it was the same old trouble that always seemed to plague Mellanie's and my relationship. I came close to telling her what had happened the night before. But I decided against it because I understood that long ago someone must have hurt Mellanie too.

I had to go back to my group home on Boxing Day. Cara was already back when I arrived there. Her home visit hadn't gone well, and she was angry and unapproachable. Her sour mood lasted for a week.

In early January Cara and I grew tired of waiting for the guys to call us. Cara said she knew where RJ might be and that once we got there RJ would be able to reach Jeff.

Since I was no longer on probation I had nothing to lose by leaving. I was tired of the humdrum of normalcy anyway. So when she came to get me later that night we decided that we would leave through the front door instead of crawling through windows and sneaking away out the back.

Joan was the staff member on duty that night. When she saw us heading for the door she tried hard to reason with us. "Do you know what time it is, girls?" she asked us. "It's past curfew."

We ignored her and slammed the door behind us.

Cara and I walked down Fifteenth Street and headed for the Lions Gate bridge. I had never walked across it. Nearly deserted, with almost no traffic, the city at its quietest, it was breathtaking. The ocean was outlined dark on the horizon and the water itself looked crisp and clear. There were only a few ripples gliding across its otherwise still surface. I was overwhelmed with the feeling of freedom. I stared across at all that vastness of space that was far from empty. Whole worlds rest in that ocean.

Cara and I had no money; we had planned to walk all the way to Mick's house. I realized it was farther than we thought and once we began to trek through downtown we started to get tired.

A dark brown sedan had been creeping along behind us for almost two blocks. A very large round elderly-looking fellow was driving. He kept signalling that he wanted us to come to his open window. Cara, finally getting upset at his relentlessness, went over to his window. After talking to him for a few minutes she came back to me. "Wanna make an easy hundred dollars?"

An easy hundred sounded really good to me. Then we could take a cab.

So we climbed into his car and he drove us to his apartment. By the time we got there, there was no doubt what we were going to have to do to earn our "easy" money, and I was feeling a little sick. I convinced myself that if Cara was willing to do it then I could do it. I wanted to get it over with so I told Cara that I would go into his room first.

In his bedroom the man pulled from his wallet two crisp one hundred dollar bills and gave them to me. I racked my brain trying to remember if I had ever held so much money in my hands at once. I knew that one bill was for Cara. I put them both in my jeans pocket.

The man got naked quickly, and was obviously quite excited. I told myself to just strip naked and get in that bed. He put on a condom and started to climb on top of me. I just prayed that he would hurry up and that it would all be over soon. Within seconds it was. I got dressed and went into the next room to send Cara in. When she walked past me to go into his bedroom I wondered if it would still be Cara who came out.

I knew that I didn't feel like me anymore. I knew that something in me had switched off and that I would no longer hurt myself at night. I had found something better. I had found a new way to hurt myself.

The next morning Cara and I made our way to the house where Mick was couch-surfing. I was excited to see Mick; I hadn't seen him since we had shared that brief hello in YDC. Mick offered to let us stay there with him that night since his friend was going to be away for that particular night.

RJ showed up at Mick's not too long after, and he and Cara began to argue almost immediately. Mick and I stayed in his room and let them have it out. Eventually they stopped arguing and more intimate sounds became audible. I eyed Mick, who looked pained. I felt it too. He would have been much better for Cara.

I was able to see Jeff the next day. We met him at Metrotown mall. I ran straight to him when I saw him. He wrapped his big muscular arms around me and we just stood like that for a while.

Cara was starting to get a tad crabby, which usually meant that she'd been hungry two hours ago and was near starving now. She became almost intolerable if she didn't eat. Mick said that he knew where we should go for some money and that it would be easy and quick.

"Easy and quick" usually meant we were going to steal what we needed. Cara and I had money in our pockets, but we wouldn't be able to explain where we'd gotten it. Trying to quiet my guilty conscience, I fell into step behind my friends.

We went to the Canada Games Pool, a short SkyTrain and bus ride

away. The guys told Cara and me to take a seat on some stairs about half a block away and wait for them there. They were gone for about twenty minutes and when they came back they had four wallets.
Cara and I saw our opportunity, and slipped the money we had made the night before into one of the wallets.

Pocketing the cash, we left the wallets on the stairs and made our way back to Metrotown, where we headed for the food court. In the mall parking lot I noticed a large bin for recycling newspapers. A man climbed out through a narrow slot where papers were thrown in. Feeling sorry for him, I took ten dollars off Jeff and handed it to the stranger as he unceremoniously hit the ground. The gesture did little to make me feel any better about RJ and Jeff having stolen those wallets. But I knew that no one was going to just give us money or miraculously show up with food to quiet our tummies. I thought of what Cara and I had done the night before. It had been repulsive, but I reasoned that compared to thievery, it was a victimless crime.

We stayed together the entire day until Jeff had to go back to his father's place. Mick's roommate was going to be home that night so we were unable to stay at his place either. Cara and I were on our own for the night.

Jeff took us to Lesters, an arcade off the main street by Metrotown, and said we could stay there all night if we made our money last. After promising to come back in the morning he left us there.

When Cara and I ran out of money it was nearing 4 a.m. We walked out of the arcade and found it had begun to rain. I remembered the man who had climbed out of the newspaper bin earlier. I led Cara back to it and we climbed up and inside it. We wrapped the newspapers around us to stay warm, and fell asleep—until someone dumped a phone book by Cara's head, startling her awake.

For the next few days, Cara and I hung out in Lesters as late as we could and retreated to the newspaper bin for a warm dry place to sleep. By the end of the week we were starting to think of the bin as ours.

We got a kick out of throwing the newspapers back out of the bin at the people who threw them in. Some screamed and ran, and others banged on the walls and yelled at us.

No one ever asked why there were two kids living in a dumpster behind the mall, although if anyone had we would have had to say by choice. We just ignored the voice of reason that plagued our every waking moment. We felt wronged, ignored, and mostly lost. We didn't want an adult to fix us or claim to understand us. We didn't know what we wanted and we didn't give it a lot of thought; we just knew we needed something to be real and ours. For Cara and me, at that time, that something was each other.

More than two weeks after Cara and I had crossed the Lions Gate Bridge, we were still sleeping in the bin, showering at the Canada Games Pool, and hanging out with the guys during the day. Late one evening, RJ and I were wrestling and playing around outside Lesters Arcade. I had RJ in a pretend headlock and he reached through my arms, grabbed my wrist, and twisted. There was an odd crunching noise and then pain shot through my entire body.

Horrified, RJ immediately let go of me and stared at me open-mouthed. I could tell he felt horrible. Jeff looked angry enough for both of us, though, as he shoved RJ aside and came running over to my side.

We went to the hospital. X-rays showed that my wrist wasn't broken. I had a hairline fracture in it, though, and had pulled a tendon.

The hospital called the group home and Tracy came to get Cara, RJ, and me. This time we left Jeff staring after us as we drove off back to West Vancouver.

RJ waited on me hand and foot for the next few days. In a way it irritated me. I had to keep reminding myself that he was only trying to be helpful because he felt so bad for what had happened.

My wrist was healing quite nicely, but I was still wearing a bandage on it when once again I ran afoul of the law.

Cara and I had run out of cigarettes, so we'd gone to the store, and raced to get back to the house by curfew. I was thirsty from the run and wanted a drink of milk. One of the group home rules was that no one was allowed in the kitchen past 10 p.m. It was five after ten.

Janet was the counsellor on shift that night. She was not a very pleasant person—word around the house was that Janet was on the night shift because she wasn't suited to actually have to talk to us kids.

I listened carefully but the coast seemed clear as I made my way down the hallway and entered the kitchen. I was reaching into the fridge for the milk when suddenly the door slammed shut against my wrist and I felt a stab of pain. I screamed, grabbing my arm, and stepped back from the fridge. Janet stood staring at me angrily. When I could finally muster words I shrieked at her, "Who do you think you are?!"

Janet yelled back at me about the rules and started to walk away. I told her that this was my home, not hers, and that if I wanted a glass of milk then I was going to have a glass of milk. I opened the fridge again. This time she grabbed me. She had me in a headlock, and I began to panic. Her grip was unyielding—the more I struggled the harder she squeezed. She left me with no other way to defend myself. I bit her.

Screaming in pain, she let go of me and ran to the office. She locked herself in and I could hear her on the phone to the police.

I was scared. I didn't know what to do. Run? Stay? What was going to happen now? In the end I waited and the police came. After questioning Janet at some length, they came and put me in handcuffs. Once again I was arrested and put into the back of a squad car.

I would spend another night in holding and stand in front of another judge who would decide my fate.

Janet was crazy. All I had wanted was a glass of milk. Who made up those stupid rules anyway?

 # Chapter 7

I MADE AN APPEARANCE AT the Youth Detention Centre for the weekend, till my case could be heard the following Monday.

There were still some familiar faces in Magnolia; there were also some new ones, but I wouldn't meet any of them. I spent most of my time in my cell, with the door open, staring into space and sleeping. I didn't want to talk to anyone. Even Midget tried to poke her head in once or twice, but I would just roll away and face the wall.

I thought of many things that weekend. I pictured my grandfather's face if he were ever to find out I was in jail. I thought about all the times my granny had yelled that I was a demon and rotten in some way. She had been right. I thought about Mom and Dad and how disappointed they must be in me. What if I never saw them again? I pulled the grey itchy wool blanket over my head and cried.

Court on Monday was quick. The lawyers and the judge discussed additional court dates for me to appear on the new charge of assault causing bodily harm. I signed some official documents that stated I understood I had a court date and would appear if released on my own recognizance.

TJ Kwan stood waiting outside the courthouse when I came striding out the doors. I had spotted him in the courtroom, so I'd expected to see him there. He smiled encouragingly at me and for a second I smiled back. Then I remembered that I hated him, and the smile disappeared behind my glowering eyes.

I climbed into his Jeep with a weary heart. It seemed he always came with bad news lately. I told him my tale, protesting my innocence and deriding the vicious staff members. He listened quietly, nodding agreeably while he drove. When I finally stopped talking he told me that I was no longer able to live in the group home. Although I was relieved that I wouldn't have to see Janet again, I couldn't help but feel resentful that it was I who had to move and not she. My hands shook with the bitterness creeping down my spine, and I had to sit on them. I wondered if Janet had a home, and if she had ever been forced to leave it.

I knew it was easier to move me than her, and I knew it was going to be that way until the day I turned eighteen. It seemed like such a long lonely time. Self-pity overwhelmed me.

I thought about a recent conversation I'd had with Mom. We had been keeping in touch regularly while I was living at the group home and I'd kept her updated on almost everything I was doing.

She had told me that if I adhered to the rules of the group home it might show that I would be willing to obey the rules at home now too. It had sounded reasonable to me, so I had been going to school every day and had been coming through the front door by curfew every night. By not running off even when I had known the police were coming, had I not shown that I was truly making an effort?

I began to hope that maybe TJ had seen it too. Maybe he was going to let me go back to Mom and Dad's house. Maybe he was finally going to let me go home.

But it turned out my efforts had been in vain. TJ had made arrangements at yet another group home that was in Vancouver. "Why can't I just go back to Squamish?" I asked quietly.

He took a deep breath, and I saw him steel himself before he spoke. "We've decided that going to live with your parents isn't going to be an option for you any more. The file's been closed on your appeal. You're going to have to continue to reside in structured group home environments because of the benefits they're providing for you." His tone left no room to argue.

Up until that moment I had thought I was just biding my time until TJ saw the light and let me go home.

Inside I was screaming, *"Home!"* It felt as if I was always screaming. Nobody ever heard me.

That afternoon I started to see TJ in a new light. Suddenly he didn't appear so new to the job. In fact, he was beginning to look arrogant. He was certainly making no secret of the fact that it was he who had pushed for that decision. I saw a man who was absolutely certain his actions were just.

It was obvious to me for the first time: TJ was sitting in the driver's seat in more ways than one. The man really did hold all the cards. I could never win.

He lived a different life than mine. His decisions wouldn't eat him alive every day because he was separated from those he loved or who loved him. He would go home, to *his* home, and this day would be over when he went to bed. For me, it would just be the beginning of another phase of uncertainty and instability.

In that moment I realized TJ was much smarter than I had thought. Now that he had finally been able to give positive feedback about my behavior to his superiors at Social Services, I had made him look as if he had made the right decision. Now he had the backing of his higher-ups, perhaps even of Freddie Lavin, to permanently keep me in group homes.

This wave of realization was followed immediately by a tide of rage and mournful hysteria.

Suddenly I saw myself as a file number discussed by a group of adults all with yellow notepads on their laps and coffees in their hands. Decisions about *what to do with Tara* made over coffee and doughnuts.

I was just part of the morning shuffle of paperwork. They thought they had a plan for my future and could file me away.

I told TJ he had just made the biggest mistake of his career. I would make sure I was dead before I let him control me. I repeated the word, DEAD. Leaning in towards his ear, I shouted, "I'm going to leave until they force me to come back and then I'll leave again. One day I might never be found! And you'll have to live with never knowing what became of the little Indian girl you once knew." Then I called him names and told him that he was probably the stupidest social worker that ever was.

TJ drove wordlessly this whole time, barely blinking at my verbal assault. Time dragged in the uncomfortable silence that followed my outburst, until he pulled into an alley off Knight Street in Vancouver.

He led me into a group home. True to my word, I waited for him to leave and then stormed out the back door.

I stood in the alley and thought about what I should do next. In order to live I needed food and shelter. For those things I needed money. I needed to find Granville Street. That was all I knew when I made my way to 41st Avenue and began to walk west towards downtown.

I made it to a pay phone on Fraser Street, where I called Mom and told her what had happened. She said TJ had already told her that if she and Dad opened their door to me they would lose their foster home status. Then I would never be able to come home. "Go back to the group home, Tara," she urged. "I'll look into what we can do in the morning."

I assured her that I wasn't going to get into any trouble and that I would keep in touch. She must have heard something in my voice, though, because she told me that some things couldn't be undone once they were done. I ended the conversation by telling her that I loved her and that I would solve this one my way. I stared at the phone for a few seconds after I hung up, then walked away from the phone booth feeling empty and alone. I wanted to go home. I wanted warm milk or hot chocolate at my mom's kitchen table. More than anything, at that moment I wanted a hug.

As I walked, I started to mentally prepare myself for what I was about to do. I felt as if I had no choice.

I thought about that night with Cara when we had met that man who had taken both of us to his house. It really hadn't been all that bad. He hadn't hurt us. I told myself that he had just been lonely; that we had helped him and he had helped us. No one was going to get hurt by my doing this, not like when you steal other people's memories in their most cherished possessions. I didn't have the stomach for robbing people or participating in that kind of crime any longer. I convinced myself there was only one way for me to survive. I upped my pace and kept walking towards Granville.

From Granville, I found my way downtown to Nelson and Seymour. I stopped, sat down in an alcove, and tried to collect myself. I thought of my grandparents, and of what they would think if they saw where I was and what was becoming of me. I was alone. It felt as if I was sitting on the edge of a cliff and was really going to jump. I started to cry. I cried for my childhood that was officially gone. I cried for the little girl I was no longer going to be, but most of all I cried for who I was going to become. I knew I couldn't do what I was about to do and come out unscathed.

I cried for a long time, until the sun had moved farther down in the sky and had started to paint the west in bright red and singed pink hues.

When I emerged from the alcove, though, I just glanced at the sunset and turned my back. To me beauty no longer existed ... no more flowers; no more whimsical breezes. *Toughen up. Life's about to get dangerous: you need to stay on your toes if you hope to have a chance of surviving.*

I was scared, though, and didn't know what I was doing. Every time a car came around the corner and the headlights hit me I would run back into the alcove and hide. A man even pulled over and tried to talk to me. I told him I was waiting for somebody. He looked at me, confused, and drove away.

I began to wonder if I could do it. I knew I was never going to make any money if I wouldn't even talk to anyone. I thought of mothers and daughters seeing me, regular people who went by with regular motives—driving home from the office, or heading to meet friends, just living normal lives—and I was embarrassed to be me. I wanted to be them so badly, to have a home and a family waiting. I knew that those who looked at me harshly were judging me, and that to them I was already gone. Those who looked at me with sympathy were even worse because that meant they understood and had forgiven me in some way. It hurt me that I would feel relief at receiving forgiveness from a stranger.

I was startled by a voice behind me asking for a cigarette. I turned and saw a young woman standing there. She was close to my age from what I could tell. She had on a very short black miniskirt, a tight-fitting low-cut tank top, and a purple sweater that covered it all, even most of her thigh-high suede boots.

I still had the package of cigarettes that TJ had bought for me, so I offered her one. Taking the cigarette, she scrutinized me closely. "You're new around here," she observed. Afraid to say anything, I just nodded.

She introduced herself as Shelly, and after we had talked for a while I found myself telling her that I had come from a group home I couldn't go back to. I told her about not being able to live with my parents, and that I had no idea where I was going to live or even how to do what I had come to that street corner to do. I realized I was almost begging but I couldn't help myself.

Shelly studied me for a few minutes. Then she turned her attention to the street. I was worried I had turned her off somehow, and was starting to feel a little awkward standing there, when she suddenly went out into the road and flagged a silver car down. She opened the passenger door, turned to me, and said, "We have to do something about your wardrobe. Get in." I took about two seconds to think about it before climbing into the back seat of the car.

Shelly introduced me to Steven, who was driving the car. He had tightly curled brownish-blond hair and the bluest eyes I had ever seen. I didn't look too long though because it was obvious that he and Shelly were together. Shelly told him how we had met and a little of my story. She said she had clothes I could borrow and that I would be welcome to room with them until I could find my own way. "That's how it is out here. We all have to look out for each other, because no one else will," she explained.

Shelly promised that changing my attire would help me to stop feeling as if I had to hide. "When I dress the part, it makes it easier for me to play the role." She said that that's what we were doing: we had a paying role that should last for no longer than fifteen minutes and should never pay less than eighty dollars for that fifteen minutes of role play. I was stunned. Eighty dollars for fifteen minutes! Why wasn't everybody doing this?

Steven and Shelly had a small room in a hotel at Broadway and Main. It had one small window, a couch, and a bed. There was a photo on the radiator of what looked like a happy family with two little girls. One appeared to be around two years old and the other maybe five. They were standing next to a woman I suspected was their mother. The woman was beaming with love, her eyes sparkling. When I asked Shelly about the picture, she said it was just some people she used to know.

Shelly began to dress me up. I imagine it was like having a full-size Barbie for her to play with—I could tell she was having fun. Steven made us some drinks and rolled us up a joint while Shelly did my makeup. Some primping and a few rum and Cokes later, we were ready to head out into the streets once again.

I was tipsy that first night. Shelly helped me gain confidence, although I'm sure the wig I had on helped too. I felt like I wasn't me. It made it

.easier to look at people in cars as they drove by.

I don't remember my first "date" that night, or any of them in the next month. I lived with Shelly and Steven in their hotel room. I slept on their couch and paid for my own food and clothing. Shelly took me shopping, expertly helping me pick out the clothes that would enable me to draw in the dates. I was going to buy my own wig but we couldn't find one that felt comfortable on my head. Hers was quite itchy as well but the ones we tried on in the stores felt as if they were made of straw.

One night when I was sleeping, Shelly woke me up and told me that I'd been screaming in my sleep and had scared them awake. Apparently it wasn't the first time. She wasn't angry—in fact, she was looking at me with sympathy, and seemed genuinely concerned.

I hadn't known that I was still having nightmares. I hadn't thought about them in some time, so I had just assumed they had stopped. I told her I was sorry for waking both of them. Shelly seemed content to leave it at that.

Shelly and I liked to get it over with early … I think because we didn't want to be there when the rough crowd of girls came out. They had pimps, and they seemed meaner because they had someone to answer to. Shelly and I, both considerably younger, got picked up quickly, and I think that frustrated the girls who had pimps.

Shelly always warned me to stay away from them. She said that the girls would use me if they could to buy their way out of their current situation. Apparently a young girl like me could buy them their freedom from their pimps.

Shelly was not only street-wise, she was beautiful, with her long black flowing hair, clear complexion, and naturally red lips. I wondered who had hurt her so badly that she was living in a dingy old hotel room instead of in the real world, which she so obviously coveted. I felt as if the real world would find a place for someone as special and intelligent as she seemed.

"The real world" is what Shelly called the normal nine-to-five world, and the name had stuck with me. When we went out for dinner we would overhear conversations at the surrounding tables—people talking to their children about report cards; husbands and wives chatting about their workday; couples on dates sharing quiet giggles and sideways glances. We called those people "the real-world people."

They seemed brave, to have so much to risk losing. I didn't dare fantasize about myself in the real world. I knew that the path I had chosen did not include a white picket fence or PTA meetings.

Shelly once said that we should never think about where we could be because in our world, daydreaming could cost you all you had left: your life.

"Hope makes you do stupid things," she'd say. Then she would tell me to snap out of my reverie, because our life was waiting.

I'd been staying with Steven and Shelly for about a month when Shelly got a phone call. She hung up the phone and did a dance. Whooping and hollering, she yelled for Steven to get out of the bath he was soaking in. When Steven came out of the bathroom, Shelly announced that her sister was days away from being released from prison.

I hadn't known she had a sister. When I asked her about any family she might have had, she would tell me that I needed to know that normalcy was an illusion and that the general public used it to shield their eyes from the truth. The truth, according to Shelly, was that no home was immune to loss and disaster. I suspected she was referring to what had happened to her own family, but I knew better than to push her for details.

It turned out, though, that she and her sister had come here from a prairie town, and that when her sister had gotten into trouble three years ago and been imprisoned, she had to stay in Vancouver to be near her. Unable to leave her sister, Shelly had met Steven, and they had taken care of each other ever since.

Later that night, I was struck with the thought that her sister would need a place to stay and that that might put me out on the street. I would be okay, I thought. I would have to save some money and get my own hotel room. I could manage anything now.

I was feeling powerful because I had survived this long. Maybe that was why I wasn't as careful as usual that night. I ignored the warnings in my head as I climbed into a beige station wagon next to a man who had not even looked right at me when we had had the chat—a definite sign that something was off with him.

"The chat" is what I termed the discussion we had with dates before we went with them. Most of the men who picked us up were older middle-class men who smelled of money and normalcy. I imagine most of them had wives. We told ourselves that they would cheat on their wives anyway, so why shouldn't we make our survival off it?

I didn't know it but I was losing a piece of myself every time I got into a car with a strange man. I was getting very good at turning myself off while they did what they needed to do. I didn't cry about it anymore. But I had stopped handing money to people who were begging on the streets. I thought if they knew what I had done to get that money, they wouldn't want it anyway. I was ashamed and disgusted with myself.

The man drove to the now-abandoned Expo site. It provided perfect privacy for what we were about to do.

This man was younger than the usual men who picked us up. When I glanced at his ring finger and saw it was bare I was surprised. Some men told us it was variety that they missed in marriage—spontaneity and the thrill of the chase. That apparently wasn't the case with this guy.

Men would talk to me about their misery and I would listen quietly, always hoping that maybe if I listened well enough they wouldn't want to do anything to me anymore. It gave my fourteen-year-old soul hope.

I even asked him why he was picking up hookers when he looked like he could get what he wanted from the bar. He said he did it for the convenience. I remember wondering what could be convenient about having to drive around and pay for it. I didn't ask.

He found a spot by some abandoned steel trailers under the First Avenue viaduct, where it was the most desolate and dark, and stopped the car. He turned in his seat so he could look at me as at least forty men had done before him. I was feeling confident and secure. After all, I was now a pro. I had just over thirty days' experience, and I wasn't afraid anymore.

I reached into my small shoulder bag for a condom—Shelly and I were both adamant about using them—and he reached into his pocket for his cash. When he saw what I was holding in my hand he said he never used condoms and that he should be able to pay me extra to not use it.

Shelly always said that all we had was our life. That was why we had to stay away from drugs (excluding marijuana, of course) and why we always used condoms and never told much of our stories to the men or allowed the men to become intimate with us.

"Never be afraid to walk away from the money," she would say. "You can make more if you're still alive." I hoped this wasn't going to be my chance to see what she was talking about.

I told the man there was going to be no date without the condom. He had already given me the cash and I had stuck it in my shoulder bag. I was suddenly very aware of the isolated spot we had driven to. Civilization was just above our heads but I knew that it was actually far away.

The man spent some time trying to convince me. Finally I told him to put the condom on or I was leaving. He became irate. "You're nothing anyway," he yelled. "What are you so concerned about?"

I realized nothing was going to work with this man and I probably should just give him his money back. But I didn't. I opened the car door and ran like hell. I ran for the wall that led up to the First Avenue overpass. When I reached the wall I began to climb the ivy that wound its way down it. I was halfway up when I felt something whip past my head. He had thrown a rock at me and missed me by a mere inch. With renewed desperation I climbed faster. When I was only about two feet away from freedom the first of the prickle bushes began. My hands were getting cut up and sliced by the prickles, but I didn't care. I just kept grabbing and climbing.

But then I realized that the bushes stuck out just enough to keep me from the top. I was stuck—there was no way I could go back down, and I didn't know how much longer I could hold on. I started to pray. I was begging and promising this and that. The man was still throwing rocks and I could hear them hitting the wall.

I was crying and wailing, clinging on for dear life, when all of a sudden two hands reached down from the overpass and grabbed me. They pulled me up and over the wall as if I weighed no more than a bag of apples. Then I was on the ground, trying to collect myself. I looked up in time to see a man I recognized walking away. Shelly and I had seen him around a lot, mostly at night when we were making our way home from the corner. He had beautiful long black hair that he covered with a bandana. He had on a deep purple dress shirt and what looked like knitted chaps covering black jeans. He covered it all up with an oversized black trench coat.

I wanted to shout after him as he walked away. The man had saved my life, or at least saved me from possible brain damage. I shuddered when I thought of how hard the rocks hit the wall, acutely aware it was my head that had been the target. I didn't know what to say though. The man seemed almost unreal to me, and I was intimidated.

I didn't start to feel safe again until the adrenaline had ebbed and I was walking on Granville, surrounded by people who understood me. Slowing my pace, I managed to light a cigarette.

Panhandlers I was on a nod-my-head basis with and homeless tin chasers who would normally give me encouraging smiles were the people I now felt the safest around. Their faces were familiar to me. I felt they were the ones who really knew me.

It wasn't until I was in this comforting milieu that I felt the pain in my upper back. I went into the bathroom of the local Burger King and took off my shirt to inspect my wounds. A large angry red welt was already turning an ugly shade of purple right below my neck, between my shoulder blades. Through sheer luck, a rock must have missed my head by inches. I hadn't even felt it hit.

I knew this incident was going to be my secret. I told myself that I had to learn to survive on my own and I couldn't run to Shelly with every little thing anymore. And Mom could never know what had happened to me; it would scare her. I put my shirt back on and turned from the mirror, vowing never to think about that night again. It never happened, I told myself, closing the bathroom door behind me.

Later that night Steven picked Shelly and me up and we went to the Knight and Day buffet as usual. There I learned that Shelly's sister was going to be arriving the following day in the early afternoon. Steven and I decided we would make ourselves scarce until early evening. We wanted to give Shelly some private time with her sister. They had three years to catch up on.

The following afternoon Steven and I went out and played pool. I really enjoyed myself. I discovered that I had a natural talent for pool—I was winning almost every game. I started trying some of the trickier shots, like rebounds. When it was time to head back to the hotel, I was feeling quite proud of myself.

In the hall outside our hotel room we heard muffled voices coming from inside. Shelly's sister was still there.

When we opened the door I just stood there in the doorway with my mouth hanging open. It was Midget sitting next to Shelly on the couch. I was tongue-tied. Midget saw me, jumped off the couch, and hugged me hard. I was still staring when she began to laugh. She had lost some weight since I had last seen her but she looked really good and really happy.

I found out that her real name was Erin and that she had just been released that day. Erin explained that she had to stay at a halfway house for at least a year. After that she'd be on parole for the next two years.

During that time Erin would go to school. The plan was that when she was done her parole she would also have earned a certificate in something or other. I was impressed; it sounded as if she had given it a lot of thought.

I turned down their invitation to go out for an early dinner with them. I had been thinking for a while that I was growing somewhat dependent on Shelly and Steven. It was time for me to try to find my own way.

I went out alone that evening. When I was done work I decided to change gears a little and walked up Davie Street. I found a cafeteria-style restaurant called the Fresgo Inn. After eating there I walked back to Granville and was thinking about what to do next. That was when I saw him—the handsomest guy I'd ever seen, and he was looking right at me.

He had short neatly cut dirty-blond hair, serene brown eyes, a strong jawline, and clear skin. I was in love. I actually felt my heart skip as he strolled over to me and said hello. "Hello," I replied.

Hours later we were sitting in his hotel room drinking beer and listening to music. I'd found out that his name was Jamie; he was from New Westminster, and had been living on the street for two years.

He said he hustled pool and did other things to make money as well. I didn't push him on what the "other things" were. I told him I was a working girl, although I was sure he had already picked up on that from the way I was dressed.

Jamie did seem a little surprised when I told him that I was fourteen going on fifteen. He was older than me by almost three years, and that bothered him. But that night we talked until the early morning, and when the sky became blue with the waking day we had sex.

I even let him kiss me, and I kissed him back. He held me as we drifted to sleep. It was like I had seen in the movies—like I imagined the real-world people did with each other. In the afternoon when we got up he took me out for a late lunch, to a dive on Granville that advertised the cheapest food in Vancouver.

Later that evening, agreeing to meet again the next night, I left Jamie at the local pool hall and made my way to the corner, alone.

After my first date I saw Shelly. She was angry. She and Steven had driven around half the night trying to find me when I never showed up at the hotel. Shelly had even considered calling the police.

I was elated. She cared! I just hugged her, giggling, until eventually she calmed down enough that I was able to tell her about meeting Jamie.

Shelly wasn't as excited about Jamie as I was. She got very quiet as I told her about the previous night and that I was going to meet Jamie later to smoke a joint in his room. "Be careful," she told me. "I've heard of him. He's not the kind of guy to be with only one girl."

I ignored her warnings. As she climbed into a car, I shouted that I would see her later that night, or else show up at her place the following morning for breakfast.

It was midnight when I arrived at Jamie's hotel and the night manager wouldn't let me in. He said he would ring Jamie's room and see if he wanted to come down. Jamie came down seconds later and after motioning for me to walk with him he led me down to the beach at English Bay.

It was freezing cold and he held me really close, tucking me into his jacket. We sat like that for some time. Then we were approached by a group of girls who asked if we had a rolling paper for their joint.

Jamie was very happy to oblige, and soon they joined us. As soon as they sat down he let go of me and zipped his jacket back up. Now he was paying a lot of attention to two of them in particular, and I felt humiliated.

I argued with myself for some time, then decided I'd had enough and got up to take a walk, heading towards the ocean. There was a bitter wind that night that bit my cheeks and whipped through my hair. After I'd wandered for quite a while, Jamie came running over to me. I thought he was coming to get me, but he had other plans.

He looked pained while he explained that he felt our ages were too far apart. "It doesn't feel right. You're not the street-kid type—you belong at home. You should get as far away from downtown as you can."

I was disgusted. He was such a liar. I knew he wanted to go with those girls. They were standing up, looking as if they were ready to leave— just waiting for him.

After he left I sat by the water and cried. I had really liked him. I had really thought that he liked me, wanted to be with me. Knowing he had left me because those other girls were offering themselves to him made it even worse.

I realized it was almost two in the morning and I had nowhere to go. Shelly would long since have fallen asleep and I didn't feel right about waking her. I decided to go out to the corner and at least try to get into a warm car so I could think about what I was going to do. None of the hotels would rent me a room, because I had no identification, and I was still too young anyway.

That's how I met Doc. He pulled over in his gold four-door Taurus, and we hit it off right away. He appeared to be about forty years old. He wore glasses, and was very friendly and chatty. He asked me if I minded going back to his place. I accepted gladly. I was so cold by then that I would have gone with him had he been dressed like the Grim Reaper.

When we arrived at Doc's, he asked if I would like to smoke some crack.

No one had ever asked me that before and I took a long moment to think about it. Shelly had always said that drugs were the first step into self-destruction. At that particular moment, though, I was feeling so lost and alone, and I knew that if I joined him I would have someone to hang out with until the morning. That was irresistible. "Yes," I said, and followed him down a hallway into a kitchen.

"I'll just get the treats ready," he said.

I sat on one of his bar bench seats and watched as he took out a test tube, dropped some powder in it, and then added some cocaine. He had a boiling pot of water on the stove and after adding some water to the test tube he held it in the pot with tongs. In a few minutes he had a rock. I was shaking and really nervous as I watched him maneuver around his kitchen grabbing this and that. He told me he was making a pipe for us to smoke the cocaine in. I just kept talking. I told him about Shelly, saying she would be really angry with me if she knew what I was doing. Doc said that some things were better kept to oneself. I wasn't sure if he was talking about me not telling Shelly or if he meant that I should shut up now.

A few minutes later he handed me the pipe and said that he would handle the burning part. I was to just trust him and suck. So I did.

The first wave drained me: I felt all my energy leave my body, and was left with a sensation of floating. I let my arms fall to my sides and relaxed fully in the chair. Suddenly nothing else mattered. I wasn't talking anymore. I was too busy soaring.

Needless to say I didn't sleep that night. I didn't leave Doc's house until the following afternoon. He gave me his pager number. I told him he could always find me at the corner or wandering the streets at night.

I was still high when I arrived at Shelly and Steven's hotel room. I knew Shelly was going to be really upset with me. I had forgotten until I was standing in front of their door that I had promised to be home by morning at the latest. I was fairly confident I would be able to hide the fact that I was still high—but that was probably because I was still high. Steeling myself, I knocked on the door.

Shelly was still in her nightshirt when she opened it.

A few minutes later I was out cold on their couch. I vaguely recall Shelly saying goodbye when she and Steven left but I was so tired I couldn't open my eyes to acknowledge her.

I slept through the entire night. I finally managed to wake up at about 10 a.m. the following day, sad and depressed. I was kicking myself for having gone to Doc's. To make matters worse, I had given money to Doc that night to buy me more cocaine. I couldn't even look at myself in the mirror, I was so disgusted with myself.

The first thing I did that morning was to get into the bath. I lay back in the water with my head propped against the soft bristles of the back scrubber, listening to the silence. This time it wasn't welcoming. I was scared of what Shelly would have to say.

With good reason, it turned out. Steven left the hotel room on the pretext of getting us coffee and doughnuts for lunch, but I caught the meaningful glance he gave Shelly on his way out the door, and knew I had spent my last night on their couch.

When he'd gone, Shelly sat down heavily on the bed and patted the spot beside her, inviting me to take a seat.

She started by telling me that she knew I was on drugs. She thought I understood her feelings on the subject. I could say nothing. I knew I had made a big mistake, and now I was going to lose a very good friend.

Shelly gave me her backpack for my stuff. "Go to the group home," she urged as we said our goodbyes. We promised to meet for dinner sometime, and then I was out the door.

I never did get to say goodbye to Steven. It was a horrible way to leave things. I loved Shelly. She had taken care of me when I had no one and she had tried to share with me her wisdom for survival.

When we parted I could tell she was sorry to see me go, which made the whole scene even worse. I had let her down. It was another bleak farewell on what was turning into a very long list of goodbyes.

# Chapter 8

WHEN YOU'RE NOT LIVING in the real world, as Shelly would have put it, time doesn't really exist except as night and day. There are no dates because there are no appointments. There are no real days because they all blend into one. There is no real tomorrow or even yesterday, just loss and change.

Because I had lost so much and everything always changed, to me there was no such thing as stability. I was starting to realize that I was going to have to take care of myself and provide my own security.

I headed for the city bus depot, where I changed my clothes in the washroom before putting my bags inside a locker and clipping the key onto my bra.

I had put on a short purple dress with a long black sweater that was more like a trench coat to keep my legs warm. New black pointy-toe boots that I had just bought on my last shopping spree completed my outfit.

Ignoring the stares from people around me, I headed for the door.

I was early for my shift on the corner that day. I was glad, because it meant chances were that I would be gone before Shelly came. I wasn't ready to face her so soon after my shameful departure.

I hadn't been there long when I first saw a police officer in a cruiser drive by me very slowly, staring right at me. I turned from him quickly and headed down the alley at as brisk a walk as I could manage in the boots that had long since squeezed the blood from my feet.

I hoped he would get a more pressing call and have to leave. I hoped he would just keep on driving and forget that he had even seen me.

But he wasn't going to ignore me.

I was almost on the other side of the alley, heading towards Davie Street, when the cruiser turned towards me into the alley. I knew it was too late to run and hide. The police officer drove right up to me and stopped the car, lights flashing. He got out and stalked over to where I stood by the hood of his vehicle.

Visibly shaking, I gave him my name. He ran a check in his car and told me there was a warrant out for my arrest.

I felt the blood drain from my face as I realized I had forgotten to show up for my court date on the charge of assault causing bodily harm stemming from the incident at the West Vancouver group home. Obediently I placed my hands behind my back while the police officer put handcuffs on me, then waited patiently while he went through my pockets and purse. Then he made me climb into the back of the cruiser, holding my head down so I wouldn't hit it on the car door frame.

I was humiliated at having been arrested right on the street, and I wanted to hang my head and wallow in self-pity for a while. But the officer talked to me all the way to the police station. "What were you doing out there?" he asked me.

"What did it look like I was doing?" I retorted snippily.

I regretted it the moment I said it. I knew he was trying to be nice to me and I wasn't reciprocating. I didn't know how to feel about this latest chain of events. I was still reeling from having screwed up my relationship with Shelly and having been shamed by Jamie, not to mention from the effects of slowly selling my soul in my still-new chosen profession.

I began to think that maybe getting picked up by the police was not the worst thing that had happened lately. I started to answer the police officer in a quieter tone when he talked to me.

Some time later I found myself alone in a holding cell, lying on a wire cot in the corner. I stared at the ceiling and tried to think what to do next. I concentrated on the only thing I knew I really wanted: to be in Squamish with the people I called my mom and dad. I couldn't fight Social Services on my own. It seemed there was no hope of making them see that they had made a big mistake.

I truly believed that if I had been living with my parents I wouldn't be where I was. I thought about everything I had done in the last month. I was starting to understand what Mom had meant when she said that when some things were done they couldn't be undone. In one month's time I had slept with men for money, had a one-night stand with a boy, and done cocaine until the early hours of the day. I had lost a good friend because of my own mistakes, and once again I was sitting in a four-walled cell waiting for someone else to tell me my fate.

Facing what I had done to myself in those last few months almost made me abandon the idea of going home. I wasn't who my parents thought I was anymore.

If life was a game, I was losing.

I began to see that I needed help. How had I ended up in another cell when only a short time ago I had been basking in the freedom of not having probation hanging over my head?

The terror I had felt when I was desperately trying to escape from the man throwing rocks at my head at the old Expo site came back to me, and I began to cry.

I flashed on John Moralice's menacing grin as he tossed his jacket on the bed, and my tears turned to loud sobs. I saw Louie Childers's disgusting sweaty mug on top of me, and finally the shadow man who appeared in my sleep and tore my peaceful dreams away.

Eventually I cried myself to sleep, only to dream of broken wings on dying birds and dark grey skies with black foaming oceans raging against the land.

When morning came, I was led to a courtroom through the maze of cement walls and locked metal doors.

I had a short two-minute visit with a lawyer. "Keep your mouth shut and don't make any gestures in front of the judge, and I just might be able to get you out of here today," he quipped.

He didn't want to hear anything from me, it seemed, because he gathered his belongings together, nodded at me in dismissal, and made his way over to another client. I was left wondering what he thought I might say—what kind of gestures he thought I might make. Wasn't everyone afraid of the judge?

Minutes later I was standing before a judge I had never seen before, and within seconds he was releasing me back to the group home and it's rules. The judge and my lawyer had spoken so fast and used so many unfamiliar words I didn't even realize I was being released.

I was surprised and disappointed to find that I still had a bed at the Knight Street group home. Upon arriving the first thing I did was have a shower. I made my way to bed and slept for two days.

When I finally did get up it was past noon. I made my way up the stairs to the main level. It was quiet; I could tell I was the only kid there. I found a staff member in the office, who told me that the others were in school and that they would be back later. The following day I was to go to school with them.

The staffer's name was Kim. He was a large Native man with long black hair. Reserved and quiet, he smiled little, but he was gentle when he talked. He seemed a little shy. I decided I liked him. I asked him questions about the other kids who lived there and what days pizza nights and movie nights were.

I had almost started to think the place might not be so bad. I had to remind myself that it didn't have Mom and Dad.

The next morning was Kim's day to take us to school. We all piled into a minivan and headed out to Kingsway. It was an alternative school housed on the second floor of a building, above a hot dog house and beside a pool hall.

When I attended class, I was a good student, and I really did love to learn. Because I was never in school long, I was glad to find I could work at my own pace with the alternative program. I launched myself into my split studies. I was still struggling with grade nine in general and grade eight math—they had changed me from modified into repeating grade eight because I was in alternative school. Almost a full year behind, two in math, I wanted to try to catch up to where I was supposed to be. I brought work back to the group home and studied until bedtime.

I kept to myself a lot, going out of my way to avoid the other kids who lived there. I ate separately from them except at dinner. There was a set schedule for it, and we had to sit at the dinner table together.

I would listen as the others talked and teased each other. I shrank farther from the table, distancing myself from their camaraderie. They would try to coax me in by asking me questions about myself. Not wanting to be rude, I would answer them, but in a manner that left little room for more queries. They even tried to woo me with movie night, saying that I could pick the movie even though I wasn't signed up on the sheet, but I wouldn't bite. I would hide away in my room when I wasn't in school, only coming out when my mother was on the phone, or to eat.

When I wasn't studying I was lying on my bed staring at the ceiling, wondering what I was studying for when I was so obviously going to wind up nothing when I grew up. It seemed no matter how I strived, I always stumbled, and alone I would never be able to pick myself up.

Again I thought about the night at the old Expo site—the man who had reached through the prickles and hauled me over the wall. I knew I had been alone, unable to save myself. Deep inside I felt that divine intervention had sent that man to that exact spot that night. If I believed that, there must also be a reason that God needed me to be saved. I became aware of my responsibility to try to do better at everything, and launched myself off the bed and back into my studies.

For a while, studying kept me occupied, until one early afternoon at school I finally broke down in front of one of the teachers.

Miss Cardaro had seemed to take a shine to me from the start. She was a small lady with a surprisingly booming voice. She seemed to sing everything at you. At first I had found her irritating and tried to avoid her singsong voice in the morning. "What do you think we should do today?" became a rendition of "The Teddy Bears' Picnic," and "Good morning" was delivered as if we were on a game show. Miss Cardaro had a scar on her left cheek that hinted at a violent past, but somehow that scar kept me from being outright rude and turning my back on her. Miss Cardaro was also very touchy-feely, and she liked giving hugs. It made me feel weird at first but it wasn't long before she had even me trained and I was hugging her back.

A while earlier, she had suggested that I should take some time off the math that I was drowning in and do something else, like art. Art was not on the curriculum I was following to get my grade nine, and I wasn't really excited about getting off track. But she seemed keen on showing me the glass art that she had just purchased for the school. She gave me first crack at it.

I learned how to do glass etching, and I was hooked. Miss Cardaro had no way of knowing that shadows plagued my dreams and chased me into darkness in my sleeping world, but she gave me a huge gift by teaching me to manipulate and create shadows.

This particular afternoon, etching together, I began to tell her my story … about my grandparents and how I came to meet my mom and dad; about TJ and how he had removed me from their home. I explained how I had tried to make my point by leaving the group home, and how in the end I had not accomplished anything with my social worker. "I miss living with my parents so much," I confessed.

Miss Cardaro listened in silence as I rattled on, telling her bits and pieces of my life. I cried while I talked and she gave me Kleenex. Exhilarated to finally be able to get so much off my chest, I was also humbled to realize how the things I had done sounded out loud. I went on at great length about how frustrated I was that I was not at home, and that TJ got to go home to his life and was unaware of how horribly affected I was by his decision.

That was how we came up with the idea of writing a letter to pass out to the public. In the letter we passionately urged people to write the minister for child protective services and inquire about the large number of youth living on the streets, and to demand change to a system that left social workers with their hands tied in terms of the range of options for their clients. We added the address for child protective services in Victoria and the name of the minister.

Everyone at school supported our cause, especially the other kids, and we took an afternoon off to hand out the letter on Granville, making our way to Hastings. It was an amazing experience. I felt people looked at us differently after reading the letter, and it gave me hope that maybe someone would help now that we had raised our visibility.

Two weeks after we handed out the letter I started to notice that things were going missing from my bedroom. I had a strong suspicion who it was, but no proof. Troy, one of the boys who lived upstairs in the group home, was a large boy, older than me by at least two years. He hadn't been living there long, and it was widely known that he had itchy fingers.

One night I came home from a late-night jaunt to the store and found my bedroom door half open. I knew I had shut it behind me. I knew even before I went into the room that it had been invaded. I had a fur jacket that had been given to me by my grandparents. It was too small on me so I just kept it in the closet, but it meant a lot to me. Swinging open the closet door, I saw immediately that it was gone. I ran up the stairs and slammed my hands against the staff office door. When Kim answered, I wasted no time blurting out the reason for my outrage. The staff decided to have a room search, and all us kids including Troy were herded into the living room while the staff went through every room in the house.

Then it hit me. I excused myself from the living room and made my way to the front door, where I put on my shoes. I quietly shut the door behind me and began to make my way around the house. Just as I had thought, I found my jacket lying in a huge puddle in the rain. It was directly under Troy's bedroom window. In that moment, I knew my guess had been right.

I ran back inside, straight into the living room. Troy had recently broken his leg and was on crutches. When he saw me coming he started to get off the couch but I was faster than him. I threw the jacket at him, and he laughed at me; in turn, I slapped him with my open hand and called him a thief. I started to walk away, yelling for Kim to come and deal with Troy. I had my back turned so I didn't notice Troy raising one of his crutches over his head. It came down on my shoulder. The first blow knocked me to the ground. Reeling from the pain, I was defenceless against the second blow. It came down on my right upper thigh.

When I tried to crawl away I saw that Kim was standing at the living room entrance. "Why aren't you helping me?" I screamed. A third blow hit me in the centre of my back, momentarily paralyzing me. When I could move again I curled up in the fetal position and waited for Troy to tire himself out. Finally he stopped. I saw that Kim was holding his arm and taking the crutch away.

Troy had tears streaming down his face. I could hear wailing and screeching, which I eventually realized was me. I tried to move. Finding nothing broken, I crawled to my bedroom. Troy was being led from the living room to the kitchen; I heard them tell him to sit and wait and that they'd see what was going to happen next. I began to throw a bag together and then decided that I didn't even care anymore; I just needed to get out of there as fast as I could. I grabbed my purse and made my way out the front door. I couldn't move very fast and I really just wanted to try to recover, but I kept seeing the image of Kim just standing there while I was being beaten and knew I couldn't stay there.

Kim chased me as I made my way down the street. "You need to be looked at by a doctor," he called. "We can deal with what happened." "You did nothing!" I yelled back. Finally he could follow me no further and had to return to the group home. I just kept moving. I was carrying my shoes—I hadn't even stopped to put them on—but suddenly I couldn't make it another step. I thought there really was a chance my back was broken after all. My whole body hurt. I dug Doc's number out of my purse. I didn't know where else to turn. He remembered me right away, and when I told him I was in trouble he asked where I was and picked me up within minutes.

Doc drove me to his house first, where I took off my clothes. He and I did an inspection. We decided I'd have to go to the hospital to have my thigh looked at—he thought I might have a small fracture. My back and shoulder were already turning a deep shade of red, almost purple, but my thigh was bruising differently and it was ugly. At the hospital I lied, saying I had been in a fight with some girls from school. After I was X-rayed the doctor told me I had a bone bruise. He said there was a hairline fracture that wasn't really serious. Although painful, it would heal on its own. I was to stay off my leg for at least two days. No one ever asked about Doc's relationship to me; I think they just assumed he was either a foster parent or a group home staffer.

Doc seemed happy to have me around. We spent that first night hanging over his stove and sucking on a pipe. I didn't care anymore—I was getting high. I was tired of trying to fight, tired of losing every battle I took on. I could never win. I couldn't shake the image of Kim just standing there while that third blow came down. I took another hit from the pipe, and another, and another.

I stayed with Doc for at least two weeks. He would drop me off on the corner and pick me up. I would give him my money and we would get high. I lost a lot of weight while I was living with him. I was too busy getting high to eat.

It was some time before I finally called Mom. She was relieved to hear from me. "I've got news. Call Social Services right away," she said. She said I couldn't talk to TJ anymore because he was no longer my social worker. I was ecstatic. Did this mean I was going to get to go home?

Mom wouldn't tell me; she said that there had been some developments, and that I really needed to talk to Freddie Lavin, who was now a supervisor at Social Services in Squamish. Hanging up, I already knew what the news was going to be, because Mom had said that she would see me later.

It was too late to call Social Services but when I got hold of them the next day, Freddie Lavin and I talked as if he had never stopped being my social worker. He listened sympathetically while I cried when he told me the news. My letter had reached the provincial government in Victoria and Victoria had made the decision that sending me home was what was best for everyone. I couldn't believe it; writing the letter had worked! It bothered me that my pleading and eventually running away had not been good enough, but yet a letter sent out to the public had changed the way Social Services looked at my situation. It felt as if Social Services had once again needed paperwork to add to their files.

Despite that slight disillusionment, Freddie Lavin seemed so different to me from TJ. In that moment he was telling me what I wanted to hear and that made him my champion in the social worker world. But Freddie could have made all the same mistakes as TJ and somehow they would have been less insidious.

I moved back in with Mom and Dad in Squamish in time to join them for their move to Richmond. They had bought a quaint little two-bedroom float home in a small marina just off the Fraser River.

When I first moved home I spent a lot of my time trying to convince my parents that I was trying to change. They had trouble trusting me, and would warn me that if I were late for my curfew or had any trouble following the rules, it would jeopardize the arrangement. At first I understood their worries and lack of trust. I knew I had to show them that I was going to change.

I surprised my dad one afternoon by returning from an afternoon bike ride with a job at the local McDonald's.

It was summertime, so lots of kids my age were working at the franchise. I made friends with some of them. They knew nothing of where I came from. But my parents knew, and sometimes I felt that my mother especially had a hard time forgetting where I had been. I think she wanted to trust me, but I had let her down so many times she was afraid to let go of her anxieties about me.

I met a boy at work named Julian. He came from a good home and dreamed of being a pilot. He was an honour roll student and was very well-liked, especially by the girls. He took an immediate interest in me, which flattered and amazed me. He lived with his parents, sister, cat, and two dogs.

I told Mom about Julian—that I really liked him and that it seemed he really liked me. When I introduced her to him, she asked me how I had ever got a boy like that to go out with me. The comment took my breath away. I realized then that I could never emerge from the shadow of my past, and a stab of regret gouged me.

I worked the summer and gave notice to McDonald's when school was just about to begin. I cried the last day I worked there. My work friends threw me a farewell party at one of their houses. It was a bittersweet goodbye. They had given me one of the many gifts I would cherish forever: a taste of what it would be like to have a normal teenage life. Mom and I were still very close. I knew she loved me because she told me almost every day and she still talked to me all the time. She was my best friend and the person I was closest to in my life.

I decided to ask Social Services to find me a new foster home. Not because I wanted to leave, but because I wanted to keep my relationship with Mom. I knew it was going to hurt her, but it was something I had to do.

I phoned Social Services one afternoon when I had the house to myself and talked to my new social worker. It was strange to have them listen to me—it made me feel powerful. I had always been so shy and I was used to feeling as if I didn't matter, but it seemed that since writing the letter I did matter. I had a new confidence that had not been there before. I found I could be assertive if I needed to be. I was convinced I was doing the right thing.

When Mom came home from work that night I told her what I had done. She immediately called my dad into the room. Mom was more upset than I'd thought she would be. When I told her that I thought that she couldn't let me just be a kid, she got angry and told me that I was not seeing things as they were. "I never meant to hurt you, Tara Lee," she said.

"You didn't, Mom," I assured her. "I know what I'm doing, and how bad it must make you feel."

"Dad and I fought for you to be able to come home!"

"I know. I fought to be here, too," I said. "Life's not about being right." I remembered a bumper sticker I had once seen on a car that read, "Life is what happens when you're making other plans." I almost laughed out loud because it perfectly explained our situation, and yet it would have felt callous to say it to Mom as an explanation.

We talked like that for at least an hour and in the end Dad was looking at me differently—in a good way, I think. He seemed to understand what I was trying to say and why I had done what I did. Mom was hurt by my decision, though. I think she didn't understand it at all. I'd known there was a chance she wouldn't see things my way and that maybe she would let me go. Although our relationship was strong, I was still acutely aware I was not her flesh and blood. I needed her, though, and I didn't want to lose what we had. Back then I had no concept of forever, nor that she'd offered it.

I moved out of Mom and Dad's one afternoon in early September of that year, and moved in with a woman named Lucia Vaw, who lived in North Vancouver. Lucia had a large house above the highway off Lonsdale. She lived with her sister and their two Dobermans. The dogs were beautiful and I fell in love with them right away. For the first couple of days they trudged after me everywhere. I think they were confused about where I had come from.

Lucia said I could wait until that following week to start school if I wanted. I didn't. I went the following day and enrolled at the alternative school a short bus ride away.

When I'd been at the school a few days, I heard a voice in the art room calling my name. I looked up to see a face that I recognized but couldn't quite place staring at me. I racked my brain, retracing my memories all the way back to when I lived with my grandparents. At one point, my granny and I had stayed with my uncle in North Vancouver briefly. *That* was where I had met this girl! We had gone to school together and been good friends. She lived right up the street and we spent our weekends climbing the trees in her complex and swimming in its pool.

I had some trouble placing her name, though, and got it wrong at first. "I'm Sherry," she reminded me, smiling.

From that afternoon Sherry and I were inseparable. She came over to my house and we had waffles smothered in syrup, a daily ritual for as long as we were in school together.

I spent a lot of time at the local pool hall. I loved playing pool. I took great pleasure in surprising some of the men, who would pick up a cue thinking they were going to kick the kid's butt only to have me teach them a thing or two.

Billy had a James Dean look about him, and I was shy at first when I met him at the joint-smoking pit out back of the pool hall. I was attracted to him immediately and found myself checking how I looked every time he was around. I began to work part time at the pool hall waitressing, renting out tables, and doing general cleaning. Billy was friends with the owner, my boss, and now that I was staff, he began to talk to me.

I was wiping down the tables one night after close when he came up to me and told me that he was going to an after-hours restaurant and that I could join him that evening. Before I could reply he said he would wait outside for me, then walked out the door. I was elated. He had finally noticed me and talked to me.

I finished what I was doing, yelled goodbye to my boss, and ran out to Billy's Jeep. He pulled out of the parking lot, still without a word, but he held my hand for the short drive. I knew from watching him that he was picky. In fact, I had seen many girls act all giggly around him, but he hadn't left with any of them. And now here he was holding my hand.

When we arrived at the after-hours he climbed out of the Jeep with a curt "Wait a second," came around to the passenger side, and opened my door. I remember thinking, "How classy is that?"

He bought me a drink and managed to find us a table in the packed restaurant that was mostly standing room only. But when his friends greeted him he turned his back to me. He looked over at me occasionally and smiled approvingly as I sat and sipped my drink. When it was empty he was quick to get me a refill, but mostly he ignored me.

Later that night we made our way to Billy's friend Farid's house. When we got there everyone was getting high on cocaine, and it seemed only natural to take a straw and help myself when it was offered. After drinking and doing coke all night long, Billy and I left. The sun was up and normal-people life was in full swing. Billy didn't even ask me what I wanted to do; he just drove to his house.

Inside, he stopped in the kitchen to grab us some water, and then we made our way down the hall to his bedroom. "Take your clothes off and let me have a look at you," he demanded. It felt clinical. There would be no wooing or romance that time. When we were done having sex he reached over me for his pants. I thought he was going to get dressed, but he didn't. Instead, he handed me twenty dollars. "Take a cab home, baby," he said. "I'll see you later." Taking the money, I started to get dressed, choking back tears.

When I left his house I decided he was a jerk, and that I would ignore him the next time I saw him at the pool hall.

It was eight in the morning on a school day when I arrived home. Lucia was just on her way out the door to work as I came in. She said little to me, although she must have known that I was not going to school but to bed. I was a little worried about what she might say because we had a deal about my working at the pool hall. We had agreed that I could work there as long as it didn't interfere with my school schedule. I did have a little bit of leeway, though, because I was way ahead on most of my subjects and was still a really good student. I brought a lot of schoolwork home with me, and would spend hours sitting at her kitchen table trying to get through a whole section on one subject or another.

During my next shift, Billy came in the back door. He glanced in my direction and went into the back office to hang out with the owner. At the end of the evening, I had already shouted my goodbye and was lighting a cigarette outside when Billy came out behind me. He scolded me for taking off and said for me to get in the Jeep. Although his tone irritated me, I decided it would seem argumentative to point out that we hadn't made any plans. I just climbed in.

We drove straight to Farid's and stayed there late into the night again. When we left we headed to Billy's. This time when we walked into his room I started to take my shirt off without being told, and Billy smiled his approval. He was gentle with me that night, silently letting me know that I had pleased him.

When we were done he handed me another twenty and I took a cab home. Our relationship would continue this way for some time.

I was still in touch with Mom and Dad. When I told Mom about meeting Billy, she said he sounded like trouble, and that I should stay away from him. "You don't know him, Mom," I'd protested. "He's a great guy. If you met him, you'd like him." Of course, first you'd have to get him to talk to you, I added in my head.

I also still talked to Doc and we would occasionally get together. We hung out at his place, still mostly leaning over his stove while he cooked us up some cocaine. Somehow I was keeping my secrets well throughout this double life, and my daytime life seldom spilled over into my nighttime life. I stayed in school and despite my busy social life still managed to find time to study at home. I worked Thursday, Friday, and Saturday night and saw my parents on Sunday. My habits were getting expensive; I needed to get Doc to drive me to the corner at least one night a week. Billy kept me high on the weekends but now I needed to stay high throughout the week too. I didn't think of myself as an addict. I told myself I was just experimenting.

Christmas was coming. It was early December when Doc told me he was going to buy me a car for Christmas. He said driving out to North Vancouver all the time was making him crazy—every time he came to pick me up he had to do it four times in one night. He said if I had my own car I could drive myself out to see him.

I couldn't believe it. My own wheels, I thought, how cool is that?

When I told Lucia she couldn't believe it either. She had never really asked about Doc before—maybe because he had always just been there when she got to know me. I think until that moment she had assumed he was related to me. When I told her about the gift, though, she asked me a lot of questions about him. I was cryptic, telling her little more than that Doc had been in my life for a long time and that he had helped me when I really needed it.

That didn't quiet her down, though. "Let alone that you don't have a licence and aren't even old enough yet to get a learner's permit." I leaned over the couch and kissed her cheek. "Okay, let's let that alone then," I retorted cheerily, and took off down the hall to my bedroom.

Billy and I split up before Christmas that year—if we'd ever really been together. It started one night when Billy hurt me while we were in bed together. I didn't complain to him; in fact, I did my best to show little emotion when he took his penis, poured lube all over it, and began to push against my back door. He got inside and began to pump into me, holding my hips so I couldn't move away. I just bit the pillow and waited for him to finish. That made me see that he had no real respect for me at all.

The next night, Billy and I were leaving Farid's house when Billy asked me if I would sleep with his friends for him. At first I thought he was joking and almost retorted with a smart remark, but when I looked at his face and saw the sincerity, I was horrified.

"What makes you think you can treat me like your property?" I asked.

"You're a woman," he laughed. "You have a place in the world, and it's not at a man's table."

I was disgusted. I had had no idea he felt that way towards woman in general. Now the ugliness of his beliefs struck me. "Well, then you shouldn't be living in Canada, because the women who live in this country have rights," I shot back angrily. As soon as I said it, I knew from the look on his face that he was done with me. He didn't want anything less than total compliance.

I walked away from him and made my way home. Lucia was surprised to see me. We made what turned out to be a nice evening out of it, eating cake and watching rented movies.

I met Doc a few days later and we discussed a car that I had seen parked on the road. It was a Datsun B210 hatchback; I had fallen in love with it right away. It had a sign in the window that said it was for sale for five hundred dollars. There was something unique about that car. It was all beat up on the outside but the engine still ran like a charm. I knew I could trust that car to take care of me. Doc bought it for me that very day and we spent the afternoon getting insurance— in Doc's name, of course, because I didn't have my driver's licence. He explained that he didn't mind paying for the insurance but that I was going to have to get my licence as soon as I turned sixteen so he could put the insurance into my name.

After Doc bought me the car we went to his place. This time he did something different: he asked me for a cigarette. I knew that Doc didn't smoke so I found this strange, but I gave him one. He proceeded to take the filter off and break off part of it. I watched as he took a spoon out and put some cocaine on the spoon. He added water, mixed it all together, and then took out a syringe and sucked it all up.

As soon as I saw the syringe my heart rate sped up and I began to panic. I was screaming inside, No! This isn't what I wanted. I don't want to throw my life away. Then Doc asked me if I trusted him. I did—it was the cocaine I didn't trust.

I told Doc that I trusted him with my life. He smiled as he walked over to me, taking off his belt. A second later I was standing up and starting to pace. I was higher than I had ever been in my life and I didn't like it at all. I thought my heart was going to explode. But minutes after that I was asking Doc to do it again. That night would last for a week.

When I left, I took more than the drugs home with me; I took a whole paraphernalia kit.

Lucia was furious with me for not calling to let her know I was okay. She stormed past me in the hallway as I made my way to my bedroom. I heard her mumbling about how concerned she had been.

I hated myself. This was obviously what I deserved. I didn't deserve the life I had somehow been creating for myself. Couldn't everyone tell that I wasn't worth all the time and effort they were putting into me?

For the next couple of days when I woke up the first thing I did was climb into a bath. There I found the privacy I needed to pull out the little bag of cocaine and the spoon that I would carry in with me. I was losing more weight and falling behind in school. I had quit my job at the pool hall because I didn't want to have to see Billy again. Oddly enough, once the drugs were all gone it didn't bother me that much, and I soon found myself wanting to be normal again.

I met Thane about a week before Christmas—I don't remember exactly how, but we became a couple almost immediately. He was a really nice guy who had a normal life. He worked a nine-to-five job, liked beer on the weekends, and represented everything that I wanted to one day have. He dreamed of a wife and kids and a white picket fence. He already owned his own apartment. He drove a beat-up car, but he came from a family of means and had high hopes for his future.

When I met Thane I made the decision that I had to let Doc go. I knew if I really wanted these things out of my life I had to stop hanging around people like him. I managed to keep him at bay for some time and almost become a normal kid again. No more Doc; no more Billy; and I was clean except for marijuana and cigarettes. I didn't even like to drink all that much. I hated the feeling of being completely out of control.

Christmas came and I spent it in Richmond at my parents' float home. Soon after New Year's my sixteenth birthday came, and it was a big one. There was snow on the ground that January, and Thane and I made a snow couple in front of Lucia's house. Sherry spent the night and we watched movies and were allowed to drink wine in the house with Lucia's permission. It was a really nice peaceful birthday.

A few days after my birthday I went out to my car and found that the licence plates were gone. When I paged Doc he called back and said that he had removed them the night before. Since I was no longer seeing him, why should he continue to pay my insurance? It hadn't really occurred to me that he might stop paying for it. I decided it didn't make sense to stop seeing Doc. I could do both worlds. I would just tell Doc that he could no longer use drugs around me, or at least that he had to go do it somewhere other than right in front of me. I wanted what I had already done in the way of drugs to be all I ever did in my life.

Hours later I was standing up Thane who was waiting for me downtown for our dinner date. I was getting high with Doc. My arms were horribly bruised the next day from trying to find veins in the darkness of the car that night. I had told Doc I wouldn't go to his house because I was afraid that if I did it might be too tempting to get high with him.

I had fought with myself for at least an hour before getting high. Doc had been stopping at almost every gas station and running in to use the washroom. I had known what he was doing. I felt sick inside.

When I finally did arrive home Lucia was up with her sister waiting for me. She took my bag when I walked in the door and began to rifle through it. Looking past her to the kitchen I saw that there were two large official-looking men standing by the counter. On it lay a sandwich bag that had syringes in it. I recognized the bag as the one I had hidden in the crawl space above my closet until I could get to the police station and give it to someone who would know what to do with it. Suddenly, I felt nauseous, and knew I was close to fainting. Lucia took my purse over to the men in the kitchen and gave it to them. I sat down on the couch and sank into it. Obviously I need help, I thought. I had so much I wanted to do with my life. I was still losing this game.

Lucia's sister brought me over some tea. She sat down across from me and Lucia came and sat next to me. She said that I was going to sleep off the night before right where I was but that the next day I was going to a teen detox centre.

Lucia then introduced me to her new friends, Officer Nelson and Sergeant Schraeder. Sergeant Schraeder came and sat on the coffee table directly in front of me. He was very large but not threatening. He looked serious, but then I guess the situation called for it.

He started by explaining that he was with children's vice in the West Vancouver Police Department. He said that they had been investigating the situation with Doc and that they had some questions for me. I told him how we had met and how Doc had helped me when the group home hadn't.

"I do nothing with him that I don't want to do," I assured them.

"That may be so, but Doc isn't who you think he is," Sergeant Schrader said. "You're only a teenager. You need to be protected from him."

"When did you start smoking cocaine?" Officer Nelson asked.

I wanted to be vague and not mention Doc's name. I thought that if I told them that it was after the incident with the crutches in the Knight Street group home, I'd be able to steer the conversation away from Doc. Lying to them about timing didn't seem like too big a deal. Except they asked all the right questions, put two and two together, and figured out that the first time I had ever smoked cocaine was with Doc.

The sergeant was the one who did most of the talking; the other officer just sat and listened and stared at me. Neither was anything but kind and gentle with me, and I found myself liking them. By the time they left I trusted them. Lucia stayed with me that day.

In the evening I asked her if she would drive me down to Thane's so that I could explain myself to him. Lucia said she didn't think it would be a good idea, and that I would be able to see him when I returned to her place. I couldn't wait though. I begged her, and in the end she took me to see him.

Thane answered the door at his place looking really upset. I found out he had called Lucia late the night before because he had been so worried when I hadn't shown up for our date. I found myself scared to tell him the truth. Deep down I knew this was goodbye.

I couldn't find the words, so I showed him my arms. There was hurt that I had never seen before in his eyes, and I realized that he had really cared about me. I didn't mean to hurt him; it hadn't occurred to me that what I had done would cause him pain. I don't know what I had expected—maybe anger and disgust—but I was unprepared for the anguish I saw in his eyes. I could say nothing when he asked me to leave. I made my way down to Lucia's waiting car and climbed in.

 # Chapter 9

I WOULD SPEND FOUR DAYS and three nights at the detox centre. There were both adults and teens, but we were separated by hallways. We had group sessions together and single counselling sessions with a one-to-one worker.

I felt like an unwelcome outsider in the centre. Most of the people there were older than I was. They had been doing drugs for a long time, and had lost homes and marriages as a result. Some of them seemed to scoff at me when I started to tell my own story.

I was really shaken by an incident involving a boy who was around my age. Two uniformed police officers brought him in, and he was taken to a room that had padding on the floors and walls. He screamed and yelled about giant purple mushrooms and bugs the whole night. I felt so sad for him; I wanted to go and lie on his floor. I remember thinking that leaving him all alone would only add to his fear, which is what I heard beneath his haunting cries.

That felt like a first-hand look at what would become of me if I kept making the same choices. I saw the gruelling physical effects some people had to suffer just to be able to wake up normal again someday. I knew from listening to their stories that I was following in their footsteps. I realized I was sitting on a teeter-totter that really could go either way.

Late one night I was lying on my bed staring at the ceiling of a rectangular cement room. There was a steady, dependable ticking from a large white clock high above the door. The rhythm lulled me into thinking, remembering ...

I thought about Doc and those police officers that had gotten me into the treatment centre. I thought about my parents and what they would say to me if they could. I knew my dad would ask me, "Why?" I knew that once again I would have no answer for him.

I knew I had made the choice to stay with Doc in his kitchen that day. I had just sat there and watched as he prepared our "treats." I could have left—there'd been nothing stopping me.

It was overwhelming to think of all the dangerous choices I had made. And the fact was, a lot of the time it would actually have taken less courage, not more, to have said no to temptation, given how hard I had fought with myself before succumbing.

I thought about the Knight Street group home, remembering the night Troy had beaten me with his crutch. I could still picture Kim's face when I had looked for someone to help me and had seen him just standing there. Resentment surged up that Troy hadn't even been punished as far as I knew. I was overcome with anger. I thought about the incident at the West Vancouver group home with Joan, flinching at the memory of her powerful grasp around my head.

Somehow the ticking of the clock sounded as if it was speeding up, keeping time with my rage as it intensified.

I couldn't remember what Robert had looked like, but I could picture Janine's pinched-up face, tight lips, and cold eyes. My reverie catapulted me forward again and I could hear a song I thought I'd long since banished from my memory ... "What I am is/What I am," the voice so clear I could feel the rough hands groping at my thighs. Oh god, I thought, I'm losing my mind, and suddenly I was crying and wailing.

I was so charged up with rage that the room felt too small to contain me. I turned my head into my pillow and bit it as hard as I could. I was afraid if I screamed into it someone might hear me. I must have fallen asleep like that, because I don't remember coming back up for air.

When I woke up in the morning I felt empowered. I had made the decision never to go near another needle. I was choosing life. At the time I didn't know what I had to live for, but that morning I felt renewed hope. I also decided that I would never tell another living soul that I had ever even tried drugs that way. It would be my secret forever.

I suddenly thought about Thane and how I had shown him my arms. I hoped he still respected me enough not to have gone and told everyone we knew. Perhaps Lucia had been right about going to him so early. I felt a pang of regret. I hoped Thane hadn't been my only chance at a normal life.

But even that regret couldn't lessen my sense of change that morning. I felt lighter in my skin, as if I had forgiven myself. For what reason exactly, I didn't know, but my thoughts felt clearer to me and I felt like I understood better who I was and what I expected from me.

I had high hopes when I left the detox centre. But when I returned to Lucia's house it wasn't long before things began to fall apart again.

One night at the dinner table, Lucia's sister was putting salad into her bowl and we were all laughing at something someone had just said, when Lucia casually mentioned the possibility of moving to the Interior of BC.

For me, that one sentence meant everything was about to change again. Lucia was going to leave and then there would be a new home, a new face to get to know, a new life to get accustomed to. Lucia continued to explain that it was just a thought and definitely not imminent, but I don't remember hearing anything through the buzzing in my ears that had become loud and frantic.

Soon after that, maybe even the next day, Doc called me at the house. He told me he had been trying to reach me for weeks, and asked me to meet him so he could talk to me. He explained that two police officers had come to his house and threatened him with a search warrant.

When I tried to apologize he stopped me by saying that he didn't care about all that. He said that they had said some things about my condition that made him feel sick and that he had to see me to know that I was all right. After a few short minutes, I gave in and agreed to meet him.

I left the house right away in case Lucia came home and saw me leaving. I told myself it was because she would then worry about nothing, because I wasn't going to get high with Doc. I was just calming his nerves.

Hours later I was still out with Doc. He asked me to drive and I was only too happy to oblige. He looked terrible—his skin was pale and clammy; he complained that he was cold, and that the bumps in the road were hurting him.

We got a motel room on Kingsway in Vancouver. He told me that he had cocaine I was welcome to do, and pulled a jar out from under his car seat. I grabbed it from his hand and led the way to the room from our parked car. By now I was cooking it up myself using a spoon and a lighter.

While Doc slept I got higher and higher. At about 3 a.m. I decided I wasn't getting enough of a rush anymore. My answer to this was to start snorting the coke as well. I carved myself out a large line from what had fallen off the spoon onto the table. As soon as I did it I felt a burning sensation cruise all through my body and settle in my chest. I knew I was in trouble. It was hard to even breathe. I stood up quickly from the table and began to pace the small room. I was more scared than I'd ever been in my life. In that moment I knew it wasn't that I wasn't high enough; I was too high.

I opened a window but it did nothing to help me take in any air, and the burning in my chest intensified. I could feel the darkness taking over my vision as it moved through my blood and into my head. Bright orange pain exploded deep behind my eyes. In a panic I threw open the door of the motel room and ran outside. I was scared that my legs wouldn't carry me to the road but they did. I collapsed on the lawn underneath a big sign that had the number "2400" on it. At the time, though, that didn't register.

I thought I was dying. I closed my eyes and lay in the grass until the dew made its way to my clothes and I could finally feel the cold crispness of the morning air. The occasional car went by but nobody stopped. Maybe they didn't see me.

Eventually I managed to pick myself up and make my way back to the motel room. I put the lid on the jar and cleaned up the mess I had made as best I could. Then I sat on the chair by the window, fighting the urge to pull out the jar and make a new mess.

Hours later, the sun high in the sky, I became aware of the bustle of another day's activity outside.

Doc woke up, and, feeling better, went straight to the shower. While he was in there I came to the realization that there was only one way I was going to get away from him.

My heart pounding, I went to the phone and dialled. Seconds later I was talking to Lucia. I told her I thought I had almost died the night before and that I was scared. I told her I needed help. "I'm sorry," I sobbed.

Lucia listened to me, not saying much, but I could tell I had her full attention. I could still hear Doc in the shower, the water loudly splashing. I almost hung up but a voice in my head urged me to stay on the phone, telling me I wasn't going to survive this life; that I would die if I stayed. I kept looking at the cradle of the phone. I could almost see the receiver sitting there—all I had to do was lower my arm.

Lucia asked me where I was. I told her about the sign I had seen while I was lying outside the night before. She gave me orders to stay in the motel room no matter what, and said that someone would be there to get me soon. "I'll call Sergeant Schraeder right away," she promised, and hung up.

When Doc came out of the shower he said we needed to get something to eat. I sat and watched as he gathered together our meagre possessions and began to load up the waiting car. I immediately regretted having called Lucia. Doc wasn't hurting me; I was hurting myself. It just happened the most when Doc was around. Didn't that make it my weakness and not Doc's fault?

"Hurry," I said, grabbing the bags from him. I climbed into the passenger seat and we made our escape. I would learn later that we missed the arrival of the police by minutes.

I stayed at Doc's house for a few days. It was different, though. Doc did more cocaine but somehow I managed to stay clean. Every day I felt a little bit stronger.

I was sorry I had even come close to betraying Doc. I knew he was my friend and that he had never meant to do me any harm. I knew deep down that the truth was that he was lonely and that when I had joined him he had become less lonely.

I spent a few nights sleeping on Doc's couch, but eventually I did make my way to the corner. I wasn't going to go back to foster care. I convinced myself that I was going to try to save enough money to rent my own apartment. Maybe I would find a roommate so I wasn't alone all the time. Then I would go back to school and eventually I would find that normal life I coveted so much.

Time flew past, and before I knew it a month had gone by.

I was alone now, and I was starting to like it that way. I was a lot older than my barely sixteen years. I had been around enough that some of the other girls were used to seeing me and left me alone most of the time.

I was always careful to stay in the same block and to only be in the area for two hours a day. Some of the other girls Shelly had warned me against had begun to smile and nod in my direction. I felt they weren't so different from Shelly and me. I wasn't thinking of hanging out with them, but I saw that they weren't as scary as they had first appeared. But then, I was getting older and the age gap was closing. I was starting to get used to the life.

I stayed on Doc's couch at night and when I wasn't on the corner I wandered the city streets, watching people, imagining what their lives were like. I would go to the normal places in town—Gastown, Granville Island. I would watch people with their kids and invent their children's life stories in my head. Their lives were always full of love, laughter, and warm milk with their mothers.

One day, on the corner of Nelson and Seymour, Jamie happened to pass by. I had seen him once before but I had managed to duck around a corner and he had walked past me unaware. This time I didn't see him until it was too late and he was already approaching me. I met him with a cold glare and turned to walk in the opposite direction. He followed me.

He still had the same effect on me: I felt light-headed and heavy all at the same time. I was nervous and unsure of myself when he was around.

He fell into step beside me. "Where have you been all this time?"

"Living my life," I shot back. Despite my snippy, bitter tone he kept walking beside me.

Two blocks farther on I stopped in front of a pharmacy on Granville.

Jamie reached into his pocket and showed me a hundred-dollar bill. "Come on, I'll even pay you if I have to," he said.

I laughed at him. "You're hardly the kind of guy that would need the services of a hooker." I started to walk again, heading towards Davie Street.

I was walking fast and he was almost running to keep up with me. Suddenly he grabbed me. "Stop. Look at me," he implored me. He said he didn't need the services of a hooker; he needed to be with me, and if paying me was the only way I would talk to him then he was willing to do it.

Jamie's persistence paid off. I let him lead me to a hotel that was just off Granville. He already had a room rented so we just walked right in. Inside, he sat down at a small table and just gazed at me. "What are you staring at?" I demanded.

"The most beautiful Indian I've ever seen," he retorted. It had been a long time since anyone had referred to me as an Indian, and I'd never heard it without cringing. I knew he meant it as an endearment, though.

He had called me beautiful, too. I didn't see myself that way. I knew I was pretty because I made money on my looks. Beauty to me, though, was something that came from inside, and Jamie certainly didn't know me. I didn't know me. I didn't know if I was even human underneath all the regret and loss that had plagued my life.

While my mind was spinning, my heart confused, Jamie got up from the table and walked over to me. He stood behind me and turned me towards the mirror. "Look, Tara Lee," he said. "You've become a woman. You didn't look like this when I last saw you. You're breathtaking." He added that there were two good-looking people standing in this room and that they shouldn't be standing. Cheesy as the line was, it didn't make me choke with laughter when he said it. I just stared back at him in the mirror.

Then he kissed me. It was deep and passionate. No one had ever kissed me like that before. It felt like a real adult kiss, the kind seen in soap operas. It made me weak and I allowed myself to be led to the bed.

Some time later we were lying naked, facing each other, spent and satisfied. Well, he was satisfied; I was happy just to have had some real human contact. We talked for some time like that. He told me about his family and I told him about mine. I told him how I was living with Doc right now because of what I had done to Lucia.

"Have you even talked to her since that morning with Doc?" he asked.

"No."

"Well, we're going to fix that today."

I started to get up, confused. I had spent a few hours with him, not even a night, and he was starting to talk as if we were together or as if something more had happened. I had learned my lesson the first time with Jamie—I was not going to be used again.

If I leave right now then it'll be me who used him, right? I thought to myself.

Jamie got up with me. He too began to dress quickly. That was when he told me he was going to move to Calgary. "I'm sick of Vancouver. It's doing nothing to help me get to where I want to be."

"Where do you want to be?"

"I don't know," he replied. "I just know it's not in Vancouver."

I remember thinking well, there it is. There was always a reason I couldn't have what I wanted, and distance was a pretty large barrier. I grabbed my purse and jacket and headed for the door.

Jamie grabbed his jacket and stalked after me.

We were walking down Granville when Jamie grabbed my hand. I decided I would allow him to feed me and then I would leave. He took me to Fresgo's on Davie. Once we were seated and I was eating my burger he asked something no one had asked me in a long time.

"Will you go with me, Tara?"

I said nothing as he explained that he did have a plan. He said that together we could make enough to rent a suite as soon as we got there.

"I make really good money hustling pool. And I know you make good money doing what you're doing." He added that together we could conquer our demons and find a way to live a normal life.

I stopped in mid chew. He had said the magic words. He had offered me "normal." Or at least that's what I chose to hear.

I explained I needed to feel I could trust him. I reminded him how he had left me that night for the other women and that I had been humiliated and left on my own in the middle of the night.

"Did you really look in the mirror this afternoon?" he asked me. "There isn't a woman in the world who can sway me from my beautiful Indian."

I asked him to stop referring to me as an Indian—even as an endearment, it wasn't a word I wanted to hear very often. Not wanting him to see that he was getting anywhere with me, I made no reference to his request.

Undaunted, Jamie kept talking. He told me how much bus tickets were, and that we could leave the following day. We could use tonight to get more money and be on a bus the following afternoon.

I began to get excited. It wasn't such a bad idea. I could get away from Doc and start over. Maybe I could even go back to school and get a real job with wages; start a normal life.

I finally agreed to Jamie's idea only after he assured me that he would not leave me in a strange town, and that he would stick it out no matter how many blondes offered themselves to him. I told him I needed to go and see both my mom in Richmond and my foster mother in North Vancouver before we could leave.

We made a plan to borrow a vehicle from one of Jamie's friends for the running around I needed to do, and to meet up again around midnight at Fresgo's. He went his way to make money and I went mine. We would catch the six o'clock bus the following evening.

Hours later I was just getting ready to head up to the Fresgo's to meet Jamie when I heard him calling my name. He met up with me on the corner.

"I can't wait for you any longer, baby. We're just going to have to make do with the money we have." He said he was scared something would happen that would wreak havoc with our plans. I saw he was genuinely afraid for my safety and agreed that the money I had made would have to do.

We sat in Denny's on Burrard Street all night, eating burgers, drinking coffee, and talking. We planned what we would do when we arrived. We talked about what I would need to do in order to get back into school. I had never been on welfare before; Jamie explained how to go about applying. He said that Social Services in Calgary would know how to get me back into school, and might even help me find a job.

I was having trouble keeping my head up, I was so tired, but I knew that at six o'clock that night I would have thirteen hours in which to get some sleep.

Later that morning we made our way to Jamie's friend's place. Jamie left me outside while he ran in and borrowed the keys to the car that sat in the driveway. First stop, we decided, would be North Vancouver— since it was Saturday morning, Lucia would be home.

Lucia didn't seem surprised when she opened her door and saw me standing there. She nodded a hello at Jamie and beckoned us both in. She had to lock her dogs on the porch because they took one look at Jamie and began to snarl and growl. I chalked it up to Jamie being a stranger, but Lucia seemed more concerned about it, eyeing Jamie more closely.

It took me a while to get up the nerve to tell Lucia I was leaving for

Calgary. When I did, she followed me down the hall to my room and watched me pack a bag with clothes and another with photographs and my poems and unfinished books I was working on.

She begged me to change my mind. She said I was still taking myself with me, so there would be no real change in Calgary, except that I really was going to be alone there. I told her that I wouldn't be alone; Jamie was coming with me.

"Sounds more to me like Jamie's taking you there," she said pointedly. "If you hadn't met him, we wouldn't be having this conversation."

I thanked her for everything she had done for me and apologized for all the trouble I had caused her. I told her she didn't need to worry anymore because I was now going to be no one's problem but my own, as she had so kindly pointed out.

"You're twisting my words, Tara Lee!" she shouted.

"Isn't that what everyone does when they hear what they don't want to hear?" I retorted.

She was momentarily stumped. I rushed past her back into hall with my bags slung over my shoulders. Jamie had left the house and was sitting on the front steps well away from the dogs and their menacing growls. When I opened the door he stood up, took my bags, and headed for the car. I turned around and saw Lucia standing in her living room staring after me, looking as if she might cry any minute. I immediately softened and went to her. I gave her a big hug, realizing it might very well be the last time I would ever see her. I looked into her eyes. "You've been wonderful to me, Lucia. I know you're trying to help me. You'd do better to help someone who deserves someone like you in their life."

She was still standing in her living room when I shut the door behind me and headed for Jamie in the waiting car.

The next stop was Richmond. I was shaken from the encounter with

Lucia—I could only imagine what she must have thought when I closed the door and walked away from her. I knew my mother would not react well, and might even take Jamie's head off.

When we arrived at my parents' float home I told Jamie, "I don't know how long I'll be, but I really think it's best you wait in the car."

As I made my way down the docks I thought about how I would tell my mom. When I finally stood in front of the house I was almost too scared to walk in.

Hearing nothing in response to my knock, I went in to find no one was home. I went up the stairs to my parents' bedroom and sat on their bed. Maybe I wasn't going to get to say goodbye after all. Self-pity dragged me down. I lay back and thought for a while. I'd really wanted to say goodbye and have one last hug with them. I thought about Lucia and how sad she had looked when I had shut the door. I realized that maybe it was for the best that Mom wasn't home.

Getting up, I made my way over to my mom's photo cabinet. I pocketed at least ten photos that day. Most of them were of her and Dad; some were of Mellanie and Ellena.

Back downstairs I sat in the kitchen with a pen and pad that I had found and began to write a letter to my parents. I was almost done when I heard my parents' dog on the docks and knew that Mom was home.

I stood up and walked to the door, opening it for her so she didn't have to put her bags down.

Mom was surprised to see me. I almost never visited on Saturday. She immediately saw that I had been sitting at the kitchen table, a silent indication of trouble.

Saying she needed a minute to put the groceries away, she chatted about her day. I could tell that she felt uneasy; somehow she knew that I hadn't come on a Saturday with good news. I can't remember in what context but she called me "Pookey" that day before she finally joined me at the table.

She went quiet, waiting for me to tell her why I was there. I could think of no easy way to say that I was leaving so I just blurted it out. I told her Jamie was in the car waiting for me and we were taking a bus to Calgary that night. When I had said it, Mom sat and looked at me from across the table for a long time before she said anything.

She asked me when I had come up with this idea. I told her I had been toying with it for a long time. Mom stood up and moved chairs so that she was sitting right next to me. She turned me to face her and said that I was about to hear something I wouldn't like.

She said that she was sorry to have to be the one to tell me but that it was something that I should only ever hear from someone who really loved me. She asked me if I believed that she loved me. She was holding my gaze and I was only able to nod in recognition. She asked me if I had ever heard of shin splints.

I was confused. What did shins have to do with my leaving town? "No," I said. "I haven't heard of them."

Mom explained that shin splints were something that runners got when they ran too long and too hard, and didn't have enough muscle for what they were doing to their bodies. She told me that shin splints could come on suddenly, or they could sneak up on you; either way you could end up crippled, with legs that would never run again.

I began to see where she was going. Still holding her gaze, I replied that I knew what I was doing was risky, but that I would always have myself to fall back on. "I trust myself, Mom," I insisted.

"Most runners do. But you're always trying to run farther and farther away, Tara Lee. All these aches and pains you're having growing up are the shin splints sneaking up on you. The only way you'll stop the pain is if you stand still long enough for everything to catch up."

I must have looked at her as if she was crazy. I stood up and told her that I had made a decision and that my mind would not be changed.

Mom resorted to begging. She cried that she needed me there. She said that my family needed me and I needed my family, whether I knew it or not. I cried too while she pleaded with me to not give up. "I'm scared that if you walk out that door today, Dad and I are going to be planning your funeral one of these days. I love you, Tara Lee. You can have a normal life here." She said a lot of the same things that Lucia had said, but what stuck with me the most was the shin splints metaphor.

My mother must have felt she was fighting for my life. I felt as if I was fighting to *find* a life.

I left her in no better condition than I had left Lucia. I was a mess when I made my way back to the car. Jamie sensed that I needed silence and said nothing as we began the drive back into Vancouver.

We dropped the car off first, then headed to the bus depot. Jamie carried his one bag and one of my bags. We said very little as we trudged through the rain towards the depot.

After we bought our tickets we still had two hours before our bus was scheduled to leave, so we headed for something to eat.

We hardly had any money left, and knew we were going to want to eat at least once along the way. Still exhausted, I decided to order a coffee and a burger. While I ate I began to feel rejuvenated and hopeful. It occurred to me this might be the last burger I would ever eat in Vancouver. Then I heard my mother's voice and the thought was immediately followed with a darker one: I hoped it wouldn't be my last burger in Vancouver because I died.

Jamie and I were the first to board the bus. We made our way right to the back. Using his leg and my jacket for a pillow I fell into a deep sleep. I don't even remember the bus leaving the depot. I was disappointed when I woke up because I had wanted to be awake for the leaving

Vancouver part. I had envisioned myself leaning my head against the window with my Walkman on listening to Bryan Adams once again sing me out of town.

# Chapter 10

T HE SMELL OF MANURE from acres of fields populated by cows and horses wafted through the windows as our bus glided past. There were snow patches in the dark night sky that up close appeared to glow and farther into the fields became black blobs.

Jamie told me that the cows were sleeping. While he rattled on about cow tipping I kept my eyes to the road. I was overcome with anticipation and excitement. I searched the dark early-morning sky for the city's silhouette, but I could see nothing of it yet.

The headphones of my Walkman were resting on my shoulders but I could still hear Starship singing about how nothing was gonna stop them now; they were going to sing their song forever. It made me smile. Jamie mistook my smile for interest in what he was saying and talked more avidly about what it was like to live on a farm. He had never lived on one himself but knew people who had. He seemed untouched by our arrival and had little interest in silence. I was finding him irritating.

I returned my gaze to the window and concentrated on the music.

Soon the houses were getting closer together and we were crossing train tracks. We drove through what I would describe as a rodeo suburb. It had such a country feel that I wouldn't have been surprised to see a horse and buggy, or witness a shootout in the streets. But it was far too early in the morning; the streets were deserted. After that came an industrial area where we passed trucks and eighteen-wheelers being loaded for deliveries.

Then I could see it: a tower against the sky that reminded me of Harbour Centre in Vancouver. I saw tall dark skyscrapers reaching up through the night. The forever lights of the city seemed to call out to me, beckoning me as they had for as long as I could remember. I wanted the bus to stop right there and let us off so we could begin exploring this new city.

The feeling lasted right up until I stepped off the bus. When I took my first breath of air and it momentarily shocked my lungs, I buried my head in Jamie's shoulder. I don't think I had ever breathed air that cold before. I don't know what the temperature was that morning but there was a definite bite I hadn't been expecting. It was a different kind of cold than I was accustomed to. The air felt crisper and drier than the salty sea air of the West Coast.

The sides of the road were piled high with snow from previous clearings, and slush on the sidewalks made walking hazardous.

Jamie and I trudged through the city for blocks and blocks, quietly soaking in the differences. We had no idea where we were going.

We passed very few people in the city that morning. I didn't even see any homelessness as we trekked.

I was excited and scared at the same time. I told myself that somewhere in this city my new home awaited. My new friends were here too, and I promised myself that a new, better life would be mine.

We stopped in a small alcove of a high-rise, hiding from the bitter wind that had picked up while we were walking. We could feel heat seeping out from under the locked door, and I desperately wished we were on the other side.

Jamie began to empty his pockets and I went through my purse. When we had finally pooled our money we had a bleak sixty dollars. Jamie said that the first thing we should do was to find a hotel that rented by the hour. I didn't relish that thought. I had been in hotel rooms like that before and they made me feel afraid to touch anything.

It began to snow while Jamie and I huddled in the alcove. I decided that gloves and a scarf were going to be the first things I bought.

We did find a hotel that rented by the hour in a less savoury area of town. Jamie took the room until ten in the morning. It bought us three hours to refuel and figure out what we would do next.

Jamie had grabbed a newspaper from one of the boxes lining the streets, and we looked up the rental rates in Calgary. We figured out we would need somewhere around seven or eight hundred to rent an apartment. It appeared we would need first and last months' rent up front, but the rents were cheaper by far than in Vancouver according to Jamie.

While Jamie and I crouched on the bed leaning over the paper, a very large, hairy, almost naked man walked right into our room. When he saw he had the wrong room, he grumbled an apology and left. Jamie and I looked at each other and laughed. We wouldn't spend another penny on a place like this, we decided.

Jamie left the room to go in search of more money. We arranged that I would stay in the room as long as I could; then I would head to the Centre Street Café, a small coffee shop we had spotted just outside the hotel.

Jamie promised me that he wouldn't be any later than noon. I didn't ask where he was going to find money at eight in the morning on a weekday. I must have known, though, that I really didn't want to know.

By three in the afternoon I was beginning to panic. The man working behind the counter at the café had taken one look at me lugging our three bags in and had known right away that I had no money. He said that the tea would be on him. I could tell that he felt sorry for me on some level, but when three o'clock rolled around he was looking somewhat concerned as well.

I got the impression that if closing time had approached he would not have been able to leave me out in the cold and live with himself. I didn't reveal anything to him, but I could feel him watching me. He must have known I was waiting for somebody.

As bad as waiting and watching for Jamie was, the worst part was being in a café where I could smell the food cooking and watch others eat it. Now it was becoming unbearable. Jamie had taken the last of our money with him, saying he needed it to get more money.

I hadn't noticed anyone else watching me, nor had I seen the man approach me. I had been silently crying, wiping my tears away before they made it down my cheeks, staring out the window anxiously praying for some sign of Jamie, money, and food.

When I looked up I realized there was someone standing beside my table. The man, who was managing to smile while frowning, asked, "Can I sit with you?" I was glad for the distraction; I just hoped he wouldn't eat in front of me.

I found out his name was Darren. He had noticed me earlier in the day when he had come in for his morning coffee and was surprised to still see me there all this time later. I explained I was waiting for my boyfriend to come back for me. I told him we were fresh off the bus from Vancouver and that we knew no one in this strange town. Somehow from the moment I started talking to Darren I trusted him. He had kind and thoughtful eyes. When he looked at me I felt he really saw me.

I was surprised minutes later when the man behind the counter stepped out and approached us with two plates of burgers and fries. He winked at me when he put them down, and left. Darren explained that I had looked hungry and that he'd figured I'd say no if he asked me whether I was. I liked him even more after he said that.

Darren sat with me for over two hours. Suddenly I noticed it was almost seven. I had barely been conscious of the time passing, and had even managed to stop staring anxiously out the window. There were the sounds of closing time coming from behind the counter— money was being counted, the music had gotten louder, and chairs were being put on the tables in preparation for mopping the floor.

Darren asked me if I would like to go to his place. He held his hands up in a silent pledge, insisting I'd be safe and could just have a shower there and collect my wits while I figured out what I was going to do.

I was relieved at the invite. I knew that Darren meant me no harm. I felt connected to Darren, not in a romantic way, but almost as if we had met before and already knew each other. He was a lot older than I was but he had a very friendly, happy face. A larger man with a round beer belly and tattoos on his meaty arms, he had salt-and-pepper hair and a moustache. His face was expressive: he had round cheeks that became small red mounds when he smiled. I couldn't help smiling back.

Taking one last look through the bay windows, I rose and started to gather my belongings. Darren reached under the table and took one of my bags. He charmed me by holding the door open for me as we made our exit.

I was not surprised to see that Darren drove a truck—better that than the motorcycle I had envisioned, I figured.

Darren lived on the thirty-second floor of a very tall skyscraper in the middle of the city. Offices occupied the first thirteen floors, and above that were apartments.

I was nervous. I didn't like being that high in the air, and I couldn't stop thinking about what would happen if there were an earthquake or a fire. Almost a year later I would be playing cards at Darren's table and notice that the chandelier was swaying. He would tell me that it was the building swaying in the wind and that for some reason or other it was a good thing it did that. He'd have his work cut out for him getting me to believe that one.

After having a shower I sat with Darren at his kitchen table. He had rolled a joint and poured me a glass of Coke while I was in the bathroom. I knew when I came out of the shower and saw him waiting for me at his kitchen table that he and I would be good friends.

It was almost ten at night when Darren offered to take me driving around to see if we could find Jamie. I accepted gratefully. We lugged the bags back into the elevator and to the truck. We had been driving for almost an hour when I decided to stop at the hotel Jamie and I had stayed in that morning. I jumped out of Darren's truck and ran inside. But a brief conversation with the desk clerk was fruitless.

I was just running back out the door when Jamie came in, almost plowing into me. I could tell he was relieved, and I was ecstatic. I almost cried.

I led him back to Darren's truck. I was surprised when Jamie barely mumbled a hello and began to grab our bags from the back of the flatbed. I had to stand on the curb to lean in the window and say thank you and goodbye to Darren. He gave me a joint for the road and started his truck. I watched as it disappeared around the corner. I hoped I would see him again.

Unaware that Jamie was angry with me, I blabbered on about how I had met Darren and how nice he was to me. I was saying that Darren had given me a joint and that we should find somewhere we could be alone and I would smoke him up, when Jamie turned on me. "I've been looking for you for hours! Didn't I tell you to sit in the Centre Street Café?"

His anger took me by surprise. It wasn't so much his words as the searing look in his eyes that scared me.

I had thought I was being really big by not letting him have it for leaving me at the café for the entire day. He's yelling at me because he was so worried about me, I told myself. Touched, I leaned in to kiss him. He shoved me away, almost knocking me off balance.

I decided to let him go on his tirade about why it was so important that I listen to him when he told me to do something. While he was talking we made our way to another hotel. It wasn't much nicer than the hotel we had stayed in the night before. This one did not rent by the hour, but it did rent by the month based on welfare rates.

I went straight for a bath when we walked into our room. Jamie said something about getting dinner and left. I hadn't expected him to be long but by the time I had finished my bath and was lounging on the bed, he still wasn't back.

I took out my writing pad and wrote a poem. When I was done that I began to read a book. Still no Jamie. I was getting really hungry and was starting to worry. I lit the joint that Darren had given me, deciding it wasn't my fault that Jamie was taking all night to find some food.

Hours later he finally returned. He had no food with him. Instead he had bought something else for us. He was standing at the chest of drawers by the end of the bed. He had his back turned to me so I didn't see what he was doing right away.

When I realized what he had on the table I was enraged. I couldn't believe it. I was starving, and he had to be hungry by now, but instead of buying food he had bought cocaine.

I peeked over Jamie's shoulder and watched as he emptied at least half of the flap he carried onto the table. What happened next is a bit of a blur, but things got ugly.

Overcome with anger, I took a huge breath and blew with all my might. Most of the devil's dust scattered and fell to the carpet behind the table. Jamie retaliated. I ended up on the floor with him on top of me. He had a hold of my hair and was banging my head over and over again on the carpeted floor, scraping my cheek into the fibres.

Suddenly there was a very large black man grabbing Jamie and holding him at bay while I tried to stand up and right myself. I ran out of the hotel room in my underwear and T-shirt. Not knowing where to go, I ran down the hall and hid behind a wall in the corridor.

I don't know how much time had passed when I heard Jamie calling me. He must have known that in my underwear I wasn't going to go very far. I let him begin to wander the halls away from where I was hiding before I ran back to the room and locked the door behind me. I grabbed my belongings and stuffed them back into their bags.

I was scared and angry. I didn't know where I was going to go but I knew I had to get away from Jamie. He was a monster who wanted to destroy me, and the only way to protect myself was to get away.

Soon Jamie was yelling at me through the door to let him in. He didn't sound angry anymore. He said that he was sorry and to please just let him in so we could talk. I looked over at the table that still had traces of cocaine on it and ignored him. I could hear Shelly's voice warning me that no woman could compete against the power of the stuff.

Only when I was dressed and ready to go, with both my bags packed, did I open the door. I pushed past him out into the hall. He followed me to the beat-up old elevator. "I'm sorry, baby. I know why you did it. I get it. I'll go get you some dinner right now," he pleaded. I told him the trouble was bigger than dinner and that he had hurt me.

We stood like that for some time, me inside the elevator crying and him in the doorway begging me to give him another chance. In the end he changed my mind. I allowed him to lead me back to the room and again he left, this time in search of food.

For the second time that night I found myself sitting alone in the hotel room. I told myself Jamie hadn't meant to hurt me—I had started it by blowing what was essentially cash across the dresser. I told myself it was just a passing moment. But I missed my family and friends very badly that first night. I had no one to tell.

The next day was mostly spent asking strangers on the street where the girls went to make money. It was an embarrassing question to pose; we had to feel people out before asking. We did eventually find someone who even walked with us to where the stroll was, near the edge of the city itself.

I would find my comfort zone on the city block that was between a Native friendship building and a cultural centre. There was co-op housing and a park nearby, and it would become my routine to smoke a joint there before heading to the stroll.

The first week we were there we concentrated on making the money to rent a suite. We went to the welfare office and Jamie left that same day with a small cheque. We would both go back the next day for our full cheques.

That night Jamie and I had a talk. He said that we had our start-up money now and all we had to do was maintain. We decided that I could stop doing the big-money stuff and stick with the safer things that men would pay for, like blow jobs and hand jobs. I was ecstatic. I was aware that every single time I finished doing up my pants and a car door slammed, I was a bit different. We had our big-ticket needs taken care of now, and I could work on the corner less and not be so vulnerable out there. I hoped that maybe we had just taken a baby step towards normalcy. Maybe we were one day closer to not living this way anymore. I hugged Jamie real close and I told him I loved him.

"I love you too, baby," he said wholeheartedly, and we kissed passionately.

When we went back to the welfare office the next day I was told I needed to talk with a worker alone. They were willing to cut me a cheque for that month, but after that they wanted me to enroll in a program at the vocational college nearby. The school had an incentive program that paid more than welfare. I couldn't believe my ears—I would get paid to attend school! The woman gave me contact info for the vocational college and coached me on what to say when I phoned there. I left her office feeling really lucky and extremely blessed. The welfare worker didn't know it but she had just made me very happy. Once again I was starting to hope that a normal life was within reach.

Maybe in Calgary I *would* find a better life.

Darren found me on the stroll a week or two after we had fist met at the café, and asked me to smoke a joint with him. He took me to an amazing place that would become our spot. It was elevated and provided a view of the entire city overlooking the diaphragm. That's what we called the Calgary Saddledome. All you could see of it from our spot was the top, and that was what it looked like.

Darren and I talked as if we had known each other all our lives. He was very nice to me and seemed to know not to say too much about Jamie. I knew he didn't think that highly of him. He said Jamie was very dark and that one day I would see that. I told Darren I had already seen it and I didn't think it was anything I couldn't handle. "If you knew about the violence Jamie grew up surrounded by, then maybe you would understand," I told him.

Once when I had asked Jamie what his earliest childhood memory was, he had told me that it was of his mother crawling on the floor and lapping up the sugar she had just spilled. His father had been holding a baseball bat and standing over her while she silently cried and did as she was told. He spoke with little emotion but I thought I could sense a wail in his voice somewhere. I had been touched and saddened by his story. I had held onto Jamie that night until I had fallen asleep, hoping that my arms could comfort him as his mother's arms had at times been unable to.

Darren was unconvinced. When he dropped me back off he said he would be around if I needed him. I could tell he was sad to leave me on the stroll but he respected me enough not to make me explain what I was doing there.

The next day I made an appointment with the school counsellor and was told I would take a test to help me decide what subjects would best suit my needs. I was looking forward to the following Monday morning when the normal world would at last have a place in my life once again.

Jamie and I found a one-bedroom apartment that we could afford the following week. We moved in right away. I was excited at the idea of getting a cat, taking walks in my new neighbourhood, and mostly just having a home.

Jamie had to take care of moving all our stuff because I was starting school on our moving day. Luckily for Jamie all we had was our three bags and an old dresser we had found in the alleyway behind our new rental. When I got out of school that first day I started heading back towards our old hotel and had to remind myself that we had moved.

On the outside, the building was very pink. Inside, our unit was small and cramped. A constant draft came in through the windows, and two people couldn't fit in the kitchen at once. It wasn't really cozy at all. But that tiny suite would be home for the next six months.

When I arrived home that first night I saw that Jamie had been shopping. He had bought us plates and silverware, a small television, a radio, and groceries. I went into the bathroom and was delighted at the surprise he'd made: a steaming bath all ready for me. Rose petals drifted on the water, and lit candles completed the atmosphere. When I got into the bath I saw there was a wide variety of new cleansers, body washes, and oils lined up against the wall. Gleefully I dunked my head through the bubbles into the water, feeling like the luckiest girl in the world.

I chose to walk to school most of the time. Our apartment was on 17th Street in southwest Calgary and the school was located on 4th Street, not far away. I genuinely enjoyed walking to school, and I loved the city. I know now that what I loved was the sense of existence it gave me. Not everyone would smile and nod when I walked by but at least there was an awareness that I was there.

The college paid me a biweekly grant, so I was able to work less. I went to the corner just for enough to eat and smoke. Jamie was adamant that he control the funds that came into our household. He said it was because I was so bad with money. I would get an allowance of five dollars a day when I had school, and when I wasn't in school I was with *him*, so I didn't need any spending money then. Or so his logic went.

I began to lie to Jamie about what I made at night, hiding money under the carpet in the corner of the living room. I figured that if it was right under his nose he would be least likely to find it.

To my amazement I was making friends at school. I was hard to approach because I did my best to keep to myself. I still felt I wasn't a normal person. In fact sometimes I felt very cloak-and-dagger, as if I was leading a double life. I had secrets, and that made it hard to make friends.

I met Chantel at school on maybe my third day. My locker was only two or three away from hers, and we had smiled at each other the first few times we had seen each other. Chantel was going to be a dental hygienist; she was in her second year at the college.

The first time we talked we ended up going to the cafeteria and eating lunch together. She told me she was from Red Deer; she had moved to Calgary two years earlier and worked as a server in a local nightclub. She didn't like having her son in daycare and thought if she could find a better-paying job she wouldn't have to work such long hours. Chantel was very proud of her son; there was a gleam in her eyes when she mentioned his name. I sat across from her watching her talk and hoped that I too would have a child someday.

Chantel told me about the Calgary Stampede and how she took her son to the rodeo every year. "I'd love it if you came with us for at least one day of it this year," she said. I had never been to a rodeo before and was excited by the idea. We made a giggly agreement to go together.

Jamie found a job through a placement program. It was in construction, and he would come home dirty and smelly. He was almost always in a bad mood and wanted his dinner by seven. Before long making dinner became my sole responsibility, as did the dishes and the housework in general. Jamie would take care of the grocery shopping.

At times rushing home to make dinner would interfere with my normal life and I would resent him imposing his routine on me. It occurs to me now that I never considered Jamie to be part of what was normal for me.

Jamie and I kept to ourselves and didn't get to know our neighbours in that first building we lived in, a low-income one where tension was always in the air. We would have horrible arguments some nights; I'm sure the neighbours could hear us. We heard them arguing many times too. The police came to the building frequently for domestic dispute calls and the occasional bench warrant.

With Christmas fast approaching, I had been going to school for almost two months. I was more homesick than ever. I had never spent Christmas apart from my family, and even though I was with Jamie I felt very alone. I was glad when Jamie gave me the news that his brother Tracy was coming from Vancouver to visit over Christmas.

I hadn't known until that moment that Jamie had a brother but once he told me the news, Tracy was all Jamie talked about. He was older than Jamie by two years, and Jamie made it sound as if Tracy hung the moon in the sky.

Tracy was nineteen when I met him but he looked older. It was his eyes. They were those of an old man who had lived a long time. When a friend of mine who did tarot and palm reading met him later, she said he was an old soul, older than anyone she had ever met before. She slept with Tracy that night; I think she was somewhat awed by him.

I thought he was a bit slimy, though. I hid my purse when he was around and felt paranoid about my money under the carpet when he was left alone in the apartment. As if he might read my mind and learn it was there.

Tracy didn't go home after Christmas as planned. He had decided that he liked Calgary and that he wanted to live here. He said he had missed his brother too. He would stay with us until he found his own apartment close by.

He encouraged Jamie to go out more, and they would return home high on cocaine or drunk or both. Other times Jamie would stay home and Tracy would go out. When that happened I was glad.

Jamie was different when Tracy was around. He would snap orders at me, and shove me and push me around. Other times he would grab me and begin to roughly feel my breasts up under Tracy's watchful eye. It seemed as if Jamie took great relish in my discomfort.

When Tracy wasn't around Jamie was nicer to me. He wouldn't walk past me without kissing me or giving my bum a playful pat. I understood on some level why he was so different when he was with his brother. Jamie had to show off.

Tracy had immediately applied for welfare and was soon in his own apartment. It gave Jamie somewhere else to go, and I began to see less and less of him.

I thought I put up with Jamie because he would eventually see the light and change. He had something of value to offer the world; it was just that neither of us knew what. Jamie dreamed of being an actor so he could become a millionaire. Then for a while he talked about being a stuntman so he could become a millionaire. I thought, okay: he wants to be a millionaire.

We adopted a cat from the local SPCA and I named him Dragon. He was a red, long-haired tortoiseshell. He reminded me of fire from the moment I first laid eyes on him. He was my cat from the beginning.

If there was ever such a thing as a guard cat, Dragon was it. He would attack people when they walked by his perch on top of the fridge, sometimes seemingly for no reason. But I learned to trust Dragon's judgement after Jamie brought over a friend he had just met.

Dragon was on the fridge when the two of them came walking into the suite. Jamie walked past the fridge towards where I was sitting in the living room. His friend was following close behind. Dragon suddenly leapt off the fridge and dug his claws into the sides of the guy's head. It took Jamie and me a lot of effort to finally pry Dragon loose. I carried the cat down the hall to the bedroom.

Later that night, Jamie would come home and tell me his new "friend" had stolen all his money.

I had been going to school for almost a whole semester and summer break was approaching. One afternoon I came home and Dragon didn't appear at my feet as usual when I walked in.

I couldn't find him right away. I called his name and searched the living room, the kitchen, and the hall closets. I was starting to panic when I thought I heard something from the bedroom.

I had a horrible feeling in my chest and stomach as I entered the room. When I opened the closet door, my beloved cat was lying there on my housecoat, blood mixed with what looked like foam coming from his mouth.

I didn't pick him up right away; I ran to the phone and called Darren, praying he would answer. By some miracle, at four in the afternoon Darren was home. Through my tears I explained that I needed his help to get Dragon to the vet. Darren must have heard the urgency in my voice because I was already listening to a dial tone when I hung up.

I ran back to Dragon and tried to comfort him as best I could. I moved his head and saw that his jaw was just hanging there. He was obviously in a lot of pain. When Darren arrived I managed leave Dragon long enough to let him in. He followed me into the bedroom and briefly looked Dragon over before agreeing we had to take him to the vet. He had had the forethought to bring a box with him, with a blanket folded in the bottom. I lifted my cat into the box, cradling him carefully. I left Dragon only to get the money I had been stashing under the carpet.

Darren drove us to the local animal hospital. I felt sheepish telling the vet that I had no idea what had happened to my cat. I *suspected* what had happened but I couldn't tell him that. The vet took some X-rays and then told me that Dragon's jaw had been nearly broken and that it had to be realigned. He might not be able to come home for a few days.

I went home in a rage. I couldn't see straight, I was so angry. I stormed into the house and was disappointed to find the apartment still empty. It was probably a good thing Jamie wasn't there that night.

Darren picked Dragon up from the vet two days later. I didn't put Dragon down for days. I wore a hooded shirt backwards so I could put him in the hood and keep him cradled close to me.

Jamie didn't come back to the apartment for another two days.

When he did, I swarmed him. At first he acted surprised and shocked at my rage and at Dragon's condition. The moment I looked into his eyes, though, I knew he was responsible for what had happened. I began to throw things at him, blindly grabbing items from the kitchen counter and hurling them at him.

He came towards me. I saw him coming; I saw the look on his face, but I didn't relent. I upped the ante on my verbal assault, my voice getting louder and nastier, not backing down or even retreating. The bastard! He had hurt my cat and then left him to die in our closet. He couldn't be human.

Then he struck me right across the cheekbone, knocking me off my feet. He sat on me and held my arms over my head. His face inches from mine, he leaned even closer and whispered in my ear.

"You're stepping over a line. I'll only let you go so far. Do you understand what I'm saying?"

I didn't care what he was saying. I tried to kick him but it was impossible. I began to struggle to get my arms free. He just sat on me and shook his head at me, a half smile on his face. Then he head-butted me, hard. My head hit the carpeted floor I was lying on. Startled and a little dazed, I was immediately silenced. I gave up trying to fight him. Unable to hide my face, I turned my head away when the tears began.

Unmoved, Jamie kept his grip on my wrists, his head close to my left ear. He whispered that he was going to let go in a second and that I was not to move. "Keep your hands above your head and I'll back away slowly," he ordered. It occurred to me that he might be a little bit afraid of me as well.

I stayed as he had told me to while he slowly stood up, grabbed his jacket, and closed the door behind himself. When he was gone I rolled over onto my side, curled into a ball, and sobbed. Eventually I went and got Dragon, who was sleeping in his new box, and cradled him while I cried silently in front of the television.

I went to school the next day and when I arrived home Jamie was on the couch with Dragon on his lap. He said that he had some amends to make with the cat and with me too.

I interrupted him, saying that it had to have been an accident and that I hadn't even given him a chance to explain. I told him I was sure he was feeling guilty enough without my having added to it by yelling and throwing things. I was almost afraid to ask. "How did it happen?"

Jamie told me that Dragon had been begging him for food when he had come home to eat his lunch. He shoved the cat away three or four times, but Dragon was persistent. The phone rang and Jamie answered it. When he got off the phone he found Dragon had taken apart his sandwich and was making his own meal out of the meat in the middle. Jamie picked him up and threw him against the wall in the living room.

I couldn't believe I was hearing this from Jamie's own lips. I said nothing, but I was scared.

Jamie told his tale of spontaneous violence very matter-of-factly, seeming focused on his own frustration.

"You need to train Dragon somehow not to irritate me and beg for food. That cat is violent himself. He needs to learn that humans are the dominant species," he said.

"Well, he's never been 'violent' towards me or any other woman," I retorted. I didn't mention that Darren had been over to the apartment several times and had never been attacked either.

Neither of us mentioned the glaring bruise in the centre of my forehead, nor the bruises in the perfect shape of his hands that scattered their way down my arms.

That night I knew that our relationship had taken a turn. I no longer looked at Jamie the same way. I was scared of him, and yet I made no plans to leave him.

Except I did. For some time after that night I worked more than I needed to. I told myself that it was because I was replacing the money that I had had to take from under the carpet for the vet.

Chantel and I had been studying together after school ever since we met. She turned out to be a great study partner and she seemed to understand that I never really wanted to go right home after school.

I told her almost nothing of my home life, steering her away from personal questions. But she noticed some of the bruises I was unable to hide. I had seen her disapproving, concerned frown.

We were friends for some time before she ever met Jamie. He finally made a very rare appearance at the cafeteria during lunch. He didn't like that I was making friends outside of his life and said that he wanted to meet these people I was surrounded by during the day. Chantel disliked him almost right away. She said I needed to be very careful. That made me realize that if she knew what I did in my after-school life she would never stay my friend.

One afternoon, the Friday just before a long-weekend break, Chantel found me and told me that some friends were getting together that weekend for a drive up to West Edmonton Mall. They would love to have me along. I was excited—I had never been there, and I really wanted to go. Chantel said they were leaving Saturday morning and could come pick me up.

It was a pay Friday, and Jamie and I had a routine on those days. He would come pick me up after school. I would meet him on the corner outside the school and we would go out for dinner, then go buy groceries. We would top the evening off by renting a VCR and a movie.

I told Chantel that I would have no money and that I couldn't go. I knew I couldn't go out to work that night to make the money. I never worked later than ten at night and I would be with Jamie past that time. I also couldn't guarantee that I'd be able to get at the money under the carpet before we had to leave. This put me in a hard spot, because Chantel knew I was never broke. I had known her a long time and she had borrowed money from me in the past, sometimes as much as fifty dollars. Plus, today was a payday. Why couldn't I just use my cheque?

I had to make something up. I couldn't tell her everything. I decided telling her half the truth was better than lying to her. I told her it was because Jamie was going to take the cheque and give me an allowance. She turned her nose up at that, telling me that it was my cheque and that I could avoid giving my money to Jamie by spending the night at her house. I was unable to think of anything else to deter her, and eventually agreed.

The rest of the afternoon I couldn't concentrate in class. I knew that I was going to get my check and that I would not be meeting Jamie. The idea of deceiving him made me nervous, and when the final bell rang I was considering changing my mind.

I met Chantel outside my class and we were first in line for our cheques. Once we had them she went into the hallway first. The stairwell was right across the hall. She went and opened the stairwell door, and motioned that it was safe for me to leave. I darted out into the hall and raced down the stairs. I knew Jamie was likely still on the corner waiting for me but it was fun sneaking around. I felt like Nancy Drew. Once outside we began to run, laughing the whole way. We met up with our friends at the local bar where we gathered to study, and pulled out our books.

But while we were there I began to feel guilty about having run off on Jamie like that. After all, was it not our unofficial date night? I couldn't concentrate.

After a while I slammed my books shut and told Chantel that I had to go home. I would call her later that night to arrange a ride the next morning.

"Okay … I'm sure I'll hear from you then," she replied. I could tell she meant she knew she wouldn't. I assured her I would phone her later and that I would go with them to Edmonton.

I had convinced myself that Jamie would be reasonable and allow me to work on Monday night after I got back to make up for what I spent in Edmonton. I told myself he would see that this would be too much fun for me to pass on and that he would let me go.

I ran all the way home, making up an explanation for why I hadn't met him after school as usual.

I couldn't have known he had been standing across the street watching as Chantel and I had run up the road, and that he had seen me stuff the envelope in my bag when I thought I was far enough away.

 # Chapter 11

Jamie wasn't home when I got there, and that gave me time to work myself into a frenzy worrying about how he would react. I smoked two joints, one after another, but even that couldn't calm me down.

I turned on the television, hoping it would distract me. Keeping one ear honed for the sound of the front door, I tried not to think about it anymore.

I didn't hear Jamie come in or approach me. I almost screamed when I saw him in the mirror just standing there staring at me. He had caught me off guard and I couldn't read the look on his face. I began to get up off the couch to greet him. He held up his hand, signalling me to sit down again. I complied instantly, almost falling back down onto the couch.

Sitting down beside me, he turned the television off. We sat in silence for what felt like an eternity. Then he surprised me by kissing me. After necking a while he led me to the bedroom. Relieved by the unexpected tenderness he was showing me, I went with him almost eagerly.

In the bedroom Jamie whispered that he had something he wanted to try. First he undressed me till I only had my bra and panties on. Then he pulled out my silk scarves and began to tie my wrists to the legs of the bed. I let him. When he was done he stood over me and began to take off his own clothes. His pants were undone but still on when he said, "There's something I need to teach you."

I knew in that moment that I had made a terrible mistake. His eyes were burrowing into me, and I could see the threat in them. I began to cry even before he said anything else. I knew that he knew what I had done that afternoon and that I hadn't gotten away with anything.

Wailing, I pleaded, "I can explain. *Please!*" "I understand perfectly what happened," he retorted, and left the room. I could hear his muffled voice and knew he was on the phone. I struggled with all my might to get the scarves off my wrist, wrenching my hands in every direction, even trying to rip the fabric with my fingernails. I was on the verge of screaming when Jamie came back into the room.

He sat down on the edge of the bed, looking so sinister that I shrank under his gaze. "You need to remember where you came from. I saved you. Maybe you need a reminder of what I saved you *from*. Have I done something to hurt you so terribly that hurting me like you did is justified?"

I could only shake my head because I didn't trust my voice. I thought I might scream if I tried to say anything through my desperate sobs.

"I've invited Tracy over for a little fun," he continued. "You're gonna show him a good time."

The blood drained from my head. I began to struggle with renewed energy and had opened my mouth to scream when Jamie said that we didn't have to wait for his brother, and that I could start by giving him a blow job until Tracy got there. He stuffed two of his fingers into my open mouth, causing me to gag; then shook his head at me in a silent order not to scream. Then he pulled his fingers from my mouth.

I just lay there and cried while Jamie took off his pants and stood over me with his hands on the wall and his penis waving in my face. "Do it!" he yelled. I thought about biting him but didn't. I cried and did what he'd told me to.

We were interrupted by a knock on the front door, and when Jamie was gone I made one last hopeless attempt to get out of the ties that bound my wrists. I was driven by humiliation: the thought of Tracy seeing me topless and helplessly bound was almost unbearable.

Then Tracy was standing in the bedroom doorway. He saw me on the bed with my shirt ripped open and my breasts hanging out, naked except for my underwear. I was begging through sobs by then, mumbling for him to please help me, though I didn't really expect him to.

He came all the way into the room, and I looked away, unsure what he was about to do. My heart was beating loudly in my chest and I could feel my blood pounding in my head. I concentrated on the corner of the bedroom, focusing on the electrical outlet, and tried to regain control of myself.

Tracy touched my arm. I shrank away as best I could. Then he began to untie me. He covered me with a sheet, giving me back my dignity, and left the room. Not yet daring to move from the bed, I overheard him talking to Jamie.

"You've gone too far this time, man. You really shouldn't have done that." Minutes later I heard the front door to the apartment close, and they were gone.

I got up off the bed and called Darren. He came and picked me up within minutes and took me to his place. I told him what had happened. He listened intently, allowing me to finish the whole tale before saying anything. Then he made us each a rum and Coke. I guzzled mine and he made me another.

When our chit-chat subsided and the room fell silent, Darren stood up, walked over, and sat down beside me. "Let me send you home, Tara Lee," he pleaded. "I'll buy your plane ticket. You can be home tomorrow."

"I don't want to go home," I replied. "I'm building a life for myself here. The vocational college is the longest I've stayed in school since I was twelve. I'm happy there. Most of the time I'm happy at home too," I added.

Darren raised an eyebrow and said he was sure I was mistaking co-dependency for comfort. I was insulted.

"I'm definitely not co-dependent," I retorted. "I'm making a go of my life here. I'm showing stamina by sticking to my guns, aren't I?"

Darren didn't push me. He left it by saying that he would be there when he could be and that he hoped I wouldn't need him when he couldn't.

Jamie came home days later, apologetic and depressed. I found myself comforting him and telling him not to worry; that he'd only behaved that way because of how he'd grown up. I loved the Jamie who returned once the smoke cleared—a vulnerable, wounded Jamie. We were caught up in a cycle by then, and this phase was the lock that kept me from leaving.

Summer break arrived. I had completed almost half of my subjects. I was proud because even though I had started really late I was only one semester behind the rest of my assessed class. I was hoping I could make that up the following year. I had one more semester to go before I could begin working towards my career goal, nursing. I had wanted to be a counsellor but there was a waiting list for those courses and I didn't want to have to wait another semester. If all went well I would be a nurse before my twenty-second birthday.

On the home front things were okay. Jamie seemed more relaxed and I began to remember what it was I liked about him. He was charming and chivalrous again. He gave me a promise ring that summer. It was white gold—rare, apparently. Jamie liked to surprise me. He said it kept the momentum up. I was happy to be on the receiving end.

Summer went by quickly and uneventfully right up until the end. I was with Jamie and his friends almost all the time. We spent most of the summer in the bars and nightclubs. I would dance and drink the night away. Jamie would play pool and drink the night away. Some nights we would bring home some cocaine and get high. On those nights I ended up on the stroll at three in the morning because we needed to stay high. Not only was I out way later than usual, I also wasn't very careful at such times. I was in a hurry to get back to Jamie, to order more cocaine.

One of those nights I was picked up by a man I vaguely recognized. It was nearly two in the morning and I was really high. I had brought the last of our coke with me and had just done a line in an alcove before hitting the corner.

The man drove around the corner into the alley and turned off his engine. He reached into his pocket, took out a hundred-dollar bill, and put it on the dash on his side of the car. "I want to talk to you," he said. "Will you at least listen to what I have to say?"

I nodded. I was really high, and he was making me feel as if maybe I was a little *too* high. I wasn't sure I'd be able to defend myself if I needed to.

The man asked me if I remembered him from six months previous. I looked him over. He looked like an office type, the rich boss kind. There was the odour of expensive cologne in the air. Well kempt, he wore a suit and tie with gold cufflinks and tie clip. I searched my memory. He looked familiar but I didn't specifically remember him.

He turned in his seat to look at me. "I feel very sad," he said. "When I met you the first time I felt awful, because I could tell you weren't just some hooker doomed to a life on the streets. The girl I met then," he went on, "was someone who was in trouble but could find her way. Now, looking at you, I can see the streets are eating you up. I know you're high and that you're here to make more money to stay high." He ended by handing me the money and telling me to go home, get high, and then get clean. He said he never wanted to see me out there again if I didn't have my wits about me. Then he reached across me and opened the door. "Go and kill yourself if that's what you want." When I slammed the door shut behind me he was saying something about what a shame it was.

I stood there for some time after he drove off, thinking about what he had said. My first thought was that he was weird. Then I looked at the money I still held in my hand and realized he had been trying to help me. I wondered what it was that made me different than any other girl who lived life the way I did. I certainly hadn't done anything with my life that made me special, yet people kept trying to help me.

I cried all the way home that night. I told myself I was high so I wasn't able to look at what had happened clearly. The truth was that the man had forced me to look at myself, and I'd gotten scared when I saw where I was going. At home I got high again, and in the late afternoon, when the drugs were all gone, I went to sleep. When I woke up I decided I would never think about that man again or about the hurtful truths he had revealed to me.

I spent a lot of time with Darren. I would call him before I went out to work and he would come and pick me up from the corner. He said that he would never pick me up from home when I was heading out to work because he hated the idea of taking me there.

We would go to our spot above the city and smoke a joint. Then sometimes we would go to Darren's place and play cards. Time had a way of passing quickly when I was with Darren. He made me feel normal. He let me tell him everything and never judged me. He had no trouble telling me when I was wrong or being stupid; he kept me honest.

I eventually broke my vow of silence and told Darren about my strange encounter with the man in the car. Darren admitted he agreed with what the man had said. He said he too had noticed a difference in me since we first met. He said maybe Jamie wasn't the best person for me to be with, but what I was doing to myself was far worse than anything Jamie could do to me. I ignored what he said about what I was doing to myself and defended Jamie.

"You just don't like Jamie because all I ever tell you about him is the bad stuff." I saw all the sides to Jamie, I insisted. Our relationship was volatile. Jamie wasn't the only problem. Darren just smiled.

He leaned forward and turned on the radio, adjusting it to another station. I almost didn't hear him remark that I wouldn't be defending anything if there were nothing to defend, and that if there was nothing to defend then there was also no awareness. He looked up at me then, and told me he believed I was a smart girl and that it would be hard to pull the wool over my eyes. His words stung.

That was the closest Darren and I ever got to having an argument.

Jamie and I moved to a new apartment that summer. It was a step up from where we had been. There was still only one bedroom, but it was newly painted and had all new appliances. It was on 24th Avenue, still in southwest Calgary. Farther for me to walk to school, so I had to take the bus on really cold days, but I liked the neighbourhood.

In our new apartment's living room I found a corner of the carpet that would come up for my money stash, and once my money was safely hidden I felt as if I was home.

School was set to begin that coming week when Chantel called me. We made plans to meet up that Saturday night at the bar we usually went to after school.

The Friday prior to that I had been on the corner and met a girl named Teesha and her friend Robin. I knew those weren't their real names but I joined their game and introduced myself as Sparrow. Robin and I didn't hit it off but I liked Teesha right away. Teesha ended up spending the night at my apartment.

I was glad when Teesha and Jamie hit it off, and thought that maybe I had found a new friend.

They say that bad things happen in threes. What happened one Saturday night made me think there might be some truth to that. When it was time for me to leave Teesha still hadn't left. She was in the living room, and I needed to get to the money hidden under the carpet. I thought fast and called her into the bathroom, telling her I had a face mask I wanted her to try. I had conveniently already done mine. While she was busy putting hers on in the bathroom, I went to the living room and took a fifty from under the carpet.

Teesha stayed in the apartment while I went out and met Chantel. We had a great night out, dancing and playing pool until late. We got hot dogs at a sidewalk stand and sat by a water fountain to eat. I didn't think about earthquakes and broken glass from tall skyscrapers even once that night.

When I arrived home I was surprised to find the apartment empty except for Dragon. I went straight to the bathroom and when I came out the phone was ringing. It was Jamie.

He was in jail and needed me to get three hundred dollars for his bail. When I asked him what happened he said he was being charged with assault. I promised him I would be there by noon on Monday. I told him I would work all day Sunday and all night if I had to.

I knew I didn't have to, and I thought I would just surprise him in the morning by saying that I had made all the money that night after he had called. I stood up from the couch, went to the corner of the carpet, and lifted it up. There was nothing there but the carpet underlay.

I had saved close to six hundred dollars, and it was all gone. I lifted the carpet halfway across the room to no avail. Devastated, I crawled on the carpet and cried. Everything I had worked for was gone. Suddenly all I had done to get that money had been for nothing. All the shame was now worthless. I couldn't believe it was gone and just kept staring at the corner, all curled up, hugging myself.

Months had gone by and nothing had happened to that money. I got angry with myself for not being smarter and just taking the money with me when I left—I could have hidden it again later. I became even more enraged when I thought of Teesha. I knew she was the one who had taken my money. She must have sensed something and snuck down the hall after me when I thought she was in the bathroom. I knew I wouldn't see her again but I played scenes over in my head about how it would go if I did happen to see her walking by. They didn't make me feel better. That had been the money that was going to save me one day, and nothing could make me feel better in that moment. I cried for a long time before I pulled myself together.

The following morning I woke up early. I decided I would get an early start. I was on the stroll by eleven in the morning. Because I was limited in what I would do for the money it took me a long time that day, and it was dusk before I had enough money for Jamie's bail. I asked the last man if he would be kind enough to drive me home. When I got there I realized that all I had was the money Jamie needed for bail. I decided to drop it off at home and head back out for just one more trick. Then I could grab a bite to eat on the way home and get Jamie in the morning.

It was after dark when I made it back to the stroll, and the street lights had come on. I stayed in the shadows, not wanting to be seen by just anyone. A silver truck drove by slowly. The man inside wore a pastel tie-dye sweatshirt that advertised a local gym. He turned his head to look at me as he drove by. I felt a shiver up my spine, and stayed in the shadows.

The same man came around again, and this time he stopped the truck and motioned me over. We had the chat and I informed him that I didn't do what he wanted. He then said he would take what he could get from me and that I was the prettiest girl on the block.

I was tired and starting to get cold. Against the voices in my head telling me to walk away, I climbed into his truck.

We drove for some time; I was nervous the whole way. He said he wanted to be well away from the city and from police officers used to seeing girls like me. I was insulted but I bit my tongue and let him concentrate on driving.

He stopped in a large open field. I could see no lights anywhere, not even far into the distance. I was kicking myself for letting him take me out to the middle of nowhere.

He took his seat belt off and began to take his pants down. I told him I needed the money first.

"Don't worry about that," he replied. "I'll give it to you when we're done. Girls like you have ripped me off before. I'm not gonna let that happen again."

Again, that "girls like you" thing he had said earlier. It had grated on my nerves then too.

"*This* particular girl, who you don't know at all, won't rip you off," I told him, an edge of irritation in my voice. "But I won't do anything without the money up front."

He smiled almost sweetly at me from across the seat.

"I'm gonna have sex with you, baby, but I'm not gonna pay you for it," he said. "I've done this to lots of other working girls. I won't hurt you. I just want sex." He shrugged, took a condom out, and set it on the dash.

He had been speaking so calmly and his movements were so casual that I took a few seconds to register what he was saying to me.

I stared at the condom on his dashboard, then reached for the door handle as quickly as I could, jumped out of the truck, and began to run.

He caught up with me in seconds and threw me to the ground, jumping on top of me and roughly ripping at my jeans. I kicked and screamed until I was hoarse.

"Shut up!" he ordered. "You're ruining the moment for me."

"Get off me, you rapist!" I yelled.

"Oh, you're really starting to get under my skin, baby."

"You're a sick fucker. You need help," I said. Then I descended into crying for my mom. He had still hardly touched me, though, and all of a sudden he surprised me by crawling off me.

He repeated, "You ruined the moment for me, man."

If I hadn't been so terrified I might have laughed right then, he looked so dumbfounded and ridiculous as he fumbled to fasten up his pants.

Then he stood up, got in his truck, and drove off.

Alone in the field I did start to laugh. I laughed and laughed until my sides hurt. I wasn't sure exactly what had happened.

I knew I was in the middle of nowhere and had to find my way back. I knew that I had been attacked, but what kind of attack was that?

I looked to the sky and thanked the Lord that he had sent someone human. Then I started laughing all over again.

I didn't move from there for probably over an hour. I watched shooting stars and satellites make their way across the sky. I was confused about everything. By the time I got up nothing was any clearer.

I made it back home sometime around three in the morning. I still hadn't eaten but I was too exhausted to worry about it. I slid into bed and slept with my clothes on that night.

In the morning I went to get Jamie. I never did tell him what happened to me that night. I don't know why but it was a secret I buried deep inside my closet. I didn't even tell Darren.

I was late for my first day back at school. I knew that wasn't a very good start to the year. I found Chantel in the cafeteria, though, and we began the routine we had had the year before. I fell back into normal quite easily, and even wondered a little if I was more normal than I had thought.

Jamie had found another job. I think he was bored when I wasn't home all day with him and needed something to occupy him. His last job had ended almost to the day school had got out.

I was starting to like the routine though—even Jamie's need to have supper by seven. It was dependable. The chaos seemed to be lessening.

Christmas came and once again I was sad and alone. I called my parents and cried to my mother. I told her that I missed her and that Christmas really sucked. She said that if I were at home I'd be eating chocolate pound cake. That made me cry harder and I hung up feeling worse than before.

Tracy came over on Christmas morning and the three of us had our own small gift opening. Tracy stayed for dinner. I didn't know how to cook a turkey so Jamie and Tracy played around with each other while they chopped and sliced, hard at work in the kitchen. Maybe Christmas didn't suck so badly after all.

I was arrested right after my eighteenth birthday. A man driving a blue sedan pulled over and we had the chat. I didn't catch the hints that he was a police officer. I didn't have to spend any time in jail, though. It was all very clinical and quick. They took face shots of me, did a fingerprint kit, and made a Polaroid of my face for the vice squad that worked the stroll. The officer who took my prints said that it was for them to keep on file for if I ever disappeared. I said nothing but his words stung and I felt insulted. He believed that I was a doomed soul—I could tell by his dismissive nod when he thrust papers at me to sign. The whole procedure was methodical and seemed routine. I was given a court date and released.

My double life went rather smoothly for a while. I went to school in the morning and studied in the late afternoon with my friends. Dinner would be ready for 7:00, and then I would be at work by 8:30 and home by 10:30. Jamie and I were staying away from drugs, even on the weekends, and Jamie seemed to be enjoying his job.

One afternoon he came home with a friend. Brent was a cook at the restaurant Jamie often ate in while at work. He was a fiery redhead, freckles accenting his pale skin. Brent was a regular guy, so to him our late nights and the way we scraped by financially were unfamiliar. Our unconventional, destructive lifestyle seemed to fascinate him. A week after I met him he moved in.

Brent was sleeping on our living room floor and seemed quite content with the situation, except it became obvious that he didn't like Jamie and me arguing. One night he witnessed a verbal fight between us that escalated to Jamie holding me by the throat against the wall. The next day when Jamie was out, he said, "You know, Tara, you should really stand up to Jamie more."

I explained to him that Jamie and I had found a system that worked. I did everything the way Jamie wanted it done and that made him less frustrated. "Jamie just feels thwarted," I added. "Life's dealt him a bad hand. He likes things to be a certain way. And really, most of what he asks of me is pretty reasonable. Cut him some slack, Brent."

The thing was, for Jamie and me fights like the one the night before were common, and it didn't occur to me that the normal world didn't live that way. Brent, though, looked truly distraught, and I felt a twinge of humiliation as I realized he was looking at me with pity in his eyes. It made me angry. I stalked out of the living room and away from him.

In a Calgary civic courtroom I was told by a judge that I would pay a fine for my prostitution charge. There was no probation; no threat of loss to my freedom; the judge himself didn't even speak to me. I left feeling like things had just gone too smoothly. I was waiting for a police officer to come and tell me that they had made a mistake and needed to throw me in jail.

Brent had left for just under a week, and was nowhere to be seen those nights. When he did come back he had a girlfriend on his arm. I don't remember her name but she made me feel uncomfortable when we met. She looked both Jamie and me up and down, and the look on her face told me we had been judged and had come up wanting.

Later that night when Jamie and I were alone I told Jamie that he needed to stop her coming over. We argued over it; in the end Jamie walked away the victor. I was left in a heap on the bed, hugging myself and praying that I wouldn't have to wear a long-sleeved shirt in the heat of the sun to cover my bruises. The next morning I woke to find a large bruise on the side of my head in front of my ear. I hadn't even felt that blow the night before. I could do nothing to hide the bruise, though, and I knew there would be more questions and knowing glances from my friends.

I was almost at school that day when I changed my mind and went over towards the stroll. I knew it was early, but I couldn't go to school. I couldn't face Chantel and the others. They knew already, but I had never confirmed anything. If I went to school I would be confirming it without having to say a word. They would never believe that I had walked into another door, or once again played soccer with my face. They had heard it all before and by now they saw through me.

Not only that, but I hated that the streets ate people alive and I hated that the stroll was even there; I hated that I was living in it and I hated that most of it was invisible to the average person.

It tore at my soul every day. I saw changes in myself that I feared were irreversible: I was no longer crying during sad movies; I was having a harder time connecting with Chantel and my other friends from school even when I wasn't bruised. My second life was seeping into my normal life, and school was becoming my second life.

I walked along a high overpass across a busy road and thought about my body falling to the pavement below and then bouncing and being plastered on the front of a giant truck. It was an image that left me empty. I knew I was closer to giving up than I ever had been.

# Chapter 12

NEAR THE END OF the year at school rumours began to circulate about my secret life. Somebody had seen me in a tight skirt on the stroll, and word was spreading fast.

I was in the science lab on a Monday afternoon when one of the girls in the class stopped by my desk. I think it was the first time this particular girl had ever spoken to me. I searched my mind for her name. She leaned in very close to me, her voice low with concern, and asked me if what she had heard was true. I quietly gathered my books and left the room.

All at once the little world I had created away from my life was spinning and wrenching free of me. I pulled up the hood of my sweatshirt and kept my head down, avoiding everyone I knew. By the last class that day even my teachers were treating me with kid gloves.

I was devastated. Now everyone knew my shame and people were looking at me differently. I fought the urge to leave school early.

When classes were over I went home depressed and angry at the same time. I was even incensed with God, for not letting me hold onto that tiny bit of peace I had managed to carve out for myself.

Even more than angry and depressed, though, I was scared. For the first time I was overcome with the reality that was my life. I felt the only normal thing in my life falling apart, and I was struck with the terror of having nothing but the streets left for me. It would be as if it was summer all year long.

I was at a loss when I thought about what would happen to me now. I knew I had always managed to hang in there because there had always been something in my life that I could latch onto. All at once I had lost my sense of direction. Without school, alone except for Darren, living in Calgary with Jamie the way we did, I saw no safety net. What if this was how I was going to live for the rest of my life?

I knew that it wouldn't be very long then because I wasn't strong enough to fight forever and survive. I was already losing my will. When I had nothing left to lose, what then? Maybe the next time I walked across a bridge and the idea of hitting the pavement struck me, I wouldn't have anything to hold me back from taking that final plunge.

These were the questions that haunted me in bed every night, and after that day at school they were screaming at me. I didn't have the answers. I just knew that I had always believed in me and that now for the first time I was beginning to doubt I would ever find a better life.

Chantel found me on the second or third day of school that week. I told her that the rumours were true. I tried to convey that my school life was completely separate and that I was desperate to keep something normal in my life. Sadly, she told me that she couldn't compromise her son and that I would not be able to go to her house anymore. "We're still friends, Tara," she assured me. "I'm not judging you at all." Then she walked away, headed to her next class.

I stood in the hall watching as she rounded the corner. I knew she had just bade me a gentle goodbye, but somehow I didn't cry. I realized that I had expected it to happen since the day we had met, and I understood her reasons.

I sighed wearily and told myself to get to class.

After that, when Chantel phoned, I would talk to her, but I steered clear of her after school and kept to myself. I told myself it was okay because she hadn't known me anyway. She had only known the girl who went to school every day, the girl with the plastered, stupid grin, who was full of useless hope and unattainable dreams.

I thought of Shelly and how she had said that thinking about normal could cost you. I wondered what she would say about *seeking* normal?

Finally summer came and school was over for that year. I prayed as I emptied my locker that I would be able to begin next year with a clean slate, and that no one would remember the Native hooker from the previous year.

Brent still had his girlfriend over quite often and they would keep us up at night with their squeals and cries of ecstasy. It was disgusting—I hoped that Jamie and I didn't sound like that. I would bury my head in the pillow and wait for the silence that would envelop me in sleep.

Jamie would be gone from the apartment for days that summer. I didn't know what he was doing and I didn't care. Left with the silence, I would lie back and relish it. I did nothing but think.

I would think about my nightmares and how they had started to chase me when I was awake. I thought about my grandparents and I thanked God that they weren't around to see what had become of me, their well-mannered, respectful granddaughter.

I had picked up from my dad that nothing could happen that I couldn't learn from. I thought for a long time about what I had learned from John Moralice. I suspected that either whatever path I was on now had begun the day I met him, or meeting him had given me that extra push towards self-destruction.

I thought back to living with Janine and Robert and what Janine had said about me. I was already in trouble, even back then. Whatever was wrong with me, it seemed, had always been there, even before I met John Moralice.

I believed that we all had a role in life and that even though I was on such a downward spiral, I was supposed to be there. I was struck with the thought that maybe some people are destined to make up the dark side of life. Maybe I was meant to be on the street so that people who had a normal life could say to themselves, at least I'm not *her*.

When Jamie was around, I spent my days differently. I would wake up and go to the stroll. Often Darren would find me and we would take off to smoke a joint at the top of the city. Then I would go to work for the later afternoon. I was working later and later, in violation of my safety rules, but I didn't want to be at home. I would make my money and head straight to the bar, where I would meet Jamie. We would party the night away and sometimes carry on into the next day.

Our idea of partying was slipping into the bathroom at the bar every twenty minutes or so to powder our noses, then getting a flap for home. The coke combined with the alcohol meant I was spending many evenings hiding in oblivion, unaware of the normal world around me.

I was drinking heavily and I knew even while I tipped my glass that I was nearing another very dangerous cliff. Part of me wanted to jump.

Brent was almost never home. His girlfriend had gotten her own place and he stayed there most of the time. I couldn't really blame him. Jamie and I were high on cocaine almost all the time. When we weren't high, we would argue until I went back out to work. Then the cycle would begin all over again: drink and then get high at home until the drugs and alcohol were all gone.

One weekday morning the police came and arrested Jamie at the apartment. A neighbour had called them because of the screaming coming from our place. After they arrested Jamie they took me to the hospital. The nurse at the hospital wanted to do a rape kit. Humiliated, I explained to her that it had been with my boyfriend and that it was okay that I had bruises down there. She wrote something down in my chart and left the room, taking the chart with her. I was left wondering what her notes said.

Darren picked me up from the hospital that day and we went to his apartment and played cards late into the night. He never asked me what had happened. I think he was hoping I would approach him and ask for that plane ticket, and when I didn't, it became a subject we avoided.

That summer I worked more than once with black eyes and made more trips to the hospital. I told myself it was the cocaine that was making Jamie so explosive and unpredictable. I felt as if I could never make enough money to keep us both high enough, meaning to keep him even-tempered and to enable me to forget what I was giving up.

Darren would occasionally insist on taking me to dinner. Those nights I would devour my food and more often than not I would be sick afterwards because my stomach would go into shock at having had a meal.

"I'm worried about you," he said one night. "I'm starting to worry that the world is about to lose a valuable member." I hugged him, but I didn't assure him he was wrong. I only smiled.

School began again and I missed my first day that year. I had been up half the night talking to Jamie.

We had discussed the fact that life needed to go back to normal. He and I were both lost and didn't know where to even begin. That was one talk that didn't end in an argument. I finally crawled across the bed straight into his waiting arms and he held me gently all night long. I lay there and listened to him breathe, revelling in how good he smelled when he was content like this.

I fell asleep almost hoping that things were about to get better again, and September's dependable calm did bring some peace.

Jamie was looking for work, and I was trying to talk him into taking a school course. He kept coming back to me with ideas of entering a stunt college in California or going to Asia to learn about Tai Chi so he could teach it here. I found his excitement entertaining, but I knew he had delusions of grandeur.

I felt scared for Jamie. I saw him getting older, but he still had little-boy dreams. In a way I admired him for that, but at the same time I feared it was holding him back from something really big that was meant for him. I know he felt it too. Maybe that was why he felt so frustrated: because he was so corrupted with his past that he couldn't let it go and just be. Jamie wanted everything I wanted, but he had never had anyone in his life to show him what normal was. His whole family was dysfunctional. I was beginning to see that he didn't have the tools for what we wanted to build.

School was uneventful from the beginning; no tittering followed me through the halls. Once again I began to blend in with the walls. Occasionally I would pass Chantel in the hallway; we would only nod in acknowledgement and keep walking. I was careful to make no new friends and talked to no one except my teachers.

I went so far as to ignore a girl who asked me the time. Guiltily, I stared straight ahead and pretended I couldn't hear her through my scarf. I heard her mumble something as she walked away from me to find someone else to ask. I told myself that conversations get started that way and that I had had to ignore her.

Days before Halloween, Jamie asked me to go camping with him. He had just bought a truck and wanted to take it up into the bush. He thought it would be the perfect romantic getaway.

We drove out to a secluded creekside spot Jamie had heard about that was two hours outside of Calgary. Jamie had gotten directions on how to reach it, and we followed a map roughly drawn in pencil. I was skeptical about being able to follow the directions, but we arrived and the spot was exactly as Jamie had said it would be.

We started a fire and sat side by side, eating the KFC that we had picked up earlier and talking late into the night, allowing the fire to go out so we could see the stars. It was a crystal-clear night and there were no city lights blocking out the sky. The stars were vivid and sparkling, layered across the sky. I was really happy in that moment with Jamie.

What I remember most was that Jamie was very tender with me that night. He made love to me gently and lovingly, like he never had before—like no one had. He caressed me soothingly, barely touching me as he drew his hands across my skin. He whispered that he loved me and stroked my hair, looking into my eyes. I would take that moment with me forever.

Almost a week later Jamie moved out. I don't remember what we had fought over that particular time, but all memories of that night under the stars were gone. I locked myself in the bathroom, having run in there to hide from him. He packed while I hid, and when he walked out the door he yelled, "You don't need to worry about me anymore." Then he was gone. I crept out of the bathroom, went to the couch, and cried.

Jamie was always leaving, and I knew that one day he would leave for the last time. I knew that he and I were not good for each other. Maybe we knew too much about each other; maybe we didn't even like each other. I cried for this awareness that was seeking me and that I had been trying to outrun. I cried because I knew there would be no such thing as normal if Jamie and I stayed together, not for either one of us. When I heard the front door slam I tried to gather myself together. Thinking Jamie might have come back, I wiped my tears and sat up stiffly while the footsteps came down the hall.

I slumped back in my chair. I knew what Jamie's footsteps sounded like, and these were not them.

It was Brent. He happened to decide to make a rare appearance at the apartment that afternoon, and had seen Jamie leave. He seemed relieved and tried to talk to me. He said maybe I would see that there was life beyond boyfriends. I sat smoking a joint, staring intently at the ceiling, and listened to him rattle on about the possibilities for my future.

I think when he saw how distraught I was Brent felt obligated in some way to stay home with me for the next few days. He brought me home chicken soup and bread that he had baked that day at work. He made tea every morning and got me up for school. It was strange; I felt as if I was living with a brother I didn't know. Brent said more to me in those few days than he ever had in all the time he lived with us.

Jamie called a few weeks later. He began to come over again and Brent made himself scarce. Jamie would come for dinner. Sometimes he would stay longer, but he still always left before the sun came up.

About a month later Jamie was over watching television when we had an argument. I can't remember what started it but it ended with Jamie throwing me against the wall and kicking at me while I curled into a ball. I was screaming for him to get out. After he left the unit I ran to the balcony and screamed, "Don't ever come back either!" Jamie grabbed his groin at me and flipped me the bird. It would really have been quite comical if not for the violence that had preceded it. I will forever have that image of him in my head.

In the days that followed his departure I began to feel as if I was coming down with something. I had a stomach flu of some kind. I couldn't eat, and I had no energy at all. I was missing school, even sleeping away entire days.

When he was unable to reach me via phone, Jamie came over. He made me some NeoCitran but I never drank it. I don't even remember him being there.

He came over again the following day and found me in even worse shape. He cleaned up the mess I had made in the bowl he had put beside me the day before and made me some more NeoCitran.

I think he called someone to talk about how sick I seemed to be. After making me some chicken soup, he turned the heat up and left.

Later he would tell me that something had made him call me later that same night. He didn't usually call at night, and the insistent ringing of the phone disturbed me. I finally mustered up the strength to pick up the receiver, but that depleted my last vestiges of energy, and I fainted.

I have a vague memory of Jamie and some large burly man hauling me down the hall and outside to a waiting car. They took me to the hospital. When I came to, the doctors told me that I was severely malnourished and was suffering from something called hyperemisis gravidarum.

The doctor asked me if I knew what hyperemisis was? I didn't, and was completely unprepared to find out. I was pregnant—four to five weeks along, according to the doctor. The hyperemisis was a rare complication, one that induced a permanent state of morning sickness, which was why I hadn't been able to keep any food down.

My heart stopped and I couldn't quit blinking. My only thought was, "Oh my god," and then I threw up. Not entirely from morning sickness either. I was shocked, scared, and oddly rejuvenated. There was something to do now. There was something really important to do. Somewhere inside of me a glimmer of hope flickered.

I looked over at Jamie and was surprised to see him grinning from ear to ear. I couldn't think straight. The idea of Jamie being a father scared me. The idea of me being a mother was terrifying.

I thought about a book I had once started, about a single teenage mother trying to find a job. I had written that she loved her son but that her future looked bleak judging by the Help Wanted ads.

I focused in on the doctor telling Jamie and me that there were options and that I needed to consider the risks. "You're already not handling the pregnancy very well. To carry through with it means to expose yourself to risks—risks you need to consider. You only weigh 86 pounds. That means you're seriously underweight. The chances of your having a healthy pregnancy to term are significantly less than those of a mother with an already healthy lifestyle."

I just stared at the doctor. I knew there was no option. I knew I was pregnant from that night camping with Jamie. I knew this child had at least been conceived out of love. I couldn't destroy that. This might be the only good thing that ever came of Jamie and me. It might be the only good thing that would ever come of me.

I stayed in the hospital for three days while they got my fluid levels back up and gave me some vitamins. They told me how to start taking better care of myself. A nutritionist came in and advised me not to eat solid foods right away, but to start with soups and yogurt. She explained to me about prenatal vitamins, and how and when I should take them.

With one sentence my life had changed forever. The whole world looked different. I felt hope and despair at the same time. Hope for the child I carried, that at least for him or her there might be a better life. I'd been terrified the moment they had told me I was pregnant, but at least I felt as if I had some control over the outcome of this latest twist.

One evening, a few days later, Jamie came and got me out of the hospital. We walked to the bus stop. I trailed behind him, lost in thought, barely registering as he recited names and told me the games he would play with our baby if it was a boy and how protective he would be if we had a girl. He grabbed me and spun me around, yelling into the starry sky, and I couldn't help but let out a giggle.

I insisted on heading to the grocery store right away. I was determined to get my stomach used to food again. I ate yogurt, and when it came back up I ate some more. I figured that some of it had to make it into my system. After a week of being home I began to feel like myself again.

I was definitely pregnant, though. Nothing smelled or tasted the same. I quit smoking overnight, not because I wanted to but because I had to. It made me sick to even smell burning tobacco. I did try to keep smoking marijuana because I really didn't know how to function without it, but eventually I had to give that up too—every time I inhaled I would have to run retching to the bathroom. My skin changed too; it became blotchy and bumpy. I was beginning to think that physically, pregnancy and I didn't get along too well.

When I told Darren I was pregnant he became very quiet. When he finally spoke, it was to say, "I'm not sure what you want to hear. I don't doubt that one day you might make a great mother. But I can't help but think you're not in that place yet. Exposing a child to the life that you and Jamie lead is hardly the responsible thing to do."

I knew Darren meant well. He didn't mean to hurt me, and I knew that what he said made sense. But it was to no avail. I was pregnant; I was going to be a mother and Jamie was going to be a father. Together we would be parents.

That was really all I knew that day talking to Darren. I was so confused I couldn't even stick up for Jamie and me. We hadn't discussed how this was going to change our lives and what we needed to do now. I had felt victorious because I could eat a sandwich now without running to throw up. Yet here I was, discovering I had no idea what came next.

I was sick all the time. It would come on really suddenly; I was unable to go to school because if it came over me while in class I might not make it to the bathroom.

I wasn't working either, and hadn't been able to since I had first begun to get sick. I would never have been able to stick anything in my mouth without retching, and I didn't do anything else. So money was tight, but I was managing without Jamie there. I was becoming aware of how much money he had spent on a regular basis and how much more often I had to work when he had been living with me.

Christmas was fast approaching and there was the familiar festive buzz that comes with the holiday, but I was so ill and Jamie wasn't even living with me. I would have preferred not to have known what time of year it was.

I tried to rejoin class after the holiday break. It was an effort every day. Even just sitting in class was hard for me. It didn't take much of any smell or thought to have me running to the bathroom to vomit.

Calgary was in the middle of a cold snap that February. I couldn't wait for the cold to ease up, because I had run out of food and money.

One day I ate breakfast, showered, and dressed in a tight black dress. I wore leotards, boots, and a long black wool raincoat to keep me as warm as possible. I looked myself over in the elevator mirror and assured myself that my baby hump was barely visible.

Once I was a block away the cold began to creep under my skin. It was a deep cold; I felt it sting my lungs as I breathed in. I pulled the coat tighter around my middle.

It was on that walk that I first talked to my daughter.

I called the baby my daughter from that day on. I held my hand over my belly and told her I would do everything within my power to do right by her. I promised her that I was going to give her the family that she deserved and that whatever it took I would find a better life for both of us. With one hand on my stomach in a silent vow, I assured her that we would be okay. "Hide from the cold," I urged her. "I'll keep you safe."

I prayed that God would help me to make everything I had just said real and that He would keep me safe.

Hours later my legs were ice cubes that my body rested on. The wind was blowing snow flurries and the tiny slivers of ice sliced into my skin and tore at my face. There was no alcove deep enough to hide from the fierceness of the wind. I realized I had walked out in near blizzard conditions. I thought of my empty fridge. I thought of my baby, depending on me for nourishment and food. The streets were deserted, cars passing only intermittently. No one seemed to be looking for a hooker. Most passersby just looked like they were in a rush to get out of the cold.

A family in a minivan pulled to a stop at the red light of a nearby intersection. There were kids in the back, their heads all in shadow. The wife reached her hand behind her husband's head, running her fingers through his hair. He had a vaguely panicked look on his face from the stress of driving in the blizzard-like conditions. Yet he tilted his head towards her hand. The gesture was so minor for them, yet so affecting for me, that I was overcome. I stopped fighting my tears and just broke down and wailed into the wind. I cried until my tears froze in cracked white trails down my cheeks.

I did make some money to spend at the grocery store that day. Back at home I collapsed on the couch and hugged my belly. After that I was far more careful with my money. I sat down and worked myself out a budget. I would have nothing left over by cheque issue day. But I didn't smoke, drink, or do any of that anymore, so I was really ahead.

I quit school officially in April. I was five and a half months pregnant and there was still no relief in sight from the morning sickness that I had been assured over and over again was supposed to end after my first trimester. I was sporadically sick and couldn't even focus on my classes. I was putting on weight, however, and my skin was slowly starting to clear up.

I had to apply for welfare again. This time there were no private meetings, and no one asked me if I wanted to go to school or if I wanted to work. No one really even looked at me.

Jamie still didn't live with me. I had been begging him to come home. I wanted to try to work things out. I wanted to try to have the family I had always dreamed of. I thought that if we tried—really tried—we might find a way to be good parents for our baby.

Jamie was excited about the baby and bought baby clothes from time to time. Every time he came home with a new outfit it made me sad. I didn't know why it upset me when he would bring them home. I just knew that it made me want to tear them into little shreds and let them cascade down on his head.

I finally told my mother that I was pregnant. She was very quiet and said nothing. I had learned from Darren that silence was not a good thing. I told Mom that I still had everything under control and that I would talk to her again in a week.

Mom called me back the next day. She said that she had hardly slept at all the night before. "Maybe this was meant to be, Tara, so that you'll come home," she said. "You'll have all the support you need here. Can't you see it's time to come home?"

I told her everything was going to work out and that Jamie, me, and the baby were all going to be a family. I told her to trust me and let me at least try to do this. I hung up and sat down weakly, feeling more lost and alone than I ever had.

Brent officially decamped to his girlfriend's place that week. He moved out early one morning, with no goodbye other than a note. I was relieved he was gone. He was too hard to read, and it took too much energy to figure him out. Or so I told myself.

Jamie came back to the apartment one afternoon. He just showed up with all his stuff and sat on the couch as if he had never left. We didn't even talk about it. I was left not really knowing what to think. Everything always seemed so convenient for him, and I felt insulted.

Jamie would sometimes come home after a bender, and the stench of stale cigarettes and beer on him would literally make me throw up. I eventually asked him not to come home on those nights. I preferred not knowing where he was to having him come home smelling like that.

By then I was just over twenty-five weeks along and finally showing. I had even felt her fluttering around inside of me. I woke Jamie one night hoping he would be able to feel her move too, but she settled down when he touched my stomach.

I hadn't worked for almost three months and it felt good. I could look people in the eye now, and had even started to write again. Jamie found scraps of my discarded poems throughout the apartment and made fun of some of them, but things were starting to feel the way I imagined normal would feel.

Once Jamie moved in the budget that I had set for myself needed to take care of two, and it didn't take long for the money to completely run out. I began to get increasingly nervous. Not having any food in the house was how I had gotten sick in the first place. I knew I was going to have to go back out to work if the situation didn't change, and I didn't see Jamie doing anything about it.

I was angry with Jamie. I knew he hadn't done anything other than live at the apartment too. Somehow, though, I felt as if he had let me down.

One morning I found myself staring at him as he ate his cereal and silently yelled that we had made a huge mistake and now there was never going to be a way to make things right ever again.

I watched from across the table as he chewed his food and listened in disgust as he grunted, swallowing. I felt as if I was on fire—the rage was overwhelming. I had an almost uncontrollable urge to start grabbing things off the table and throwing them with all my might right at his head. In my mind's eye I even saw blood rushing down his face.

When I realized where my thoughts were going I had to physically remove myself from his presence and seek solitude in the bedroom. I hoped it was just a pregnancy hormone gone a little amok.

My dreams that night were fitful and fearsome. In the morning I knew what I had to do. It was all so clear to me. I spent the day working myself up to what would come next.

The next day we ventured out together—I don't remember why or where. I do remember staring at the back of Jamie's head as we walked, though. I knew I was leaving him. I knew that no matter what happened now or what was said between us we could not be together with a child. No child needed to see the way Jamie and I were together.

I saw for the first time that the main reason Jamie and I stayed together was just for the sake of not being alone. Now, though, that was no longer a fear for me, and it never would be again. I had someone else who was dependent on me to not leave them and I was determined to be there.

I had no idea what being a single mother would mean for me and my baby but I knew that Jamie and I were not going to be parents together.

I thought about Chantel. She had done well for herself and her son. She lived in a co-op and went to school; was able to pay for daycare and still have somewhat of a life. She was proof that it could be done. I decided to put my hope in her example.

Later that night when dinner was done and the dishes had all been cleaned I went into the bedroom and stared around the room. I couldn't put it off any longer: I had to tell Jamie that it was over. I steeled myself one more time, looking in the mirror, before I called him into the room. He must have seen the seriousness in my eyes because he said nothing. He just sat on the bed and watched me fidget with the cord on the clock radio.

I was standing facing him, trying to muster what to say. I knew what I wanted to say but my mouth had gone dry when he had walked in.

I found myself staring at him. He was still so handsome. I thought to myself okay; one last look, then let's get this show on the road.

I broke the silence with words I had chosen carefully. "Everything has changed now, Jamie. We're wrong for each other, and we don't have the right to teach our dysfunction to another human being, much less a child. I love you, and I always will. But you have to go now."

He sat watching me. I had to check his face twice because I thought I must be wrong about what I saw in his eyes. It looked like admiration. When he said, "I've never loved you more than I do right now," I believed he meant it.

His words stabbed me like a knife. They sliced through my soul and took my breath away. I wanted to leap across the bed and claw at those eyes that oozed sincerity. I wanted to scream that it was too late for sincerity—too late for a calm and reasonable Jamie. I wanted to scream until my voice was hoarse and I wanted to kick until I had nothing left of my feet. I was aching inside and what he had said hurt me deeper than any yelling or hitting. I had even been prepared for that. But not *this*.

I slept on the couch that night and Jamie slept on the bed, seemingly unaware that I had been trying to break up with him. But the next day I would see he had been very aware of what I had been saying and had probably gone to bed seething that he had been unable to convince me to reciprocate his love.

From Jamie's point of view he had put himself out there. He had been trying to grasp at me the only way that had always worked for him in the past. This time, though, he had seen that he had pushed me further away and that now I couldn't even look at him.

I went to sleep that night trying to plan another attempt for the next day.

 # Chapter 13

IN THE MORNING, OVER our cereal bowls, Jamie attempted to make small talk with me. He asked me if I was bored at home all day since I wasn't going to school anymore; he asked me about prenatal classes; and he asked me if I had heard from Brent at all since he had left.

I could tell he was uncomfortable, and I almost felt sorry for him. I didn't know it at the time, but leaving Jamie would be a walk in the park compared to what was coming.

I decided to just ask him to leave and get it over with. I needed him gone so I could think about what I was going to do next. I had been thinking about going home and I didn't want to call Darren or my mother with Jamie listening over my shoulder.

He was just coming out of the bathroom when I made my approach. I stood between him and the kitchen he was heading for, my legs parted, leaning in towards him. I was ready for combat when I informed him that he had all morning to pack and arrange a place to stay with friends until he got himself organized. I reminded him that when it was he who wanted to leave there was always somewhere for him to stay. He stared straight into my eyes, and I saw the transformation begin.

He retreated further into himself. The coldness took over.

I knew he was going to hit me even before the blow came. I saw it coming and yet I just stood there. When he raised his arm to bring on the second blow I turned and ran for the phone. I had just reached it when Jamie grabbed me in a football tackle. I went down hard and landed on my stomach.

I screamed for the baby, and Jamie yelled that the baby was the cause of all our troubles. That was when I saw the phone in his arms. He was swinging it in a wide arc. "I can fix this problem, though!" I lay on the floor and watched as he swung the phone a final time. Taking aim for my stomach, he let go. I pivoted away as fast as I could and the phone hit me in the back. Momentarily stunned, I could do nothing as Jamie roughly picked me up and grabbed me by the throat, holding me up against the wall.

My feet were no longer on the ground and I knew he was going to kill me this time. I could see in his eyes that that was what he wanted to do. I looked at him as pleadingly as I could with my eyes bulging out and my face getting redder and redder. I felt as if my head was going to explode—I could say nothing; I couldn't even breathe. I felt the world fade and saw only black as I was violently dropped to the ground.

It seemed only moments later that I heard Darren yelling that Jamie was never to come around me again or Darren would have something to say about it.

I realized I was lying on the couch and had a blanket over me. I reached for my stomach first and felt between my legs for blood. Everything appeared okay but I was still scared. How long had I been unable to breathe? I tried to clear my throat but it was too tender. I decided that a little phlegm in the back of the throat was just enough to let me know that I was still alive.

Darren came in from the kitchen with a glass of water and sat down on the coffee table next to me. He handed it to me and told me to drink.

When I could finally speak I choked out that I was ready to go home now. Then I cried. Darren stroked my head while I cried. My voice was off and it sounded rough. It hurt, and the pain only made me cry harder. I fell asleep like that and woke up some time later to find the apartment was silent.

I called out for Darren but he had left. There was a note in the kitchen that said for me to call him when I was ready and he would come and get me.

The phone was lying on the floor, the cord obviously broken. I thought for a minute and then left the apartment and trudged down the hall in my stocking feet. I knocked on a neighbour's door and asked if I could borrow a phone cord. I must have appeared desperate because without hesitating they took the cord from their phone and handed it to me.

I called Lucia first. She was happy to hear from me.

After I told her I was pregnant and in trouble she asked me if I had decided to come back home. She told me that I could have a room in her house for a short time, just while I got welfare and got my own place. Talking with Lucia was easy, and I was relieved to know that if I did choose to return to Vancouver I would have a roof over my head.

Next I called my mom. She wasn't home and I had to leave a message. I just said for her not to call me; that I would call her in the next day or two. I didn't want her calling and maybe getting Jamie on the phone. I didn't trust him not to say something hurtful and end up in a yelling match with my Mother. He would lose—my mother would chew him up for breakfast. She had seen through him without even having met him.

My last long-distance call was to Sherry from North Vancouver. She was ecstatic and almost cried when I told her I was coming home. I hadn't talked to her in over a year but it was as if no time at all had passed. I told her everything, all about Jamie and being pregnant. I told her about the latest altercation with Jamie, and about my friend Darren and how he was helping me make it home.

I promised to call as soon as I arrived, and hung up.

For the first time I felt I was doing the right thing. When I picked up the phone for my last call to Darren I felt so relieved I was almost giddy.

I still had one more issue: Dragon. I couldn't leave him with Jamie. Lucia had offered to allow me to bring my cat if I kept him in the downstairs suite away from the dogs. She didn't think the dogs would be bothered with a cat in the house. Now I just had to figure out how I was going to get him there.

Darren and I assumed there would be a charge for transporting the cat on the bus, and I didn't really want Dragon cooped up down below. I convinced Darren that the way to handle this was to see a vet and tell him we were going on a long road trip. Hopefully the vet would give us enough medicine to make Dragon sleep, and then I could just take him in my bag.

I packed only one bag and reserved an empty shoulder bag. I took only my books and photographs. I left all my hooker clothes, hoping I would never have to wear anything like them again.

Just as I had locked the door to the apartment and was heading down the hall for what I thought was the last time the shrieking of the phone reminded me that I still had the neighbour's phone cord. I re-entered the apartment, thinking I wasn't going to answer the phone out of fear it might be Jamie.

I knew that my leaving town was probably the only thing that would stop the cycle of violence between us. I also knew I couldn't do it with him whispering in my ear. He was too good—he always knew just what to say to change my mind; to convince me we were right for each other. But I found myself reaching for the phone anyway.

Thankfully, it was Sherry. She was calling to tell me that she had called Alice and that they were going to pick me up from the bus if I called and told them what time I'd be getting there. I couldn't believe it. I still had friends, true friends who were banding together for me.

I couldn't wait to close the door behind me, and when Darren pulled up to the curb I ran to the truck.

The vet must have realized what Darren and I planned to do to get Dragon to Vancouver, because he talked to us about the dangers of over-drugging the cat. He said that thousands of animals were killed by accident or abandoned by highways because people didn't take the proper precautions with their pets. He said that he would only give me one pill, which would sedate Dragon but not make him sleep. He didn't even charge us for the exam.

When we climbed back into the truck Darren and I looked at each other in mute recognition. I was going to leave Dragon behind. Darren started the truck and we headed for our favourite park.

The tall trees, acres of wide-open grassy fields, and flowers lining the walkways did nothing to lessen my tears as I held my cat close. I prayed while I held him that God would watch over him and guide him to a new family that would take really good care of him—better care than I had.

It was some time before I opened the door and, still holding Dragon, made my way out of the truck and towards the trees. He made a sudden leap from my arms and then he was gone.

Darren and I sat in the park for a long time. I was hoping Dragon would come back because if he did, then I was going to have to find a way to keep him—it would be fate. It would be God himself telling me to hold on for a little while longer. But Dragon didn't reappear, and finally we drove away.

We went back to Darren's apartment and he made a few more phone calls. The next bus was at 7:30 that night. That gave us three hours before I had to be at the station.

I took longer to look around Darren's apartment than I had my own. His place had been a safe place for me every time I had come there, and I realized that most times I had genuinely smiled in Calgary had been around Darren.

As I shut the door to Darren's suite I stole one last glance at his chandelier, and saw that it was indeed swaying.

After dinner at Darren's favourite steakhouse we drove up above the city and sat there staring off into the distance. I was trying to piece together what I wanted to say when Darren broke the silence. "You're a good kid, Tara," he blurted. "I'm better for having known you."

I was stunned. No one had ever said anything like that to me before, and I could tell he really meant it. My eyes welled up, and I took his hand and held it.

When I finally found my voice I told him that I understood how he felt because I felt the same way. "You've saved me more than once, Darren. Today you're saving two lives. Remember, when you're alone and feeling lonely, whoever knows you is lucky to know a man like you."

He chuckled at me, reached into his bag, and took out fifty dollars. "Here's a little something to get you through the road trip," he said, handing it to me. Then he started his truck and drove us to the station.

Darren came in with me and paid for my ticket. Then he said it was time for him to leave because he hated long goodbyes. He gave me a quick hug and then he was gone—so quickly, a part of me felt he had never really been there at all. I stood with my lone bag and waited for the doors to the boarding area to open.

Once on the bus I took out my Walkman and tuned the world out, staring at the passing city through the window. I held my stomach and whispered to my baby that we were on our way. I told her that sometimes we ended up running to where we had run away from in the first place.

I did wonder where Jamie was and what he was doing. I wondered when he would realize that I had left. I knew he would call Darren; I hoped Jamie wouldn't cause Darren too much trouble. "Just let him understand for once," I prayed. I fell asleep thinking, "Here I am ... on a bus and full of hope again."

It was nine in the morning when I stepped off the bus in Vancouver. The sun was shining and Sherry and Alice were there as promised. After hugs and a lot of jumping up and down we climbed into Alice's car and drove to North Vancouver. We went to Sherry's housing complex and swam in her pool. I remember that for the first time I didn't feel the morning sickness. My baby belly was now clearly rounded and starting to expand and yet I didn't feel awkward or out of place at all.

I watched Alice and Sherry gleefully jumping on each other's heads and dunking each other under the water. I watched as they giggled and screamed in delight, and for the first time in a long time I felt comfort. The warmth from the coastal sun was hot on my back, and I tilted my head back to feel it on my face.

That night at Lucia's house there was a bit of a celebration. She cooked a beautiful multi-course dinner and invited my friends to stay. We were all happy and there was lightness in the air. I remember thinking that my baby was going to have many happy people in her life.

The next morning I made my way to Richmond, to the restaurant where my mother had been working for years as a waitress.

I had two hours on the bus from North Vancouver to think about what I would say when I arrived. I was excited and nervous about seeing my parents again. There were so many things that had happened to me and I had changed so much since they had last seen me.

I sat in a booth near the middle of the restaurant and anxiously looked around for her.

I heard her before I saw her. She was behind the partition that stood between the kitchen and the dining area. As soon as I heard her voice I sagged in my chair with relief. I was really home. Listening to her talk about eggs and toast gave me the peace that I had longed for since I was fourteen. Four years later, pregnant and in real trouble, my mother's voice had brought me a moment of serenity.

Mom finally came out from behind the partition. When she saw me she almost dropped her tray. I stood and hugged her. When I began to pull away, she held me for an extra second, and that was when I started crying. I knew it wouldn't reflect well on her for me to cry in her place of work, so I sat back down and tried to pull myself together.

After sitting with me for a few minutes she told me that she was going to be off work soon and that I could come back to the house with her. Then she got up to finish her shift.

I stared after her, my mind reeling. I was hit with the realization that I had more than just a hope of normalcy. For the first time I clearly saw that it had been within my grasp all along.

I had been afraid of my own family for a very long time. I had been afraid that I would not measure up and they would let me go, leaving me on someone else's porch step having to pretend to be strong. In that moment I understood that I didn't need it to be written down for me, and that I didn't need to be born into it: for me, family was a side effect of real love—of genuinely caring for someone else. That was what I had: a family.

That night I stayed at my parents' house for dinner.

Mom and I giggled our way through making the meal, and the three of us sat down to eat at my beloved kitchen table. After we had eaten and the dishes were cleaned and put away, Mom made me hot chocolate and herself a coffee. We sat at the kitchen table and I told her what had happened with Jamie in Calgary.

She sat listening as I talked and when I was done she hugged me and expressed relief at my being home.

Afterwards, Dad gave me a ride to the bus stop. My heart was overflowing. I was singing as the bus pulled up and with my Walkman turned up high, I made my way back to Lucia's house.

I was only able to stay with Lucia until mid-June because she was finally moving to the Interior. I was sad to see everything familiar being packed into boxes. Even the dogs seemed subdued.

Once again applying for welfare was quick and painless really, although humiliating. I was told that as soon as I found a place to live they would give me a cheque that would cover both my damage deposit and first month's rent.

While still at Lucia's I received my first call from Jamie. He had come back to Vancouver, and was staying with his grandma in New Westminster. We made arrangements to meet up in Vancouver that week.

I hung up the phone feeling exhausted and confused. I had run away from Jamie, hadn't I? I looked down and placed a protective hand on my protruding belly. "Your father called," I said in a whisper.

I met Jamie in a small café on Granville the night of the big Stanley Cup game in Vancouver. He was handsome as ever. He looked me over. "You're definitely getting bigger," he said. "That's what pregnant women do," I retorted.

After making small talk for a while, we left the café. My mind was spinning with all the violence that had plagued our relationship. Suddenly I wasn't so sure anymore that having Jamie and me for parents was the best thing for our baby.

A wave of weariness overcame me. I realized I had been considering adoption since probably the moment I had found out I was pregnant. But I had never said the word. I hadn't even admitted to myself that I would consider such a thing. For me, keeping her had meant preventing a cycle of unfamiliar faces in foster homes, or worse, group homes and social workers.

I wanted stability for my daughter so she could concentrate on real life and be able to attend school—maybe even get good grades—and have the freedom to be a real child. I wanted my daughter to play games, giggle with friends, have a first date, and go to her prom. Most of all I wanted my baby to have the freedom to love and be loved without fear. I wanted her to have the security of knowing there would always be a roof over her head; knowing that she was protected and safe, surrounded with comfort and most of all love. Jamie and I would love our baby, but I knew in that second that with us she would never experience freedom, stability, or security.

Nearly fainting from despair, I allowed Jamie to lead me down the sidewalk for a few short blocks. It felt as though we walked for hours.

We made our way to an alcove near Pacific Centre and sat in the warmth of the setting sun. I watched Jamie's eyes change colour as the evening turned to dusk. He began talking about how I could get a place in Vancouver and that when things were less chaotic we could move back in together. "I'll help with everything, honest," he assured me. "I'm sorry for all the shit that happened in Calgary." His eyes clouded. "It tore me apart when you left, baby." He said he had talked to his mother and grandmother and that they would like to see me soon too. It felt as if he was sweeping me up in his whirlwind of thoughts.

I was astonished that he couldn't see the agony I knew must be in my eyes. I held my hands up, silencing him. I just stood there saying nothing. I needed silence to hear myself think.

Finally I managed to choke out that I was seriously considering adoption and that he only needed to think about it to see that I was doing the right thing. Then I stood up and began to walk out into the crowd, heading for Robson Street.

Sweating, my heart pounding, I clutched my stomach, sure that I was about to be sick. I was overcome with anguish, but it wasn't over Jamie. It was worse than that first night in a new foster home and it cut deeper than any loss ever had. Sobs rose up in my throat and became wails. I began to run in a daze, dimly aware that I must look a sight, pregnant, dishevelled, tears pouring down my face. I turned towards the old courthouse at Robson Square. It had plenty of little nooks where I could be alone.

I sought out a secluded corner and sagged against the wall, falling to my knees in despair, weeping. I stared up at the sky and screamed at God for subjecting me to this farce that was motherhood. "Is it because I've screwed up my own life?" I demanded. "It's not fair. Help me!"

In my misery I had ripped out some of my hair and was holding it in front of me as if it were an offering. There was snot running down my nose onto my lap but I did nothing to sop it up. Somehow I knew that it was for my own loss that I cried. It was the worst moment of my entire life.

All I could do was tell my baby, "I'm sorry. I'm so, so sorry." All at once I understood what regret really was. But I clung to the knowledge that even though I couldn't change where I was in life, I could change where my baby started her life.

I don't know how long I sat there with my feet curled under my legs, staring at the sky. The sun had gone down and the crowds had thinned out. If anyone was staring, I was too distraught to notice.

Somehow I made it home to Lucia's. She was at the door when I arrived.

She had been watching for me anxiously. Apparently there was some trouble downtown, and she was glad I had made it home safely. The next day we would learn that "some trouble downtown" had turned into rioting and looting after the Vancouver Canucks lost the Stanley Cup game.

I remember thinking that if people knew what loss really was they would have staged a Rose Parade instead.

It took me a day to reveal to Lucia that I was considering giving up my baby for adoption. She surprised me by saying she was relieved to hear that I'd even been thinking about it. She then made me some tea and sat down on the couch, gesturing for me to sit next to her. "I know this may come as a surprise, Tara," she said, "but there's a family

I know of that you should meet."

I felt the room spin, things were happening so fast. I knew that the baby was due in two short months, but I was still just getting used to the idea.

I didn't know it then but the truth is that I would never get used to the idea. I would never get over the loss, or really forgive myself for the questions that I had asked myself all my life and would now pass on to my child.

I was overcome with a new wave of shame. I was letting my poor unaware baby down, even before she came into the world.

After that talk with Lucia the wheels quickly ground into motion. She introduced me to a woman named Stephanie, who took me to meet the lawyer who was going to take care of my side of the paperwork. Stephanie was also going to introduce me to the family that wanted to adopt my baby.

It was hard not to resent them even before meeting them: they had enough to be able to take care of my baby, and I didn't. I knew that they would eventually have what I would ache for the rest of my life.

My own mother wanted me to live in Richmond. She was on the phone with me that same week about a place she knew of. It was a bedroom and living room in the basement of the home of a customer of hers from the restaurant. I met the entire family that very night and moved in with them by the weekend.

Left completely alone for the first time since arriving back in Vancouver, I was hit by depression and ended up sleeping for days.

Someone must have called my mother because one day she came to see me.

I confided in her about what I had done. She cried with me, and I found myself practically crawling into her lap. When we could speak again she looked at me gravely. "Do you understand what this means, Tara Lee?"

"I do, Mom. I hope it means that I'll be able to keep the promise I made to my baby. I told her I was going to give her a family. I just didn't know at the time that it wouldn't be me and Jamie."

I fell silent, and we sat there holding hands for a long time, tears streaming down our faces.

Days later, Stephanie called me and we arranged to meet Rachel Nichols. She was the woman who was hoping that I would pick her to be the mother to my child.

So far, I had learned that she and her husband Roger had previously adopted a baby, a little girl. They were both well educated and had professional jobs. In fact Roger was extremely distinguished in his field, and I knew that financially there would be no concerns about my child's future.

I did feel good about this family. They went to church on Sundays and had picnics with friends and family almost every Sunday after church in spring and summer. Their daughter went to Catholic school and was kept busy with things like horseback riding and tennis. But most of all they were eager for more love in their house.

I wanted all of these things for my child. But most importantly, I didn't want my child's path to mirror my own. My experience with adoption, with Janine and Robert, had not gone well, and it haunted me. I knew that once I signed on the line all rights I had ever had would be gone.

It was so vital for me to make the right decision, yet so overwhelming. It felt as if there was no time for me to stand still and collect my thoughts. But I knew that I had to put selfishness aside and meet Rachel with an open heart.

I was introduced to her on a Thursday afternoon. It was bright and sunny outside the law office, an odd contrast to the darkness that shrouded me inside.

The files had said Rachel was in her late thirties. She looked at least ten years younger to me. She had a beautiful smile; I could tell I would have found it infectious if the circumstances had been different. She wore her hair just above her shoulders. It had a healthy sheen and a spring to it. My immediate reaction, though, was that she smelled like money, and that turned me off instantly. I wanted my daughter to have security, not wealth far beyond what was necessary.

I had to stop myself. I was judging Rachel. I knew I wasn't being fair. I already hated her—not for who she was, but for who she was going to be. I closed my eyes for a second and just listened to the air. Finally I rose, walked over to her, and shook her hand.

Minutes later we were sitting together and I was even giggling at something she said. I asked her questions about her religious practices, and she asked me about HIV and AIDS. It was all very clinical when we got down to the business side of things. Somehow that made things easier.

I stepped out into the afternoon sun, almost happy as I climbed into Stephanie's truck.

I called Jamie that night and told him about meeting Rachel. He was short with me. I realized I had never asked him how he felt about what I was doing. I knew that eventually he would have to talk it over with the lawyer because he too had to sign on the line, but I didn't want to be the one to ask him to, and I didn't want to be within earshot when he was asked.

The truth was that I couldn't afford to hear him say that it wasn't what he wanted and that my decision was hurting him—because if he said that, I would have to ignore his pain and do what I thought was right in spite of it.

I knew that if I was going to make it through this, I needed to be selfish in this case. *This hurts me more than it does you, buddy.*

Alice made it her personal crusade to keep me surrounded by friends. She came out to Richmond to get me at least twice a week. We would go out for lunch, or rent videos and watch them at her apartment.

One afternoon, I was shocked when Jeff showed up at Alice's apartment. He had aged by a few years, but he was more muscular than I remembered him. He hugged me two or three times before finally stepping back from me and checking out my baby belly.

Jeff and I talked avidly for the rest of the afternoon. He told me that he knew Jamie from Vancouver and didn't like him at all. He went on to say that when he had heard I was living with Jamie in Calgary and prostituting myself he had known he had to come and get me out of there. That very night he had stolen a car and gotten arrested while leaving town.

I was touched—I even kissed his cheek—but I didn't believe him. Years later I would hear from a mutual friend who had been with Jeff on that fateful night, and he corroborated his story.

When evening came Jeff drove me back to Richmond in his van—and this time he had the keys to the vehicle. I invited him in, apologizing in advance.

"I have no TV ... no place to sit ... nothing much really except a bed."

Jeff looked around my spartan suite. "You sure are keeping only the bones," he concurred.

I laughed. "I left everything in Calgary," I explained. "I've come home for a fresh start." Where had *that* come from? I didn't even know. Strange as it felt, though, I knew it was true.

My baby's due date was fast approaching and I was surprised to hear that all the papers that could be signed before the baby came were taken care of. There was very little left to do until the baby came.

I liked the family that I had chosen for my daughter but I hated them too. I knew that the closer the due date came the more anxious they became. They were afraid I would change my mind. The anticipation and excitement must have been torturous for them. They had suffered disappointment in the past when another birth mother had changed her mind. Rachel especially was having a hard time.

I knew that they were looking for me to assure them I was not going to change my mind. But nothing I said would convince them there was going to be a happy ending for them. They wouldn't be able to truly relax until they no longer had an empty crib at home.

They would have their new beginning, but I was angry that they needed me to keep reassuring them about it. Wasn't it enough that I was *doing* it?

I felt I had played a really bad game of chess and was now cornered but still had to move, knowing that I was mated in only two short turns. I was going through the motions, humouring everybody, but in truth I wanted nothing more than to be left alone to wallow in self-pity. For the time being, at least, wasn't I entitled to some tears and reassurances of my own?

One afternoon after I had been visiting my parents I was sitting on a bus near the front. Staring off into space, I was startled by the sudden wailing of a little boy of about three years old. His Native mother, who looked like a larger, older version of me, was holding him by the back of his shirt, half-dragging, half-hauling him up the stairs and onto the bus. The little boy made eye contact with me and held my gaze for a few seconds before his mother gave him a violent shove. "Hurry up and sit down!" she snapped at him.

The little boy was covered in dirt and his clothes were a size too small, but it was his eyes that would forever haunt me. There was such sadness and despair in them. I remember thinking that no child should even know those feelings, let alone be so acquainted with them that the pain was that visible in their eyes. He was such a little man. I wanted to kick his mother in the ass. Didn't she know how lucky she was that her son even knew her, that she'd been given the gift of having him with her, having him know her and love her?

That night I dreamt of that little boy. I dreamt he was covered in flowers and floating high above the clouds. In my dreams his eyes were bright and clear. He was smiling and happy.

I was dreaming of freedom.

# Chapter 14

I WENT TO THE DOCTOR'S office for an ultrasound, and it confirmed that not only was my baby a girl; she was healthy and doing well. They said her due date was August 4, 1994. I left the office that day feeling relieved that she was healthy, but also acutely aware of the inevitable passage of time. I had a date to anticipate with both dread and excitement.

I was extremely disappointed when the night of August 4 came and still nothing had happened.

I lay awake for hours, unable to sleep. I remembered having read somewhere that walking can sometimes help labour get started, so I ventured out into the night and walked around the block a few times.

That night I spent a long time talking to my baby. I told her about her grandparents, and regaled her with stories of my childhood. I told her about her father and how we had met. I recited to her what I could remember of a poem I had once heard called "Forever." The poet had written that forever was a long, long time when compared to the life of the moon and the stars.

I had succeeded at pushing thoughts of what was to come out of my mind, but as her delivery date passed I could see my impending loss coming, and at times the anxiety was overwhelming. I would cry into my pillow and hug myself close, sorrow and resentment colliding inside me.

People kept telling me I was doing the right thing; that I was not alone and that they were all with me. I was glad to have their support, but as much as they claimed their roles beside me, I knew that the moment was going to be mine to deal with and that this was a path I had to tread alone.

They would rub my back and tell me that my daughter was going to have everything she ever needed because I was unselfish enough to let her have it. I wanted to scream at them to shut up! That I was selfish, because I was too afraid to try and fail, because I couldn't make it work with Jamie, but most of all because I was unable to get myself together in time to be able to afford her the things in life that really mattered.

One afternoon I randomly opened the Bible, and the first thing I read was a verse in Isaiah that spoke of forgiveness.

> Then you will say on that day,
> I will give thanks to You, O Lord;
> For although You were angry with me,
> Your anger is turned away,
> And You comfort me.
> Behold, God is my salvation,
> I will trust and not be afraid;
> For the Lord God is my strength and song,
> And He has become my salvation.

For a moment I felt quiet and peaceful, as though God was trying to tell me that I was not alone, and that I would one day forgive myself.

That night I fell asleep still talking. When I woke up I felt as if I had been talking in my sleep.

Stephanie took me to the doctor's office that afternoon and again I was given a clean bill of health. We all marvelled at the fact that I still wasn't in labour.

After leaving the office Stephanie and I went to the White Spot restaurant in Richmond for lunch. We decided to go to a movie in North Vancouver that afternoon. It was there that I went into labour, which meant that we had a panicked drive back to Richmond in rush-hour traffic to get me to the hospital in time.

It had taken me by surprise because it just felt like a bad backache. If this is labour, I thought, then I'm going to have many more babies after this. It's a breeze.

By the time we arrived at the hospital, though, I was increasingly uncomfortable. I still wasn't in pain, but I was becoming more aware that there really was something happening.

They took me into a private room—at the time I thought because the hospital was aware of the situation, but later I would find out it was because my daughter's adoptive parents had paid for it. I was touched by how thoughtful they were.

I was lying on the bed when a particularly startling pain stabbed its way up my back. Shocked at the intensity, I told Stephanie when it was gone that it had felt like the worst menstrual cramp ever. I was crying now, and I asked her to call Alice and my mother.

An hour passed and there was no more pain. I was relieved, but the doctors seemed concerned. They decided to break my water. I was scared when I heard them say that, but by now Alice was there by my side. She held my hand and leaned over to talk to me while the doctor did the deed. I don't know what I had envisioned but I was pleasantly surprised that it was over within seconds. I hardly noticed a thing when the doctor slipped out from under the sheet covering my legs.

Hours later I was in dire pain; I remember trying to claw my way up the wall, ripping out my own hair, my whole body contorting in an attempt to escape the unbearable intensity. I took no comfort from the knowledge that many millions of women had given birth before me and survived. I knew I was dying, and I hoped the next cramp would be the one to finish me off.

Alice was nearly hyperventilating from trying to help me breathe. I think she was emotionally drained too. She kept having to leave the room for brief periods. But she put on a brave face for me. Stephanie intermittently stepped forward and gave me crushed ice to chew on.

I had been in labour for at least six hours when they finally gave me an epidural. It worked, too; minutes later I was far happier, even able to hold a conversation.

Time passed slowly. Now the only evidence that I was still in labour came from a machine that monitored the contractions. I felt the odd pang but it was a shadow of what it had been.

My mother poked her head in and sat with me for a short time. The hospital had a rule that there could be only two visitors in the room at a time; she and Stephanie were taking turns. Alice was the constant. She kept me focused and held my hand the whole time.

At another point Jamie showed up at the hospital with his grandfather. They were both very drunk. Jamie even offered me some of the booze he had hidden in his shirt in a brown paper bag. I was disgusted, but not entirely surprised. He didn't stay long. After kissing my forehead he waved at me from the door and I didn't see him again that night.

Tiffany was born at 6:42 in the morning. She was healthy and perfect with all ten toes and fingers. The nurse stood holding her in front of me, unsure whether I wanted to hold her or not. I reached for her and the nurse laid her gently in my arms.

Tears rolled down my cheeks even as I smiled down at her. She looked so peaceful. I named her Tiffany because I needed her to have a name.

The nurse placed a card on her mobile crib that had her name on it. I stared for hours and hours at the card with her name, my name, and Jamie's name on it. This was the only time I would see all our names together like that.

Something changed forever in me the moment I saw her. I know it's a cliché, but for me it was a huge shift. I looked at her face and saw me in there, and Jamie, but most of all I saw hope. That should be your name, I thought.

Tiffany spent almost no time in that crib while I was at the hospital—I held her the whole time. At about nine o'clock in the evening a nurse came in. "You need rest," she said briskly, and tried to take Tiffany from my arms.

"You can't take her before I'm ready!" I yelled. "My time's not up yet!"

The nurse looked startled. Then her gaze went soft, and she touched my shoulder. "Don't worry," she said. "I'll make a note on your chart so no one else interferes."

When she left I cried. I had only one full day with Tiffany, so it felt as though I had to tell her everything I had to say right then. I was so exhausted I couldn't keep my eyes open, which made me angry that I was going to lose some of my precious time with her. I carefully moved all the way over in my bed against the rails and laid Tiffany beside me. Cradling her head on my arm, I fell asleep.

I woke up and the room was dark except for a small light glowing in the bathroom. I had a moment of panic when I discovered that Tiffany was no longer on the bed beside me. I found her in the crib the nurses had wheeled in earlier. They had moved the crib so it was right beside my bed. I reached in and lifted her up, marvelling at how light she was in my arms. She was so tiny, her little fingers curled into fists. Like me, she was holding onto something in her dreams.

I looked up at the clock and discovered it was four in the morning. I was scheduled to leave that day, and here I had slept for almost seven hours. I could have kicked myself.

The funny thing was that every time I looked at Tiffany she rendered me speechless. I had so much to tell her. Most of it I had already said when she was in my tummy, but so many times I had envisioned holding her in my arms and talking to her face to face for the first and perhaps only time. I had wanted to have every possible minute to fill her head with the sound of my voice, hoping she would take some of that love with her throughout her life.

I was dreading having to leave. Every time the door opened my heart would beat a little faster and I would hold onto Tiffany a little tighter. I was shaking, trying so hard to be strong. I didn't want to cry while I held her. I had heard that babies could pick up on emotions, and I didn't want her to cry because of me.

With every tick of the clock it became harder. I knew time was running out and I still hadn't said anything that felt significant. I hadn't given her any advice to take with her. I hadn't told her any secrets to being a girl. I hadn't even told her to say no to drugs and to stay in school.

Jamie came in that morning. He walked over to my bedside and kissed me. When he reached out to take Tiffany from me I almost denied him—not because I didn't want him to hold her, but because I was so afraid those doors would open and someone would walk in and take her away. I didn't know how they were going to handle it, but I kept expecting someone to whisk into the room and then she would be gone.

Once again, though, Jamie didn't stay long. He held Tiffany and cried for a while, lost in his own pain. I let him take her outside to see his mother and grandparents. He was gone for only minutes but when he brought her back I realized I had been holding my breath. After he handed her to me, he gently kissed us both goodbye. Promising to see the lawyer that week and sign what needed to be signed, he left.

I looked at Tiffany and it came to me what I hadn't already said: she had saved my life.

I would have to do something with my life now because I didn't want her to just see where I had come from. I wanted her to see what I would become. She had given me something to live for—in truth it was something I had always had, but had been blind to. I was awed by what her little face and little soul had given me: so much happiness and freedom.

I was holding her close, my tears unstoppable. I could only whisper, but I thanked her for saving me and showing me what hope really was. I told her that if and when she was ready to find me I would be right there, waiting for her. It was because of her that I could make that promise and know that I was telling her the truth. "I'll never say goodbye to you," I murmured.

Then it happened—the door opened and the doctor came in, smiling. My chest heaved as she examined me to make sure I was recovering all right. Then she said the words I had been dreading. "You're fine. You can be discharged this afternoon."

When the moment came, I was dressed and sitting on a bench in the hallway. My room had been emptied of all my belongings. I was holding Tiffany, the nurse standing close by, patiently waiting but not hovering over me. I couldn't stop looking at the sleeping baby in my arms. I didn't know how to let her go. Nothing could have prepared me for this moment. It felt as if my heart was ripped wide open; I couldn't stop the flow of my tears or the wailing from deep inside me.

I looked up, begging God for the strength to hand her to the nurse. I leaned over her, rocking back and forth, crying and pleading with God to make sure her family cuddled her to sleep at night and that they would comfort her when she woke up from nightmares. I prayed that they would kiss her better when she was hurting and that she would never feel like she was nothing. Because she was my daughter, no matter where she was in the world, she would always be something to somebody. I just hoped she would know that.

I knew that she was going to have some really bad days in her life and that I couldn't protect her from that. But I prayed that her family knew how to arm her with the tools to get through them differently than I had.

I couldn't do it. I shouted at the nurse to please just give me a second. She smiled slightly and reached out to hold me but I pushed her away.

She moved off further down the hall, keeping me in her sights. I knew she was making sure I didn't try to leave with the baby. I remember thinking her apprehension was rather ridiculous since I had been the one to arrange everything. Then I looked back at Tiffany and knew it really wasn't. I wanted to do just that. I thought there has to be a way; we can do this. I'll call Jamie and everything will be the way it was supposed to be.

But then I looked at Tiffany anew. She was so beautiful. I remembered why I was doing this.

I didn't notice my mother making her way down the hall to me until she took a seat beside me. She put her hand on my back and began to rub it in a circle. I knew she was doing her best to comfort me, but I recoiled from her, irritated.

"I'm not ready, Mom," I protested.

In a soft, low voice she told me, "You'll never be ready. It's time to go now."

She was right. I held Tiffany a little harder and closer. She just lay there sleeping, unaware that her whole world was balancing on a pinnacle at that moment. I was close to standing up and announcing that I had indeed changed my mind and was keeping my baby.

My mother stood up and took my elbow, helping me to my feet. She whispered that I could hold on to her. The nurse had returned and was again standing beside me, waiting patiently. I knew she was going to take Tiffany away. This was the moment we had all been waiting for, the moment I had been dreading.

For her awaiting family it was a moment of rejoicing, a new beginning. For me, it was the beginning of the waiting: waiting to see if my doorbell would one day ring, or if there would one day be a long-distance phone call from a vaguely familiar voice.

The nurse reached through my arms and began to gently take my sleeping baby from my arms. Sobbing my protest, I stood with my empty arms up as if I were still holding Tiffany, and watched as the nurse disappeared down the long hallway.

I sagged back onto the bench and hugged myself. I was wailing now and didn't care if people were looking at me. I missed her already. It felt wrong to leave behind what was mine. I told myself that she wasn't mine now; she was theirs, but it hurt so deeply. I was overwhelmed with grief.

I finally stood, turned in the opposite direction, and began the long walk out of the hospital.

The afternoon sun glared down on me when I made my entrance into the outside world that day. Everything was suddenly different. I realized that maybe this could be a new beginning for me too.

I took one last glance at the hospital and whispered to Tiffany that I loved her before climbing into my mother's car. I blew a kiss out the window as we rounded the corner and the hospital left my sight.

I knew Tiffany was going to get a new name and that tomorrow she was going to wake up in the room they had created for her. A new beginning was waiting for her, and me, while I was driving off into my own new beginning. I was better armed to save myself than I had been when I'd felt this way in the past, and this time I had a reason to want better than I had had before.

I hoped Tiffany would one day find me. I would be waiting.

 # Chapter 15

OVER TWELVE YEARS LATER I am sitting in my living room, surrounded by family photos, kids' toys, dog toys, and wadded-up discarded paper.

Today I have told my six-year-old son I love him at least five times, and he has responded, "I love you too, Mommy." I know that by the time I have finished writing this chapter we will have said those words at least five more.

I have a good friend coming for tea tomorrow and just talked with another good friend on the phone. I am waiting for my husband to walk through the door from work so I can cover him in kisses and give him his supper before it goes cold.

There is an envelope on the table bearing a return address in Phoenix, Arizona, from my grandmother. I have begun the repair of my relationship with my granny. My grandfather unfortunately passed away before I could tell him that I appreciated what they tried to do for me. Granny has met my son two or three times now and I hope she'll come back to our city to visit us again soon.

I now understand that my grandparents made a sacrifice for me that I was always vaguely aware of. I know that their relationship with their daughter, Janine, changed forever the day they took me into their home despite her protests. They too took a chance and hoped for the best; it just didn't work out that way. They loved me, though, and I am grateful for all they tried to do for me.

I found my love of books while living with my grandparents. Through books I connected with my imagination. I think my grandparents and teachers would call it daydreaming. I would forever be a dreamer because when I had lived with my grandparents I had had the time to dream.

My relationship with my parents became much stronger too after that day at the hospital. I stopped fighting and began to accept their love. I think someone once said that there was no greater love than that which is given freely, and I can attest to the truth of that.

When I met my husband, I ran home to my dad and told him about meeting this wonderful guy who had no idea who I was. My dad was struggling with his shoes after walking the dog and didn't even look up at me when he said, "Okay, Tara. You tell me who you are, and then you'll be able to tell him." Not having an answer even for myself yet, I hoped the man who made my feet tingle wouldn't mind getting to know me together.

Four years later when I married him, my dad walked me down the aisle while my mother and a hundred other family members and friends looked on.

My parents listened to me whine when my husband and I had our first fight, and were only too happy to explain that marriage was in fact going to take work. My mom sat with me and talked about love and life and about how sometimes they were all about time. Taking time to discover we had created a past, letting time pass to reach new plateaus in our future, and allowing ourselves time to grow.

When I gave birth to our son my mother was there, bickering good-naturedly with my husband's mom over who got to sit next to me. My mom held my hand while I once again struggled through the labour pains.

My parents were both there to hold their grandson when he came into the world. I named my son after his grandfather, my dad. They have a rare camaraderie.

My mother passed away while I was recording this story, but I know she's here beside me even now as I write these final words. It is because of her that I began to tell my tale, and it may very well be because of her that I finished telling it. My mother was my best friend; I shared everything with her, and I know that she shared everything with me. I promised her I would finish my story and tell the world how truly wonderful she was. It was not a hard promise to make—she deserves so much more.

Becoming a foster parent is never an easy decision and to stand by a particularly troubled child takes a very strong, loving person. I was blessed with two. My dad and I are now very close; we share a unique relationship. A straight shooter, he keeps me honest.

I look back on my life and I am so awed at what blessings have come my way after such turmoil in the beginning.

There have been no hungry days for our son; no moments where he's had to question whether he is loved. He was born into a loving family that dreamed of him with excitement and happy anticipation. I know that Tiffany deserved no less than what we have offered our son.

I miss Tiffany. I often wonder whether she's had a good childhood, with lots of play and laughter. I hope her mom makes her hot chocolate or warm milk and sits with her too.

I wonder about her school life—which subjects are her strongest or her favourite, who her friends are, if she has homework. I wonder if she has slumber parties where they eat lots of junk food and watch movies until dawn. At those moments I whisper a hello to her on the wind.

Jamie occasionally invades my thoughts. His face will suddenly sweep across my mind. Some of the memories are good and funny, and somewhat bittersweet. Other times they leave me silent and pensive. Having not crossed paths with him in years, I don't know what became of him. I like to imagine him finding peace with himself, with Tiffany, and with me.

Time has new meaning now. Months fall into soccer season and baseball season. Our boy is asking for hockey season too. Weeks are punctuated with birthday parties, dinners with grandparents, and movie nights. Some days are a blur of frenzied events, and others just pass by with the ticking of the clock.

Mom was right: life really is just about time.

May peace and time find us all.

THE END